PAUL
XMAS 1997

**Revised
Ninth Edition**

Cruising Guide

ys

With Fl⸻ ⸻vest Coast Supplement
by
Capt. Frank Papy

1

Table of Contents

The charts in this book are artists sketches only. They are intended to give you an idea of the area, anchorage sites and marinas. Since channels shift and shoal up, for actual navigation, use the latest U.S. C&GS charts.

THE CAPTAIN

Frank M. Papy was born in Savannah, Georgia, where he began sailing at the age of 11, when his Uncle Hugh gave him his own pram, "Sea Fox." His mother helped him sew the sails, and he has been sailing ever since.

During his teens, he sailed class boats in races at the Savannah Yacht and Country Club. At 23, he began his professional sailing career, serving as first mate on a 12-meter yawl carrying charters from Ft. Lauderdale to the Bahamas. He also served on boats sailing to Panama and Jamaica.

In 1967, Frank Papy bought the first of three sloops and began cruising the Florida Keys, from Biscayne Bay to the Dry Tortugas, with frequent trips to the Bahamas. He lives the summers on Fox Island on the South Carolina coast and winters in Islamorada in the Keys doing piloting and narration work for Sailing Quarterly Video both in the Keys and Bahamas. With the popularity of his book and stories, he lectures through "Cruising World" magazines, is on the preferred speakers list, and conducts seminars for "Coastal Cruising" magazine at Sail Expo. He is a member of Boating Writers International, the Sports Writers Guild, and an Olympic correspondent for a Ft. Lauderdale newspaper.

Due to the high cost of spiral binding, we have been forced to increase th price of the Eighth Edition of the Keys Guide by two dollars. Due to th numerous request for the spiral binding, we feel that the added cost will not b too great of a burden to our readers.

This book is written, published and printed by Americans, and employ recycled material wherever possible.

This Edition of the Keys Guide is lovingly dedicated to my mother, the lat Catherine Papy. Her help and support will be missed.

CREDITS:
Author & Publisher: Frank M. Papy
Editorial Assistance by R.L. Gregg (Capt. Grog)
Photography and Illustrations: Cy DeCosse
Typing: Ellie Papy
Printing: Colonial Press, Miami, FL

CONTRIBUTORS:
Bill Behre, Clark Shimmel, John Calvert, Willia Youmans, Tom Collins, John Davis, Capt. Eddie Eguria, Dan Flanery, Capt. Sam Gehring, Tom Gibson, Dan Hardy, William Hardy, Jay Helmken, Roland Matranga, Steve Mermell, Pat and Wayne Messilia, Don Porter, Bruce Purdy, Burr Ruby, Len Sacks, Paul Shofner, Steve Salem, Dr. Charlie Scarborough, Joe Schaeffer, Bob and Anna Campbell, Mike Van Ost, Sam Wampler, David Williams, Bruce Hooke, Bob Allen, Rose, Witte, Capt. Steve Ziskind, Jack Calaghan, Ed Wiser, Russ and Christy Teal, Buddy Fripp, Steve Herold, Gordon Bok, Pete Anderson, Gary Corbin, Fred Wonderlick, Keith Douglas, Dennis and Alice Dugas, Nancy and Susan Williams, Jean Jacobs, Chuck and Corrine Canter, Shelton Adams, Nora Papy, John Ziegler.

Cover Photo By Mike Whitt, Yacht Photography, specializing in photography for the marine industry, 1550 S.E. 17th Street #3, Ft. Lauderdale, FL 33316

"Bonefisherman on the Flats, Bayside" by Millard Wells

Millard Wells
Overseas Highway
Islamorada, Florida 33036

The watercolors illustrating this book are by award-winning Florida artist Millard Wells.

Mr. Wells, the owner and operator of Wells Studio-Gallery in Islamorada, uses his lush surroundings as subjects for his watercolors. He has gained national attention for his watercolors of tropical fish, the Keys, and other subtropical islands. His skillful handling of the vivid blues and greens of the Keys area has earned him many awards. Many of his watercolors are seen in public and private collections throughout the country.

LOWER KEYS
MARATHON
ISLAMORADA
KEY LARGO

March 31, 1986

Mr. Frank M. Papy
208 Hendricks Isle
Ft. Lauderdale, FL 33301

Dear Mr. Papy:

It is indeed a pleasure as Mayor of Monroe County and
Chairman of the Tourist Development Council to congratulate
you on the fourth edition of the Cruising Guide to the
Florida Keys.

This most complete guide is filled with helpful
information regarding the Florida Keys and the waters
surrounding them.

Your generous contribution to libraries and educational
institutions is deeply appreciated.

On behalf of the good citizens of Monroe County, I wish
you well in your continued endeavors to publish this most
informative guide to convince sailors and powerboaters alike
that the waters of the Florida keys are the finest on the
East Coast.

With best wishes, I remain,
Sincerely,

WILHELMINA HARVEY
MAYOR, MONROE COUNTY
CHAIRMAN, TOURIST DEVELOPMENT COUNCIL

The Florida Keys...America's Caribbean Islands
MONROE COUNTY TOURIST DEVELOPMENT COUNCIL P.O. BOX 866, KEY WEST, FL 33041

7

THE FLORIDA KEYS

This Satellite Image Map was prepared by
the U.S. Geological Survey. Generally
clouds appear white, clear areas are white or
light gray, vegetation is shades of red, urban
areas are blue gray, and open waters are
shades of blue.

DISCOVER THE KEYS

The Florida Keys have some of the finest sailing waters on the East Coast. Navigational aids in the Keys are easier to follow than in the Bahamas, where there are only a few major lights and inadequate charts. You have to read the water, which makes it difficult to move around at night or when the water is murky. In the Keys, waters are well-marked, charts are up-to-date, and the Coast Guard keeps the channels dredged out to the proper depth. Usually, what you see on the chart is what you've got under the keel, barring extreme high and low tides at the Equinox. The Keys are a nice alternative to the Bahamas because you don't have to contend with international protocol, customs inspection, quarantine regulations and vaccinations, or extra insurance on your vessel for protection from piracy and highjacking due to drug traffic.

After traveling down with their boats from the north, many people are tired of riding in the "big ditch", the Intercoastal Waterway, with its heavy traffic and murky water. Palm Beach, Fort Lauderdale or Miami are their jumping-off spots for some serious cruising in the Bahamas. When they return, they usually have had enough cruising, and skip the Keys, which I think have more to offer than the Bahamas in the way of sheltered harbors, easily navigated and well-marked waters, food, ice and water. You can get marine parts and repairs in the Keys, but if you have a Bahama breakdown with your boat in the Central Berrys or the southern end of Andros, you're in big trouble.

The Keys are America's Out Islands, with the only coral reef in continental United States. The warmth of the Gulf Stream and seeds carried by the trade winds give them a tropical climate and vegetation. The local people are friendly. The native-born are called Conchs; others who have lived there more than ten years are called Freshwater Conchs; everybody else is a tourist.

Expert marine repair services are widely available in the Keys. If you need a replacement part, you won't have to wait while it's shipped overseas, or pay duty on it when it arrives. In case of emergency, telephones, medical aid and the U.S. Coast Guard are close at hand; this is helpful to know because of the increase in recent years of drug-related hijackings in foreign waters.

In the Keys you can cruise in any style that suits your taste. If you like seclusion, you can provision "Bahama Style", with enough canned and dried food to last for several weeks spent swimming, fishing, or exploring uninhabited islands and deserted beaches. If you like fresh meat, milk, water and ice, sometimes hard to find in the Bahamas, you can return to civilization long enough to reprovision. There are plenty of supermarkets in the Keys, many within walking distance of the marinas where you can stop for fuel, water and ice.

If you prefer resort living, you can cruise from one luxury marina to another, enjoying golf courses, tennis courts, swimming pools and gourmet restaurants. Or you can go to the old fishing camps and eat freshly caught fish, shrimp and lobster while you talk to people who have been fishing the same water for thirty years. In bars and coffee houses you'll hear old sea songs and folk music played by struggling young musicians.

The Keys are full of colorful history, from the days of the Spanish Galleons and Keys-based pirates, to the time when salvage from wrecked ships furnished the homes of Key West and made it America's richest city. The Barrier Reef, which made this one of the most dangerous coasts in the world, is now clearly marked. The U.S. Coast Guard provides weather information and immediate assistance when needed. Now days, the only salvagers are divers who still bring up treasure from wrecked Galleons.

You'll get plenty of cruising variety. You can go down on the outside and come back on the inside, where there's beautiful open water for sailing and where, if the weather is bad, you can pull into shelter. I enjoy sailing in the Bahamas and the Keys. I think the Keys offer the best part of both worlds. In this book, we've tried to share our cruising experience and give you tips on navigation, places to anchor and things to do. As you use it, keep notes on your own experiences. If you have any suggestions, please write us so we can add them to the seventh edition.

Help Us Make A Better Guide To The Keys

This is our ninth edition of the *Cruising Guide to the Florida Keys*. My wife, daughter, and I have been cruising the Keys for many years. Each trip yields new experiences. When we return from a charter or cruise we add information which we try to pass on to our fellow cruisers and captains. In this way we feel we are doing our part to promote safe boating in unfamiliar waters so they can enjoy the beauty and nature of the Florida Keys even more.

Helpful sailors who have enjoyed our latest edition of the Cruising Guide have written and called in many suggestions and good tips. We've incorporated them into the new edition and hope to continue the practice. If you have any suggestions that will help other sailors enrich their cruise please write us and we will try to include them in our next edition.

Write to:
Captain Frank M. Papy
Fox Island
Box 263, Rt. 6
Ridgeland, SC 29936

"Shrimp Boats, Key West" by Millard Wells

THE FLORIDA KEYS

While the Keys, like the Bahamas, are most accessible to boats with drafts up to 4½ ft., boats with 5½ or 6 ft. draft can cruise the Keys. Every year more marinas open deep draft facilities on the Atlantic side, as cruising the Keys becomes more popular. In the diagram, the dotted line shows routes for deeper draft boats, beginning with a cruise across Biscayne Bay to Elliott Key.

From Miami into the Atlantic there are several channels, but Government Cut would be the safest choice. Along Hawk Channel there are numerous places where you can stop. Even in the longest stretches, you would never have more than a 60-mile run to make in daytime, and most of the anchorages and marinas are close enough together so that you can take time to visit points of interest on shore or dive on the beautiful coral reefs along the way.

At Channel 5 or Snake Creek you can swing through Yacht Channel and go over to Cape Sable, which has some unbelievably beautiful beaches, then up the west coast of Florida, taking shelter in the Shark River or behind Sands Key for protection from the weather.

At Marathon most of the marinas, on the inside as well as the outside, can handle a deep draft boat. From Marathon to Key West is a good day's run, but you can put in at Newfound Harbor or Stock Island on the way. From Key West you can go on to Fort Jefferson and the Dry Tortugas, which are known as the Gibraltar of the South. It's a blue-water trip which can challenge the capabilities of the vessel, captain and crew.

As indicated by the solid line, boats with drafts up to 4½ ft. have a wide variety of routes, with interesting side trips and beautiful anchorages. Most of the marinas can accommodate you. Swing from the outside to the inside to visit places of special interest or run for shelter in bad weather.

If you cut through Yacht Channel to the west coast, stop at Lake Inghram on the way to Cape Sable. From Marathon you can go on to Key West in Hawks Channel, with several anchorages available along the way, or take the back route through Big Spanish Channel for a more away-from-it-all experience.

If you go on to the Dry Tortugas, 4 ft. can make it inside the Marquesas for protected anchorage. Fort Jefferson is on Garden Key, where the diving is spectacular. There is a well-marked underwater nature trail, fishing so easy it almost isn't sport, and a chance to observe the nesting season of thousands of migrating sooty terns.

On behalf of the charter ketch Lamara II and her fine crew, we wish all you blue-water sailors and cruisers fair winds and sunshine.

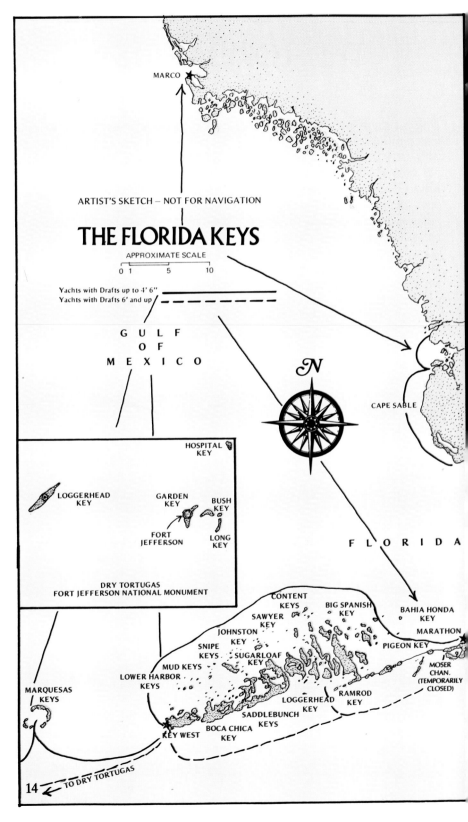

MARCO

ARTIST'S SKETCH – NOT FOR NAVIGATION

THE FLORIDA KEYS

APPROXIMATE SCALE

0 1   5   10

Yachts with Drafts up to 4' 6"
Yachts with Drafts 6' and up

G U L F
O F
M E X I C O

𝒩

CAPE SABLE

HOSPITAL KEY

LOGGERHEAD KEY

GARDEN KEY

BUSH KEY

FORT JEFFERSON

LONG KEY

F L O R I D A

DRY TORTUGAS
FORT JEFFERSON NATIONAL MONUMENT

CONTENT KEYS

SAWYER KEY

BIG SPANISH KEY

BAHIA HONDA KEY

JOHNSTON KEY

MARATHON

SNIPE KEYS

SUGARLOAF KEY

PIGEON KEY

MUD KEYS

LOWER HARBOR KEYS

MOSER CHAN. (TEMPORARILY CLOSED)

MARQUESAS KEYS

LOGGERHEAD KEY

RAMROD KEY

SADDLEBUNCH KEYS

KEY WEST

BOCA CHICA KEY

14 TO DRY TORTUGAS

FT. LAUDERDALE

MIAMI

MIAMI BEACH

VIRGINIA KEY
BEAR CUT
KEY BISCAYNE

FLORIDA

FOWEY ROCKS

BISCAYNE BAY

SOLDIER KEY

RAGGED KEYS

SANDS KEY

ELLIOTT KEY

OLD RHODES KEY

DEER KEY

KEY LARGO

EAGLE KEY

PALM KEY

FRANK KEY

ROCK HARBOR
RODRIGUEZ KEY

SANDY KEY

MAN OF WAR KEY

TAVERNIER

TAVERNIER KEY
NEW SNAKE CREEK BRIDGE
PLANTATION KEY
WINDLEY KEY
ISLAMORADA
UPPER MATECUMBE KEY
INDIAN KEY CHANNEL
LOWER MATECUMBE KEY

A Y

ARSNICKER KEYS

MATECUMBE

CHANNEL FIVE

DUCK KEY

LONG KEY

RATHON

GRASSY KEY

FAT DEER KEY

VACA KEY

HAWK CHANNEL

STRAITS OF FLORIDA

ATLANTIC OCEAN

15

FORT LAUDERDALE

Fort Lauderdale is a like a city of water, with wonderful canals, rivers and marinas. You can go to stores, restaurants and just about anywhere by boat. Sometimes my daughter even goes to school in a dinghy along the canals. It's truly a sailorman's and yachtman's paradise. It's easy to enter from the ocean. It has two landmarks—a big 18-story condominium complex with a white strobe light on top for finding it at night, and to the south of that entrance, a Florida Power and Light Plant with four red and white striped smoke stacks that stand out among the many hotels along the coastline. This entrance, called the Harbor of Port Everglades, is very easy to come into. There's 42 feet in the entrance. A lot of big ships travel in and out of there.

Heading south down the Inter Coastal with Bahia Mar Marina in the background.

Los Olas Anchorage, a popular anchorage south of the Los Olas Bridge is convenient to downtown and the beach.

Once you're inside the Harbor of Port Everglades, turn north. If you run into any trouble and have to sail in, tie up at one of the transient slips at the Marina Inn and Yacht Harbor. It's just to the east as you come up to the bridge. That will keep you from tying up where the commercial ships dock. It's especially helpful if you can't sail through the bridge. The bridge has a convenient sign that counts down the time to the next opening. This allows you to adjust your speed and prevents a bottleneck at the opening of the bridge, especially during heavy weekend traffic.

Just inside the bridge, watch for a very strong tidal rip that flows north and south with the incoming and outgoing tide.

There are three marinas here. Pier 66 is to the east, with fuel dockage, a pump station for waste, customs clearance and very nice restaurants. The Marriott Hotel is on the west side. It has a dockage on the front and a marina with a few transient slips around the corner in the inside. There's also the Lauderdale Marina with fuel and bait, 15 street fisheries and some very **nice restaurants.**

Further up the first canal to the west as you're coming in, there's a place called Southport Raw Bar. A lot of locals and yachtsmen hang out there. It's a quaint place to eat great seafood. They have three or four slips for small boats where you can tie up while you eat.

Heading into Port Everglades with smoke stacks on the left and the large condos on the right.

After you pass Pier 66, The Marriott and the Lauderdale Marina, you have a choice—you can head up the river or take the channel to the east. The channel takes you to Bahia Mar, one of the largest marinas on the east coast with restaurants, stores and yachts. It's on the starboard side as you're heading north up the Intercoastal Waterway. It's an excellent place to tie up to. It has fuel and just about everything, including a fantastic ship store that's convenient for marine repairs. A lot of charter boats and transients stop there.

If you don't want to tie up at the marina, another good choice is Los Olas Anchorage. Just as you come up to the Los Olas Bridge, which is the next bridge heading north, you'll see it on the left side of some mooring buoys. There are some sailboats there. You can tie up for a modest fee, something like $3 a day. It's col-lected by the marine patrols. They have a little dinghy ramp that's convenient to tie up to and go into the city. It's only a couple of miles down Los Olas to downtown where you'll find all the convenient stores. There are also several stores and restaurants on the beach across the bridge.

If you decide to take the western channel and up into the river which takes you into Fort Lauderdale proper, just head up, watching out for a very strong current. You'll find several beautiful parks, including one on the right side as you travel into the river. On the port side as you're heading up, Shirt Tale Charlies is another nice place to stop. It's really a fine place to have a couple of drinks and a good meal.

There are several convenient city docks along this area. Some

bridges in this area have restrictions. Check your local charts for information. One railroad bridge stays up most of the time.

Further up the river, there are some quality boat yards. River Bend Boat Yard, a do-it-yourself yard, is very good. Large tour boats also use the river; be careful to give them a wide birth. Lauderdale Self Service is another marina up that way.

In this area you can find just about any marine item, new or used. A new development is the marine flea market, held once or twice a year, where several stores including Marine Hardware and Sailorman, sell used marina supplies. You'll also find the latest developments in marine electronics, painting and hauling boats here.

LOCATION OF REEF MOORING BUOYS
Diving Tips: IN THE FLORIDA KEYS

Key Largo National Marine Sanctuary
maintains 129 reef mooring buoys at these reefs:
Three Sisters
Molasses Reef
Sand Island
White Bank Dry Rocks
French Reef
Benwood Wreck
Grecian Rocks
Key Largo Dry Rocks
The Elbow
Carysfort South
Carysfort Reef
Turtle Rocks
Turtle Shoals
Northeast Patch

REEF RELIEF,
a non-profit conservation group based in Key West, maintains 83 mooring buoys at six reefs near Key West:
Western Dry Rocks
Sand Key
Rock Key
Eastern Dry Rocks
Western Sambo
Pelican Shoal

The Coral Reef Foundation,
an upper Keys volunteer group, is in the process of installing 24 buoys at these reefs:
Pickles Reef
Conch Reef
Little Conch
Davis Reef
Crocker
Hens & Chickens
Cheeca Rocks
Alligator

SNORKELING &

Florida Keys Sanctuary, Inc.,
a private group based in Marathon, maintains 25 buoys at Sombrero Reef. More buoys are scheduled for installation.

DIVING AREA

Looe Key National Marine Sanctuary
provides 54 reef mooring buoys at Looe Key.

20

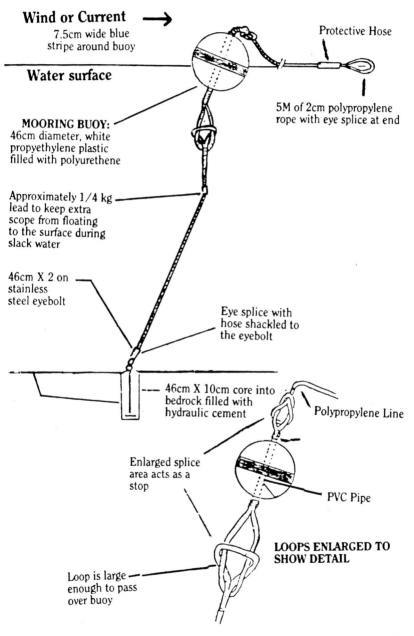

Wind or Current →
7.5cm wide blue
stripe around buoy

Protective Hose

Water surface

5M of 2cm polypropylene
rope with eye splice at end

MOORING BUOY:
46cm diameter, white
propyethylene plastic
filled with polyurethene

Approximately 1/4 kg
lead to keep extra
scope from floating
to the surface during
slack water

46cm X 2 on
stainless
steel eyebolt

Eye splice with
hose shackled to
the eyebolt

46cm X 10cm core into
bedrock filled with
hydraulic cement

Polypropylene Line

Enlarged splice
area acts as a
stop

PVC Pipe

**LOOPS ENLARGED TO
SHOW DETAIL**

Loop is large
enough to pass
over buoy

21

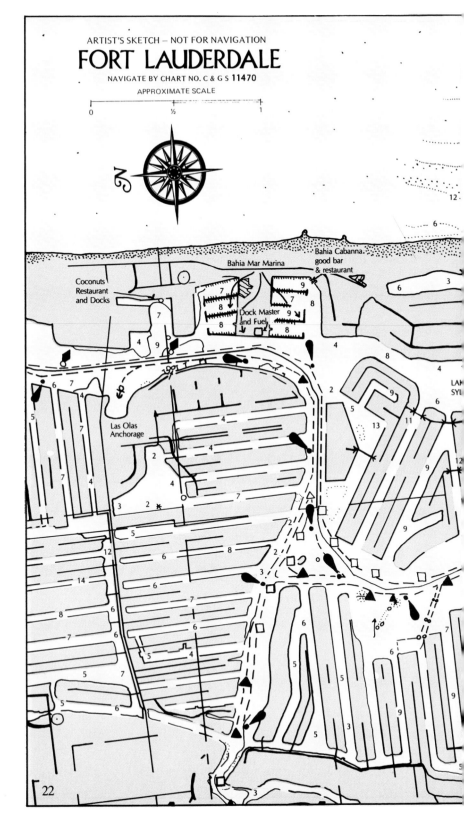

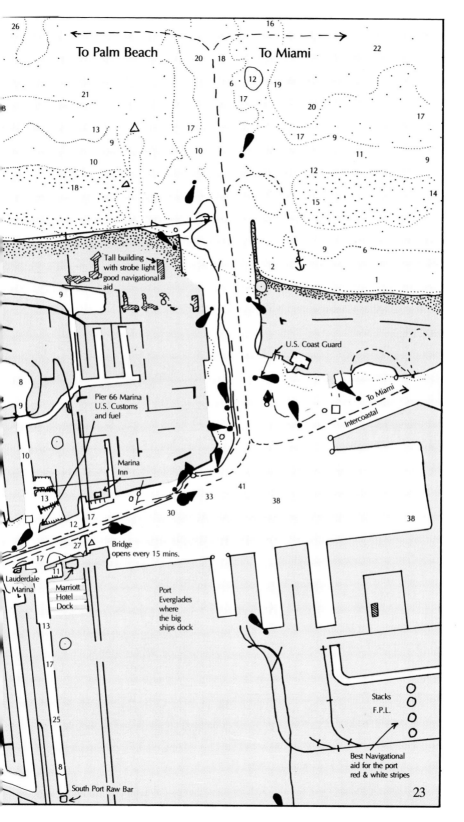

ruise the crystal waters of the Florida Keys or the Bahama Islands. We offer the finest selection of charter yachts available, at surprisingly affordable rates. Choose bareboat, or crewed yachts from 27' to 120'. We also offer American Sailing Association certification courses from basic through advanced as well as learn-to-sail vacation packages. If you are looking for a new or used boat, our friendly brokerage staff can help. We also offer the full line of Hunter sailboats for purchase or charter fleet placement. Call for a free brochure. Open 7 days.

FLORIDA YACHT CHARTERS & SALES, Inc.

AUTHORIZED
HUNTER
DEALER & DEMO FLEET

MEMBER
BUC
YACHT SALES
NETWORK™

MIAMI & KEY BISCAYNE

Most cruises of the Keys begin at Miami. Even if you've visited the city before, a yachtman's view of Miami will be a new experience. If you should need repair or hauling, the Miami River has facilities which you can find in the local directory. Just inside Government Cut is the Miami Beach Marina with a 400-slip capacity. Recently the City of Miami completed a beautiful new marina right in the heart of downtown. The Miamarina has informal and formal restaurants, a laundry and showers. On weekends, wake from power boats creates a strong surge in the marina, which causes some rolling.

You can rent a car, take a taxi, or walk to the city's principal attractions. Downtown is only a ten-minute walk, which includes an excellent public library.

Miamarina is a good place to begin or end a cruise; it's the closest marina to Government Cut if you're traveling on the outside, and it's equally accessible to the inside route. It is also close to Watson Island and Du Pont Plaza, where diesel fuel and gas are available.

From Miamarina you can go south on the inside, past Claughton Island, to the Miami Marine Stadium at Virginia Key. There's a nice restaurant there. You can anchor off, row ashore, eat and go on to the Marine Stadium where they have boat races in the daytime and occasional concerts at night. With a shallow draft vessel (4½ ft.), you can get inside and actually tie up alongside the bandstand for a seaside view.

Southeast on Virginia Key is the Seaquarium, with Loletta the Kill-

Miamarina in downtown Miami now has a fantastic new shopping plaza where you can see the trees in the upper left. Miamarina is temporarily closed for repairs.

SNORKELING & DIVING OFF SHORE - KEY LARGO AREA

Starting at the north end of Key Largo on the ocean-side, one of the spots we like for our novice divers is Basin Hill Shoals (see C.G. Chart No. 11462). The average depth is 6 ft. to 18 ft. so you can't get into too much trouble. There's lots of coral and fish and you can get fairly close to the reef with your boat.

About 3½ miles to the east lies the Carysford Light Reef. You can snorkel and scuba dive, depths range from loft to 45 ft. Anchor west of the lighthouse — plenty of fish and some of the finest examples of coral growth in the United States.

Four miles southwest of Carysford Lighthouse is a reef called the Elbow, named for its shape. It's marked by a 30 ft. structure. There are several wrecks here for exploring in 11 ft. to 40 ft. of water, but watch the current here and never get too far from your boat.

Next along the reef is Dry Rocks. There are several buoys here marking the location of Christ of the Deep, a bronze statue rising 12 ft. off the bottom. This is a "must" to see and if you have an underwater camera, make sure to get some shots. It's really spectacular. Grecian Rocks Reef is in this vicinity and is also very beautiful.

For the more experienced divers, French Reef and the Brentwood Wreck are fantastic to explore. French Reef has large caves and pockets in the reef with tremendous variety of fish and sea creatures.

Back in the shallow water, if the weather blows up a little, you can dive Mosquito Bank Reef south of Largo Sound entrance — great fun snorkeling, too. When you anchor, just make sure you're out of the channel.

In the southern-most part of the John Penecamp Park is Molasses Reef and is one of the finest with a variety of snorkeling and scuba diving. The current is strong here and it can get rough if the wind is up, but is well worth the trip. They have mooring buoys here, so don't ruin the coral with your anchor. Don't miss it! Snorkeling and diving is to live in another world under the sea.

The Miami Seaquarium on Virginia Key is linked to key Biscayne by the Bear Cut fixed bridge. Harbor at left has a depth of 5 feet.

er Whale and other aquatic attractions. Adjacent to the southeast boundary of the Seaquarium is the Rosentiel School of Marine Science. The Rosenstiel School is a world class educational/research facility and is a campus of the University of Miami.

As you will see on our chart, you can anchor on the southern side of Rickenbacker Causeway for protection from weather or go even closer to the Seaquarium or The Rosenstiel School and take the dinghy ashore. If you are visiting the Seaquarium, you can enter the small harbor and tie up on the seawall.

On the eastern side of Virginia Key is a very good swimming beach. Local knowledge will be needed here, as the water shoals off, and there's a strong current through Bear Cut.

Across from Virginia Key, on the northern end of Key Biscayne is the Crandon Park Marina. In 1987, the Marina reported a maintained depth of 6 ft. coming in and 10 ft. alongside the docks. The Marina has a restaurant and sells fuel, ice and bait. A great new restaurant and bar has been added called Sundays on the Bay with dockage and good Rum Runner Punches.

new chart editions

Biscayne Channel is a 6 ft. channel between the Stiltsville flats.

From here you could walk over to the Seaquarium or Marine Stadium, although it is quite far. Crandon Park has reasonably priced transit berthing facilities. They usually have vacancies, but during the season you should check ahead of time by calling the Dade County Parks Crandon Park Marina dockmaster.

At the southern tip of Key Biscayne is Cape Florida Park, a welcome stopping area, complete with beautiful beaches, stores and other conveniences. In the park is an interesting old tower, a lighthouse, from which you can view the entire Stiltsville area across the way. Stiltsville is a group of homes strung out along channels in the flats off Key Biscayne. The name derives from the high pilings on which the houses are built.

Cape Florida is a famous jumping off spot for the Bahamas. Boats bound for Bimini pass the time in this area waiting for favorable winds or good weather. After dark, they steer for the lights of Bimini. Ponce de Leon discovered Florida while searching for Bimini. He never did locate Bimini, but modern seamen have no problem. By sailing at night, they can steer by the lights of Miami over the stern until they pick up Bimini on the bow. There's a short space in between which calls for a compass course.

The entrance to Cape Florida Channel is pretty well marked. As you go into the harbor, make sure you follow your markers carefully. You can take 6 ft. in there with no problem. Stay in the center of the channel when entering. once inside, use two anchors. Sometimes the harbor is a little crowded; dou-

Dinner Key Marina has anchorage to the east and transient slips. Slips are also available at Monty Trainer's Restaurant, Raw Bar or at Merrill Stevens.

ble anchors will keep you from swinging badly.

You can dinghy ashore. The sea wall is deep, but you can pick up the dinghy and put it on the bank, or you can use a stern anchor. Walk through the park, explore the beaches and visit the light-house. You should be back by 5 in the afternoon, before the park closes. No boats can be moored to the shore after dark. All of this is well-marked, and easily found on the charts. From No Name Har-bor to the tip of Cape Florida there is a channel for boats up to 5' draft. It should be taken with caution. Don't touch the sea wall, but stay close enough to throw rocks at it.

Back on the eastern side of Bis-cayne Bay are two more points of interest to yachtsmen, Dinner Key and Coconut Grove. If you come in the main Dinner Key Channel,

come all the way in and swing around on the south side of the first island, as shown on our chart. It's a safe and easy way to come into the anchorage. If you swing southerly as soon as you sight all the boats anchored at Dinner Key, you might run aground in the shoal area.

The Diner Key-Coconut Grove

Entrance to No Name Harbor in Cape Florida Park on Key Biscayne.

"Looking Out From Within the Walls of Ft. Jefferson" by Millard Wells.

PROTECT OUR REEFS

Among the most popular areas for sailing and boating are the Florida Keys. The general-
pleasant weather and the beauty of the waters around the Keys make boating in the area
relaxing experience...

Unless, of course, you ignore the coral reefs below the surface of the water.

Grounding your boat on a coral reef will not only damage the boat, but will also destroy
oral structures which have been hundreds of years in the making and are very slow to
ecover.

In the Looe Key and Key Largo National Marine Sanctuaries and other protected areas
a the Keys, it is illegal to damage or remove coral by any means. *Destruction of coral for-
tations through grounding or imprudent anchoring can lead to penalties and fines of up to
50,000.* Spearfishing and removing historical artifacts in historical areas are also prohibited
a the sanctuaries.

The Looe Key sanctuary is a 5.3 square nautical mile area about six nautical miles south-southwest
f Big Pine Key. The Key Largo sanctuary is 20 miles long and varies in width from three to six
iles. It is adjacent to the John Pennekamp Coral Reef State Park and immediately south of the
iscayne National Monument.

We offer the following tips to you, so that you can enjoy your sail along the Keys and can in-
ire that others will be able to enjoy the unique and spectacular underwater world off the Keys.

"Brown, brown, run aground."

Coral reefs grow upward. When they are relatively close to the surface, the coral formations
ill make the water appear brown. Such areas should be avoided. If they are not, you can bet that
ou will run aground.

"Green, green, nice and clean."

The areas behind and to the sides of a reef are often covered by green seagrasses. The only hazard
a boat is the rather shallow water in some of these areas. Careless motoring through shallow
irtle grass beds can tear up the plants, however, and should be avoided.

"Blue, blue, sail on through."

Areas where there is deep water, such as on the seaward side of a reef, appear blue, particular-
where the Gulf Stream runs close to the Keys. When sailing in blue water, however, remember
iat coral reefs rise rather abruptly from deep water. Give yourself plenty of room to maneuver.

Before sailing into any of these protected areas, indeed into any area close to the Keys, you
iould *thoroughly familiarize yourself with the nautical charts for the area. Pay particular at-
'ntion to the symbols for reefs that are exposed at low tide and to the depth indications.* Close
p charts of Key Largo and Looe Key Marine Sanctuaries are available in local stores. Naviga-
onal and Loran charts published by the National Ocean Survey of the National Oceanic and At-
iospheric Administration are among the most reliable. For Key Largo National Marine Sanctuary
se chart 11451 or 11462, and for Looe Key National Marine Sanctuary use chart 11442 or 11445.

If you decide to anchor in a reef area, *do not anchor on the reef* itself since anchors destroy
oral all too effectively. At the Key Largo and Looe Key National Marine Sanctuaries there
re *mooring buoys* to which you can attach your boat, so that you do not have to drop anchor.
/herever possible, these buoys should be used. If no buoys are available, you should drop
inchor only in sandy areas. The bottom in sandy areas appears white.

area is one of the best spots in the south for boat supplies, seaworthy cooking utensils and clothing. You may get dock space; or you can anchor out. There's a place provided where you can tie up the dinghy on the north side of the tall white building at Dinner Key. Coconut Grove has excellent restaurants and a playhouse. It's an interesting stop before you go out to rough it in the Keys.

Now if you decide to anchor overnight in a little no-name harbor as shown on page 31, you'll find they have all kinds of regulations; how long can you stay, and you'll have to come up with some bucks. $8.40 per night, whether you have an eighty-footer or an eight-footer. Also now, if you're sailing down Biscayne Bay at night, they have put a couple of four-second flashing yellow lights. They're in deep water. I guess they're to help the less experienced boater get down to Elliot Key. If you're short of fuel and supplies, there's a new marina at Black Point. They monitor VHF 16, 8 A.M. to 5 P.M., seven days a week. We suggest you give them a hail for the latest depth's and slip availability.

Cape Florida Park and No Name Harbor located on the southern, most tip of Key Biscayne are clearly visible in this Nasa aerial photograph obtained from Eros Data Center, Sioux Falls, South Dakota.

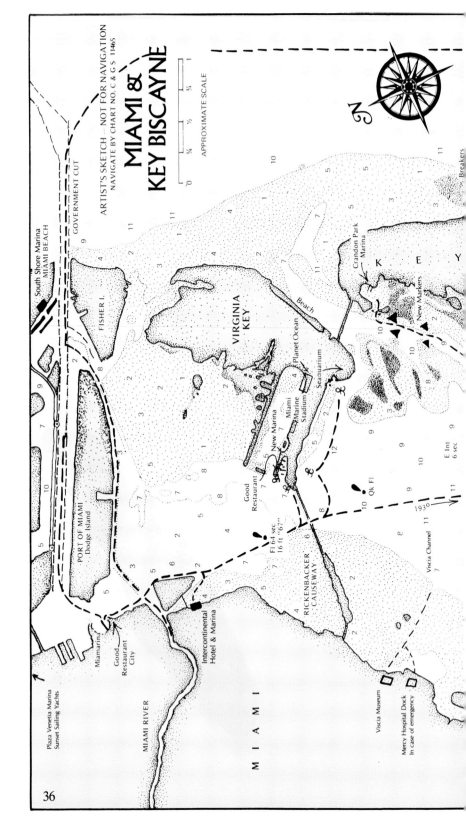

MIAMI & KEY BISCAYNE

ARTIST'S SKETCH — NOT FOR NAVIGATION
NAVIGATE BY CHART NO. C & G S 11465

APPROXIMATE SCALE

Plaza Venetia Marina
Sunset Sailing Yachts

MIAMI RIVER

M I A M I

Viscia Museum

Mercy Hospital Dock
In case of emergency

Good
Restaurant
City

Miamarina

Intercontinental
Hotel & Marina

PORT OF MIAMI
Dodge Island

South Shore Marina
MIAMI BEACH

GOVERNMENT CUT

FISHER I.

RICKENBACKER
CAUSEWAY

Good
Restaurant

VIRGINIA
KEY

New Marina

Miami
Marine
Stadium

Planet Ocean

Seaquarium

Beach

Fl 6-4 sec.
16 ft '67'

Viscia Channel

1930

10 Qk Fl

E Int
6 sec

K   E   Y

Crandon Park
Marina

New Markers

Breakers

36

37

Calendar of Events for Miami Area:

Orange Bowl Regatta . . . . 1st Week in January
Coconut Grove Art Fair . . . . Mid February
Miami Beach Boat Show . . . . Last Week in February
SORC Races . . . . Last of Feb., 1st Week in Mar.
Fourth of July Fireworks . . . . 1st Week in July
Famous Columbus Day Race . . . . Oct. 12
(Largest Sailboat Race in World)
Tentative Marine Grand Prix Sports Car Race
(Date to Be Announced)

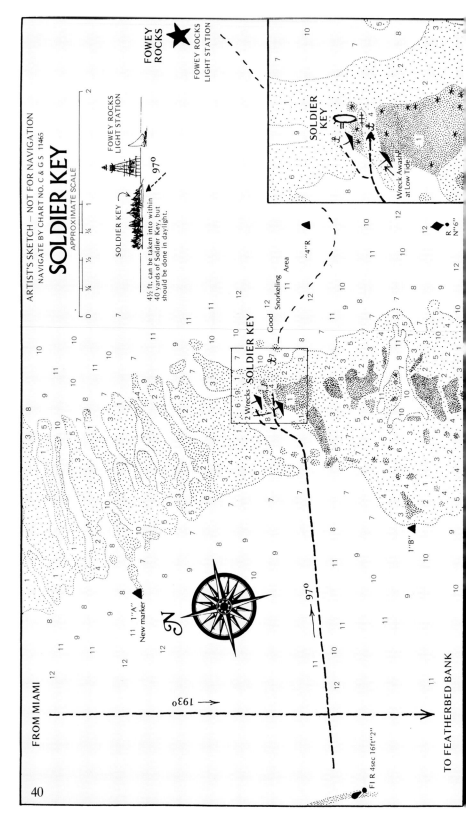

ARTIST'S SKETCH – NOT FOR NAVIGATION
NAVIGATE BY CHART NO. C & G S 11465

SOLDIER KEY

APPROXIMATE SCALE

FOWEY ROCKS
LIGHT STATION

SOLDIER KEY

97°

4½ ft. can be taken into within
40 yards of Soldier Key, but
should be done in daylight.

FOWEY
ROCKS

FOWEY ROCKS LIGHT STATION

SOLDIER KEY

Wreck Awash
at Low Tide

"4" R

Good Snorkeling Area

R N "6"

2 Wrecks SOLDIER KEY

97°

1 "A" New marker

N

1 "B"

FROM MIAMI

193°

TO FEATHERBED BANK

Fl R 4sec 16ft "2"

40

SOLDIER KEY

South of either Dinner Key or Key Biscayne, the first point of interest is Soldier Key. Steer 193° until you pick up a 16 ft. marker No. "2". She's a flashing red 4-second day marker. As soon as you get this in sight, come up onto it and line up Fowey Rocks light, off the southern tip of Soldier Key. When you get to about 97° on the bearing, steer on in to within 300 or 400 yards of Soldier Key; then you better put somebody up on the bow and pick your way in. This should be done in daylight, preferably after 12 o'clock, with the sun overhead or behind you.

If you take your dinghy, you can explore the safety valves, which

Note channel (lower right) past privately owned Soldier Key. Fowey Rocks Light is visible in background.

are cuts caused by the current. Walking on the flats, you can observe conchs and other shell life. Diving under the ledges in these cuts, you can find Florida lobster and stone crab around the rocks. Fishing is good, especially for grouper and snapper. Divers can also explore some old wrecks and the coral heads located in about 11 ft. of water.

Be careful when you are anchoring in Soldier Key Channel. A very strong current comes through here, so on the change of tide you should have someone on board to check the anchor. Hurricane Andrew knocked down a lot of trees on they island but the are grown back nicely.

My experience cruising these waters is that, when picking their way into a channel, most people don't pay attention to the bearings they have over the stern. A solution is to keep a few sash cord or diving weight with about 10 or 15 ft. of string or fine line and a couple of empty bleach bottles attached to them. As you enter a channel, throw the weights off the stern of the boat to starboard or port, far enough out to avoid the propeller, giving you a marking channel. On the way out, use a boat hook to pick up the weights and put them back on board. Biscayne Bay is a lobster sanctuary and there is a closed season on conch.

Weather In The Keys

The climate in the Keys is tropical, but around October 15 it starts cooling off. For the next two months it's pleasant.

June to September, you must be prepared for hot days, with extra precautions against mosquitos and possible hurricanes. However, weather warning systems are great, with VHF weather reports and RDF weather which are used by pilots. Frequently, rain will stay over warm areas, such as the Gulf Stream and mainland, leaving Biscayne Bay clear.

Around December 15, fronts start moving down into Florida, which result in cool temperatures and strong north and northeasterly winds for a few days, followed by warm south and southeasterly winds. If watched closely, this can be used to advantage. Winds are strongest in January. Around February 15, the fronts begin to stall in Georgia and Upper Florida, making it hard for the weatherman to predict them. The best weather for cruising is from February 15 to the end of May.

Alligator Light with Frigate Bird" by Millard Wells

SUGGESTED CRUISES

Several things should be considered when you plan a cruise. These are: how much time you have, what you like to do, the weather conditions and the speed of your boat.

Depending on the time of year and the length of the cruise, I usually allow one or two days for bad weather. From Miami to Marathon you can take either the Gulf or Atlantic side. The Atlantic side has a disadvantage, because you are going against the Gulf Stream for part of your trip. With a moderate North or Northeasterly wind, it's pleasant, but a Northerly wind over 25 knots can really make the Gulf stream rough. From Marathon to Key West you can make a long day's run on the Atlantic side, or take a couple of days and go through Marathon Trough and Big Spanish Channel, overnighting at one of the anchorages marked in this Guide.

The following cruises were taken from the log book of the Nautica, which averages 5 to 6.5 knots, depending on the wind. Using this as a point of reference, you can add a day for each stop which seems interesting. If you have a faster vessel, you can use the extra time to explore each stopping area, or cruise farther in the same amount of time.

3-Day Cruise #1

Miami to Elliott Key
One day at Elliott Key
Elliott Key to Miami

#2

Miami to Largo Sound
One day at John Pennekamp Park
Largo Sound to Miami

5-Day Cruise #1

Miami to Jewfish Creek
Jewfish Creek to Plantation Key
One day at Plantation Harbor
Plantation Key to Elliott Key
Elliott Key to Miami

#2

Miami to Largo Sound
Largo Sound to Windley Key
Windley Key to Pumpkin Key
Pumpkin Key to Miami

This cruise begins on the Atlantic side and allows one day for weather, diving on John Pennekamp Park Reef, or enjoying the Marina pleasures, restaurants and Rum Punches at Windley Key.

7-Day Cruise #1

Miami to Jewfish Creek
Jewfish Creek to Marathon
Marathon to Key West
One day in Key West
Key West to Marathon
Marathon to Largo Sound
Largo Sound to Miami

On this cruise, start the longer runs at first light.

#2

Miami to Jewfish Creek
Jewfish Creek to Lower Matecumbe
Lower Matecumbe to Cape Sable
One day at Cape Sable
Cape Sable to Duck Key
Duck Key to Key Largo
Key Largo to Miami

The 7-day cruises mentioned above start on the Florida Bay side of the Keys. This can be alternated if weather conditions are suitable for sailing on the outside.

14-Day Cruise #1

Miami to Largo Sound
Largo Sound to Marathon
Marathon to Key West
One day in Key West
Key West to the Marquesas Keys
Marquesas to Dry Tortugas
Two days at Dry Tortugas
Dry Tortugas to Marquesas
Marquesas to Key West
One day in Key West
Key West to Marathon
Marathon to Key Largo
Key Largo to Miami

#2

Miami to Jewfish Creek
Jewfish Creek to Lower Matecumbe
Lower Matecumbe to Cape Sable
One day at Cape Sable
Cape Sable to Marathon
One day at Marathon
Marathon to Big Spanish Channel
Big Spanish Channel to Key West
One day in Key West
Key West to Newfound Harbor
Newfound Harbor to Duck Key
Duck Key to Key Largo
One day diving at John Pennekamp Park Reef
Key Largo to Miami

RAGGED KEY
& BOCA CHITA KEY

The Ragged Keys are low lying and don't offer much protection from heavy winds. However, if the weather is warm, and you want a breeze, this is the place to find it. Head south until you pass marker No. "1," then make a very wide turn, and come up to a heading of approximately 42°. Work your way in past marker No. "3," checking your depth as you go.

The northernmost Ragged Key has the best holding ground, and in fine weather offers a calm anchorage with a good summertime breeze. From here you can dinghy out and snorkel or dive around the rocks on the Atlantic side.

The Ragged Keys are similar to Soldier Key, with good diving on both sides, coral heads off shore, lobster and stone crab around the islands. Keys #4 and

#5 are incorporated in the city of Islandia, a group of 5 Keys in Biscayne Bay which boasts a few residents, a mayor and a chief of police. The small private yacht club on Ragged Key #5 is now closed.

Boca Chita Key, to the south, is one of the most picturesque of the small islands north of Sands Key. It has an attractive small harbor with dockage offered by Biscayne National Park Service. The beautiful lighthouse, built in the early 1900's, makes a good landmark for navigation.

Approaching Boca Chita Key from west to east, there are some privately maintained ranged markers which lead into a channel which will take 2½ to 3 ft. draft. The channel leads around the Key in Hawk's Channel. Watch the strong setting current.

46

A tower marks the entrance to the park docks on Boca Chita Key.

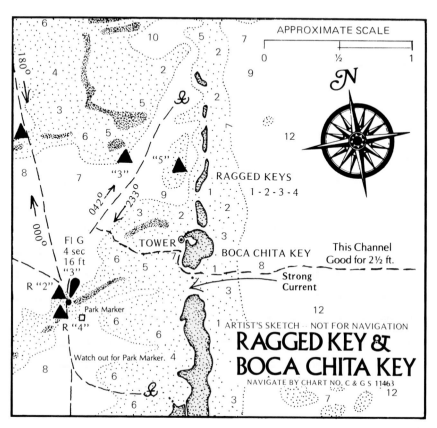

APPROXIMATE SCALE

0   ½   1

RAGGED KEYS
1 - 2 - 3 - 4

"5"

"3"

12

Fl G
4 sec
16 ft
"3"

TOWER

BOCA CHITA KEY

This Channel
Good for 2½ ft.

R "2"

Park Marker

R "4"

Strong
Current

Watch out for Park Marker.

12

1 ARTIST'S SKETCH — NOT FOR NAVIGATION

RAGGED KEY &
BOCA CHITA KEY

NAVIGATE BY CHART NO. C & G S 11463

12

47

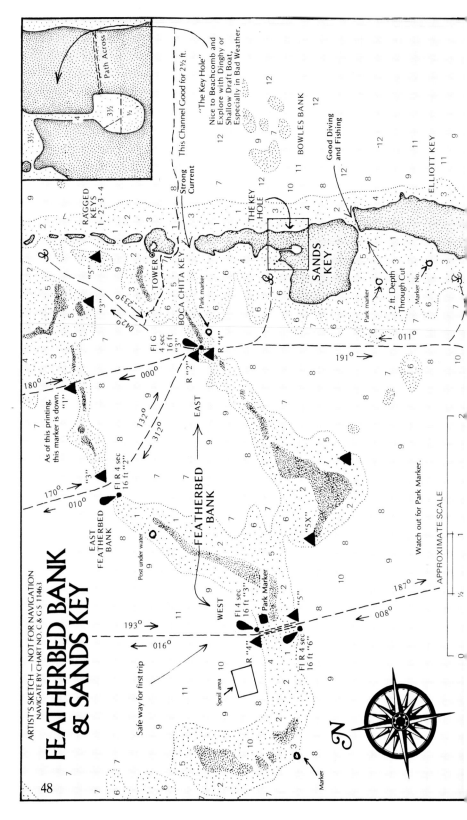

FEATHERBED BANK & SANDS KEY

South of Soldier Key are the Featherbed Banks and Sands Key. With favorable winds you can take a short cut from Soldier Key, by watching for marker No. "1B". Once you pick up that, steer 180° south, and pass privately-maintained marker No. "1". At this printing this marker was down. It has 4½ ft. of water on each side of it; pass it about 30 ft. port or starboard side. From here, on the same course, you can make it into East Featherbed Bank, although the water gets pretty shallow.

To be safer, you can swing back out and come in at East Featherbed Bank marker No. "3" and marker No. "2". No. "2" is a 2.5-second flashing white light. Once you get through these two, swing to a course of 132°, which will bring you into the Banks.

For a more sheltered area, go through the main section of East Featherbed Banks to Sands Key. There are several places where you can anchor, depending upon your draft. You can anchor fairly close to shore, and then dinghy into the small, man-made harbor. (See inset.) This harbor is called the Key Hole because of its shape. The entrance is a might hard to find. Just keep heading for the shore line and by and by you'll pick it up to the south.

Carry your dinghy across the island on the short path shown on our chart. In this way, you can use the dinghy to explore the eastern side of the island down to the southern tip, where there's a small beach and good diving and fishing. Fishwatchers should look for angelfish and triggerfish in these waters.

Right in Sands Cut, where the water is about 15 ft. deep, there's a coral sea garden which is a great spot for diving. Going into Sands Cut from either side the depth is 2 to 2½ ft., depending on the tide. A very strong current runs through Sands Cut, and on weekends the traffic is heavy with fishing boats going in and out. Be especially cautious if you dive. Beachcombing and shelling on the flats around Sands Key are very rewarding, but wear old sneakers because you'll be crossing coral.

Sands Key, Elliott Key, Old Rhodes Key are all part of Biscayne National Monument. It's a 96,000-acre park maintained by the National Park Service. Most of the park is water and reef. It extends west across the intercoastal waterway to the Florida shore, and east across Hawk Channel and includes a string of coral reefs. Plants and wildlife of both the temperate and tropic zones grow here. Along the shore mangroves spread from land to water, trapping silt and gradually building new land. You'll find tropical hardwoods in the interior, including mahogany.

49

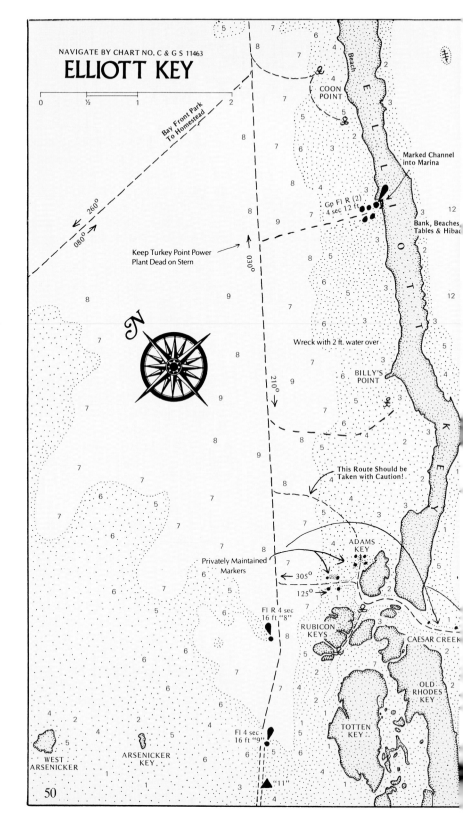

NAVIGATE BY CHART NO. C & G S 11463

ELLIOTT KEY

0   ½   1   2

Bay Front Park
To Homestead

260°
080°

Keep Turkey Point Power
Plant Dead on Stern

030°

COON
POINT

Marked Channel
into Marina

Gp Fl R (2)
4 sec 12 ft

Bank, Beaches
Tables & Hibac

12

12

Wreck with 2 ft. water over

BILLY'S
POINT

210°

This Route Should be
Taken with Caution!

ADAMS
KEY

Privately Maintained
Markers

305°
125°

Fl R 4 sec
16 ft "8"

RUBICON
KEYS

CAESAR CREEK

OLD
RHODES
KEY

TOTTEN
KEY

Fl 4 sec
16 ft "9"

▲ "11"

WEST
ARSENICKER

ARSENICKER
KEY

50

ELLIOTT KEY

On the eastern side of Biscayne Bay, as you come south from Sands Key, is Elliott Key, one of my favorite spots. On weekends, Elliott Key is pretty lively, but during the week it's practically deserted. You have the feeling of being a long way from everywhere, although civilization is near at hand when you need it. You can day sail back and forth to Miami or over to Homestead Bayfront Park for supplies. If your draft is amenable, you can go outside through Caesar's Creek for fishing, diving or sailing on the ocean side, and still come back within two or three hours for a safe and convenient anchorage.

At the north end of Elliott Key is University Dock, a small notation on Chart 11463. Just north of Coon Point is a beach with good anchorage for fishing and diving. On weekends this is a very popular spot for water skiers.

South of Coon Point is Elliott Key Park, where you can get in with a 3½ foot draft at high tide. The park has 64 slips, 55 for small boats and 9 for boats with a beam up to 12 ft. The things I like best about this marina are Head Ranger Mike Hill, who has contributed in-

Old University Dock, on the Northwest end of Elliott Key, is a popular anchorage with sand beach.

Elliott Key, where facilities have been expanded, is the headquarters and Ranger Station for Biscayne Memorial Park.

formation to *The Cruising Guide to the Florida Keys,* and the fact that it doesn't cost a dime to tie up there.

The Marina offers fresh water showers and camping facilities for boaters. Nature exhibits are provided in the recreation area, and a path across the island takes you to the oceanside picnic ground where you can barbecue. There's also a boardwalk on the ocean side.

There are 4 reefs off the eastern side of the key. Divers can get charts from the park which show the mooring buoys and help identify the varieties of coral they can find under water.

Billy's Point is not particularly interesting, but fishing is good on the flats to the south. N.N.W. of Billy's Point, about 1500 yards off shore, is a wreck with only 4 ft. of water covering it. Watch out!

At the southern tip of Elliott Key is Adams Key. You have to go through 4 ft. of water to reach it, and then you're in deep water.

There are spots 19 and 22 ft. right off Adams Key. Fishing is excellent, and you can go through Caesar's Creek to the ocean side. The current is very strong, but with a boat up to 30 ft. you can anchor Bahama style with two anchors at 180°. Use your dinghy to explore around Reid Key and the northern end of Old Rhodes Key. The deep channel is surrounded by bone fish flats.

The area around Adams Key was used for training Cuban Commandos before the Bay of Pigs Invasion. According to tradition, this was also the favorite haunt of Black Caesar the Pirate. Some people claim it still is.

With a shallow draft boat and caution you can return to the main channel by following the course marked between Adams Key and Rubicon Keys. Then head for marker No. "8", a 4-second flashing red light that leads you into the dredged channel between Biscayne Bay and Card Sound.

CONVOY POINT

The western, or shoreward, side of Biscayne National Monument begins just south of Black Point and Black Creek, where crabbing and fishing are good. They are building a 100-slip marina with transients welcome. Farther south is Homestead Bayfront Park on Convoy Point. You have about 3 ft. of water approaching the privately maintained channel, but boats with deeper draft can come within 600 yards of it in 6 ft. of water. With a hand bearing com-

Depending upon the tide, the marina at Convoy Point has a controlling depth of 3½ to 4 ft.

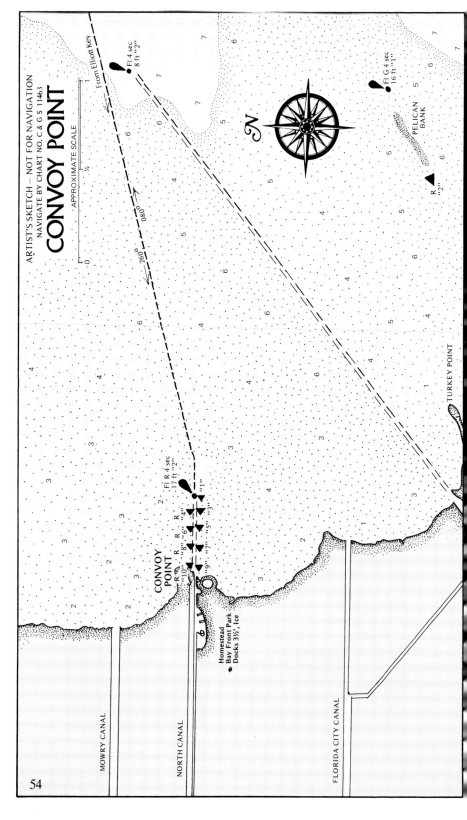

ARTIST'S SKETCH – NOT FOR NAVIGATION
NAVIGATE BY CHART NO. C. & G S 11463

CONVOY POINT

APPROXIMATE SCALE

From Elliott Key

Fl 4 sec
8 ft "2"

Fl G 4 sec
16 ft "1"

PELICAN BANK

R "2"

N

080°

260°

Fl R 4 sec
17 ft "2"

"1"

"3"

"5"

"7"

"9"

R "4"

R "6"

R "8"

R "10"

CONVOY POINT

Homestead
Bay Front Park;
Docks 3½', Ice

TURKEY POINT

MOWRY CANAL

NORTH CANAL

FLORIDA CITY CANAL

54

pass you can spot your depth all the way up to the 6 ft. depth, almost directly in front of the Homestead Bayfront Park Marina and boat launching ramps. If you anchor out at high tide, you can dinghy ashore using the markers as a guide, and replenish your supply of ice, drinks and fishing supplies.

About two miles south of the Park is the Turkey Point Power Plant. Before the hot water from the plant is discharged it must flow through a lengthy switch-back cooling canal. Blue crabs thrive in the warm water of the canal. If you have a shallow draft boat or dinghy and some chicken necks, it's worth a trip for crabbing. The canal entrance is about five miles south of the plant.

How to Catch a Blue Crab

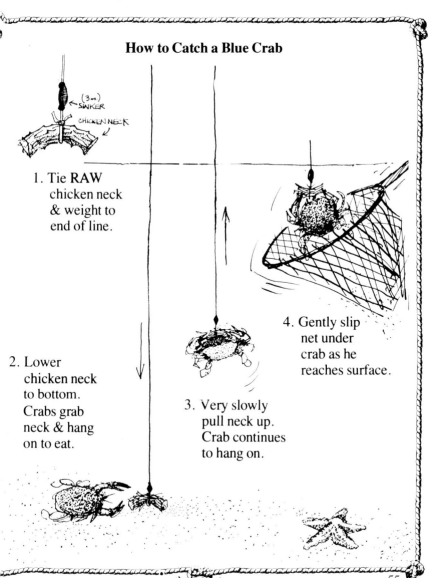

1. Tie **RAW** chicken neck & weight to end of line.

2. Lower chicken neck to bottom. Crabs grab neck & hang on to eat.

3. Very slowly pull neck up. Crab continues to hang on.

4. Gently slip net under crab as he reaches surface.

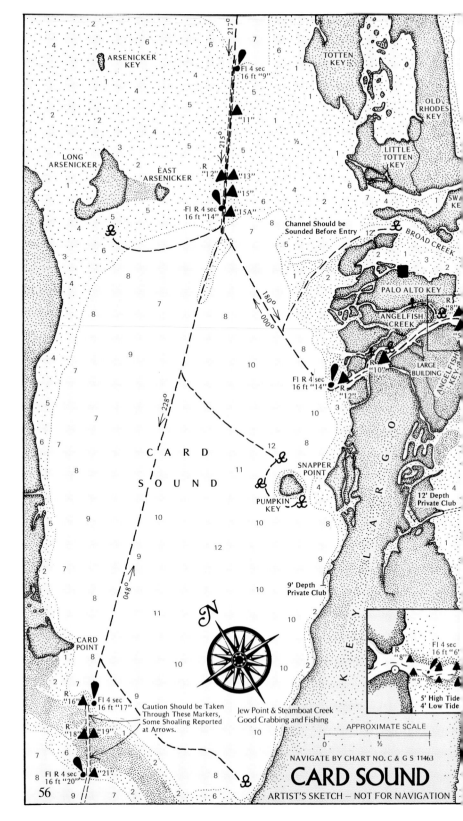

CARD SOUND

ARTIST'S SKETCH — NOT FOR NAVIGATION

NAVIGATE BY CHART NO. C & G S 11463

CARD SOUND

Between Biscayne Bay and Card Sound is a well-marked dredged channel with spoil banks on either side. These markers should be followed very closely, and you should glance over the stern frequently. A current runs through there which can set you over to one side and cause you to go aground. As you come out of the channel, the last marker you pass is another 4-second flashing red, No. "14".

From here you can swing to the west and anchor alongside of Long Arsenicker Key. This anchorage gives you 5 or 6 ft. of water and shelter from north and westerly winds. The Key is a bird nesting area. Don't go ashore without first checking with the park rangers.

Another anchorage is marked off Swan Key in Broad Creek.

Unless you have a very shallow draft boat, Broad Creek is difficult to enter, but it's good exploring in a dinghy.

Farther south there are several good anchorages at Angelfish Creek, either in the mouth of the creek, or in the entrances to South Broad Creek or Middle Creek. You have to anchor Bahama style.

Angelfish Creek has a reported depth of 4½ ft., although with local knowledge boats of 5 ft. draft go through on high tide. Boats coming down from Miami on the outside can enter the waterway here with the right timing. It's a good day's sail from either Government Cut or Biscayne Channel.

For those who want to leave the waterway and sail in Hawk Channel, Angelfish Creek is the last

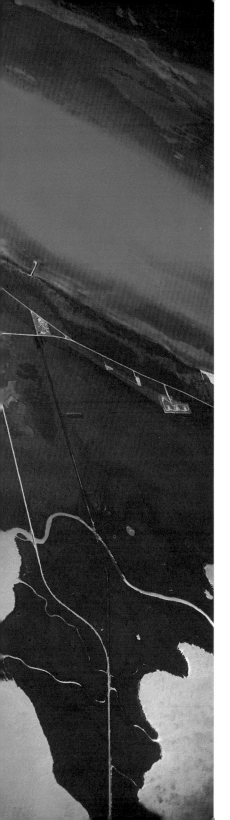

outlet to the ocean until after Upper Matecumbe Key. A detailed chart of Caesar Creek, Broad Creek and Angelfish Creek is on page 63. Charts and information on the outside of Key Largo will be found on page 74.

As the name suggests, there are angelfish in the creek, but it's also a popular fishing spot for grouper and snapper. Except for a deserted shack built on stilts, and a house, reputedly built by the CIA, the Angelfish Creek area is wild and deserted. It's easy to imagine that you're miles from civilization.

During the winter, the small tributaries of Angelfish Creek make excellent places to stay overnight. Anchor with great care because of narrow channels, strong current and rocks on the bottom.

One and a half miles south you come upon the modern residential area of North Key Largo. The contrast between these two worlds demonstrates how the Keys provide something for everyone.

Another good anchorage is around Pumpkin Key on the eastern side of Card Sound. This is a grassy area, so test your anchor well to make sure you're really holding.

This aerial view of the northern tip of Key Largo shows the residential area and the famous Ocean Reef Yacht Club.

Pumpkin Key lies due west of Ocean Reef and civilized North Key Largo, and will soon be developed.

At the bottom of Card Sound there's another good spot to anchor, at Jew Point and Steamboat Creek. Fishing and crabbing are excellent, and you can explore with the dinghy around the ruins of an old bridge. Fishermen should try for snappers, grouper, flounder and trout.

Just beyond Card Point, on the western side, is a channel to Little Card Sound, where you should be very careful. The first marker is No. "17", a flashing 4-second. The last marker on this channel is No. "20", a 4-second red flashing. This is a man-made channel which cuts across a natural channel. Water still flows through the natural channel, causing shoaling at points shown on our diagram.

"Roseate Spoonbills, Backcountry" by Millard Wells

Ocean Reef, a private yacht club with lavish facilities lies to the southwest of Angelfish Creek on the ocean side of Key Largo.

The Card Sound Bridge links the mainland with Key Largo.

Caesar's Creek has a 5 ft. depth at high tide.

Broad Creek is used, primarily by small power boats, as a pass between Card Sound and the Gulf Stream.

Angelfish Creek, seen from Card Sound, is last crossover spot for large boats from the Inland Waterway to the ocean side until after passing Upper Matecumbe. Small boats can cross at Cross Key Canal, Key Largo.

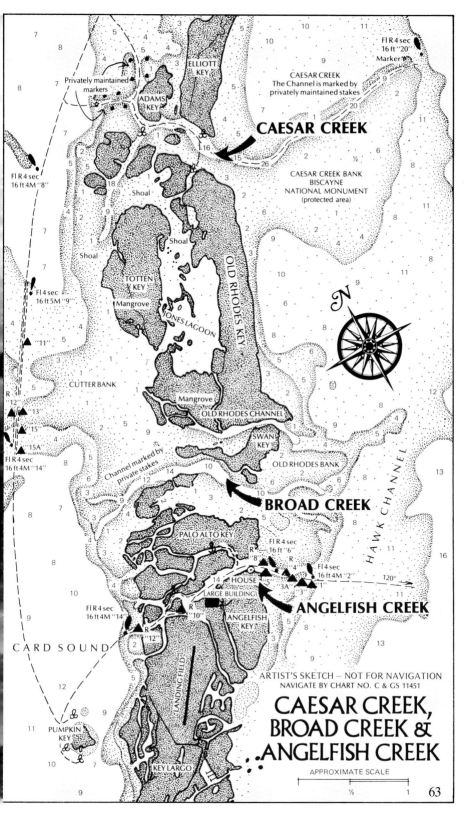

CAESAR CREEK

CARD SOUND

ARTIST'S SKETCH – NOT FOR NAVIGATION
NAVIGATE BY CHART NO. C & GS 11451

CAESAR CREEK, BROAD CREEK & ANGELFISH CREEK

APPROXIMATE SCALE

63

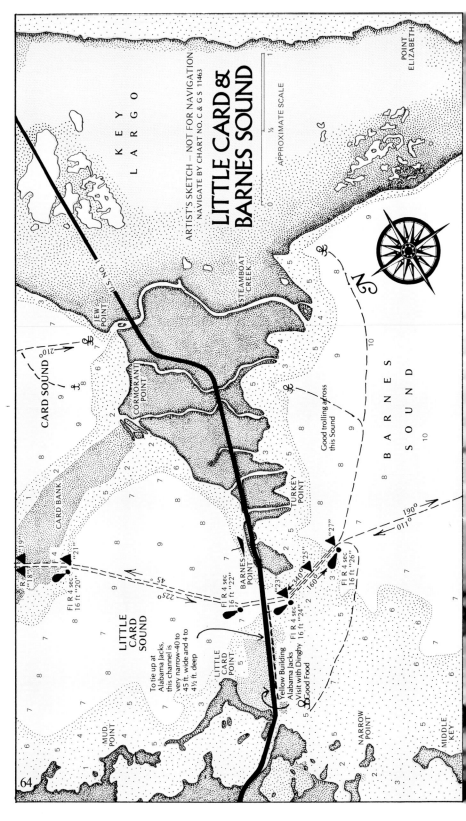

LITTLE CARD &
BARNES SOUND

ARTIST'S SKETCH — NOT FOR NAVIGATION
NAVIGATE BY CHART NO. C & G S 11463

APPROXIMATE SCALE

KEY LARGO

STEAMBOAT CREEK

POINT ELIZABETH

CARD SOUND

CORMORANT POINT

BARNES SOUND

CARD BANK

Good trolling across this Sound

TURKEY POINT

LITTLE CARD SOUND

R "19"
Fl R 4 sec. 16 ft "20"
F 4 "21"

Fl R 4 sec. 16 ft "22"

BARNES POINT

"23"

"27"

"25"

Fl R 4 sec. 16 ft "24"

Fl R 4 sec. 16 ft "26"

To tie up at Alabama Jacks, this channel is very narrow—40 to 45 ft. wide and 4 to 4½ ft. deep

Yellow Building
Alabama Jacks
Visit with Dinghy
Good Food

LITTLE CARD POINT

MUD POINT

NARROW POINT

MIDDLE KEY

64

LITTLE CARD &
BARNES SOUND

Little Card Sound has a general depth of 7 to 9 ft. until you reach marker No. "22" between Little Card Point and Barnes Point. This is a flashing red 4-second which marks the entrance to the channel under the fixed bridge. The bridge has a 65 ft. clearance for masts.

West of the Card Sound Bridge is a yellow building, which is Alabama Jack's. The atmosphere and local color are worth a detour. Alabama Jack's serves food and beer, but also sells bait and fishing supplies if you prefer to catch your own supper.

As you clear the Card Sound Bridge, swing hard to starboard and follow the narrow channel which will take up to 4½ ft. draft. Stay close to the bridge on the way in and out of this channel.

If your vessel is over 40 ft. long, it's difficult to turn here. You may prefer to go on past marker No. "24" and change your heading for marker No. "26". Both of these are flashing red 4-second markers. When you have cleared the channel by marker No. "26", you can swing west toward Alabama Jack's. Follow your chart for

"ALABAMA" JACK'S

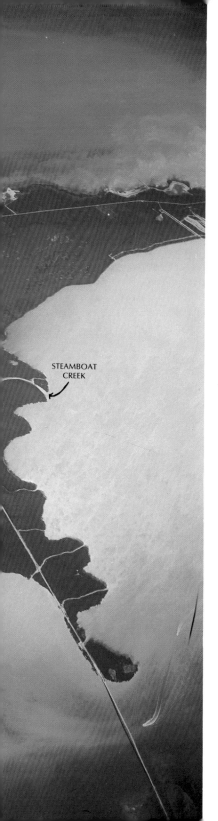

STEAMBOAT
CREEK

depths and our diagram for the route and location.

This area between Card and Barnes Sound is noted for good fishing spots. If you want to anchor and try your luck, swing east after marker No. "26", toward the southern end of Steamboat Creek. We've marked two peaceful anchorages there. Try for snapper, grouper, flounder or trout.

Barnes Sound has a controlled depth of 7 or 8 ft. all the way across. Barnes Sound has several good anchorages. If you want to explore it, use Navigational Chart No. 11463. On the eastern side there are several man-made channels cutting up into Key Largo, where you can motor in with a shallow draft boat. Depths are 6 and 4 ft. To the west is Manatee Bay, named for the sea cows which used to be abundant here. There's still plenty of wildlife, but you're more likely to see racoons than sea cows. The Cormorant Rookeries are a bird refuge. Osprey, sparrow hawks, pelicans and frigate birds share this spot with the cormorants.

Aerial view of Card Sound Bridge shows Steamboat Creek, a good area for crabbing & fishing.

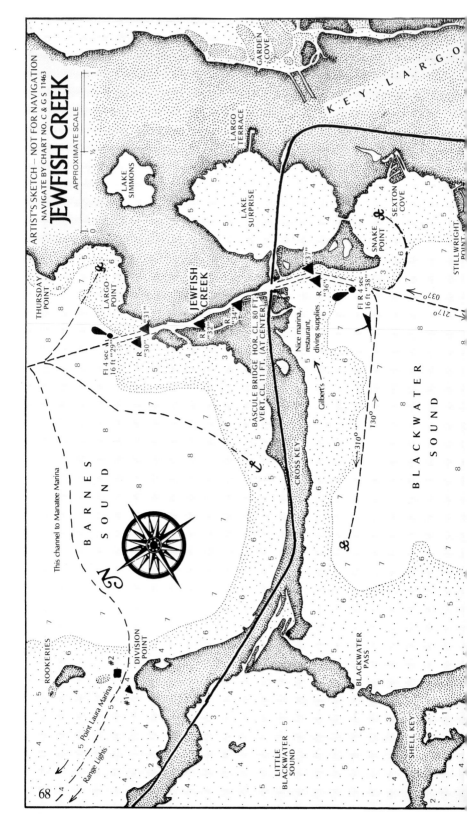

JEWFISH CREEK

BRIDGE NOTE: The Jewfish Creek bridge only
opens on the hour and half hour, Friday, Saturday,
Sunday and Federal Holidays.

From marker No. "26" at the
northern end of Barnes sound, a
heading of 191° will bring you to
Largo Point, and the entrance to
Jewfish Creek. The anchorage
marked at the southern end of
Barnes Sound is well sheltered
from the southeast and westerly
winds, if you get a blow coming
out of those directions. You can
pull up to the lee side of Cross Key
and anchor in 6 or 7 ft. of water.

As you come across Barnes
Sound, it's a little hard to find the
Largo Point entrance. You have to
get pretty close before you can see
the 4-second flash from marker
No. "29". Take a heading for the
easternmost power cable tower,
until you are close enough to see
the marker.

On the western side of Barnes
Sound is the entrance for Manatee
Marina and Point Laura. It's best
to take 3½ ft. in at high tide to be
safe. Manatee Marina is a boat
yard; the moorings and Point
Laura take transits. The Manatee
Boat Yard is owned by the sailboat
racer and builder, Dave Westfal.
It's a good yard for having work
done on your boat, or you can anchor off the entrance of Manatee
Creek and take your dinghy into
the Cross Key Marina and restaurant for limited supplies.

For local knowledge in this area,
you can call for Joe Gurger on
VHF 16. He and his wife run the
Lange Marina just taken over by

the government. Joe is a member
of the Florida Keys Towing
Association.

The first time I came through
Jewfish Creek, I felt I was finally in
the real everglades. There are high
mangroves on both sides, and
blind corners coming around the
side channels. This passage should
be navigated slowly, as all the
channels in Jewfish Creek have a
depth of 5 to 6 ft. and any blind
corners may bring you on collision
course with another boat.

Most of the time, a 1 or 2 knot
current runs through Jewfish
Creek. As you approach the
bridge, note the direction of the
current, so that you allow plenty of
time if you have to wait to open the
bridge. Bridge tenders in the Keys
are all very polite, as long as you
give them plenty of warning.
Watch for traffic on the other side
of the bridge, to make sure that the
tender is not opening for someone
else. When the house is on the far
side of the bridge, the tender can't
see you, and may close on you
unless you give a good strong signal. Always give a proper signal
and stay well to starboard when
navigating these narrow passages.

At Jewfish Creek there are
overhead cables by the bridge,
with an authorized clearance of 80
ft. from the water. If your mast is
higher than 80 ft. you can't make it
through.

Gilbert's and the restaurant at Jewfish Creek are a good supply and rest stop.

As you go beyond the bridge on the other side of Cross Key, Gilbert's Marina is on the west side.

Now under new management, it has a fantastic Tiki Bar with good Rum Runner Punches and a pool to jump into if you get too hot. They are a full service marina; fuel-tackle-marine store and an excellent stopping point. The fishing is excellent from their dock.

Across Jewfish Creek from Gilbert's is the "Anchorage Resort and Yacht Club" which boasts a full service marina (swimming pool, tennis court, electric power and water) but does not provide fuel. The Anchorage, like Gilbert's monitors VHF Channel 16.

Adjacent to the Anchorage are a restaurant, a convenience store and a boat rental facility.

Coming past the Jewfish Creek Bridge, follow the channel to Marker No. "38". This is a flashing 4-second red marker off Snake Point. From here you can pull into Sexton Cove, anchor and row ashore. Or you can head northwest after Marker No. "38" and anchor at the north end of Blackwater Sound. This is a famous fishing area and you can get fishing supplies at the marinas and shops along the creek.

BLACKWATER SOUND & TARPON BASIN

Blackwater Sound gets its name from the mangrove roots and cypress that make it look black. Bird fanciers should watch for the pink ibis. After entering Blackwater Sound, you can cut to the west and anchor and fish near Blackwater Pass. (See preceding chart.) This is a sheltered anchorage in bad weather. If you swing to the east and anchor in Sexton Cove, give Smoke Point a wide berth.

Toward the southern end of the Sound, there's a marina and anchorage on the east for boats up to 4 ft. of draft. High water is 5 ft. You can take a shallow draft boat or dinghy through Cross Key Canal into Pennekamp Park for snorkeling, scuba diving and fishing. For a description of the park and its regulations, see pages 74 and 75.

To the west of Brush Point, avoiding marker No. "40", you'll find a good anchorage if you get any westerly winds. Blackwater Sound can kick up, making it uncomfortable in a small boat. On the eastern side of Blackwater Sound is the famous Caribbean bar featured in the Humphrey Bogart movie *Key Largo*.

At Dusenbury Creek you cut through into Tarpon Basin. This is another place where you have to navigate, staying to the starboard side of the channel around blind corners and following your markers well. Watch out for large power boats which can come whizzing around a blind corner and take you by surprise. This creek reminds me of "The African Queen", because it's pretty close quarters. Speaking of the African Queen, the original boat used in the movie is at the Holiday Inn on Key Largo oceanside.

With northeasterly or easterly winds, I sail through Dusenbury Creek with the main up. You may startle a few fishermen if you have a 40 footer just coasting along with the main up. You'll see fishing boats tied up along the creek banks; it's a good spot for snapper and grouper.

As you follow the markers into Tarpon Basin, you can cut north just before marker No. "48" for a sheltered anchorage. If you have a shallow enough draft, there are two routes to the Howard Johnson Motel. From marker No. "46A" you can take a heading of 180° to a privately maintained marker. Leave this marker 20 ft. to starboard and take a course straight for the Dock Master's shack. The second route is to go a little south past marker No. "48", and make a wide circle around Tarpon Basin. At Howard Johnson's there's a bulkhead where you can tie up in 3 ft. of water, or you can pick up the float buoys and enter the small basin.

Grouper Creek means exactly what it says; there's good fishing in the creek and Buttonwood Sound. If the weather's clear, you can see right down to the bottom and watch the fish biting the hook. You'll have to anchor in Buttonwood Sound and dinghy in.

Buttonwood Sound has a good anchorage at Sunset Cove. With a larger boat, anchor off and row ashore. Four blocks away there's a shopping center with a big grocery store, drug stores and a bank. You can even get the "New York Times" and the "Wall Street Journal", this far away from nowhere.

Tips on Diving in the Keys

Diving Equipment:

In my experience, this is the amount and type of equipment charterers have found to be right:

1. Wide vision diving mask (available with prescription lens)
2. Lens fog liquid
3. Large diameter snorkel
4. Good pair rubber or cloth gloves
5. Light fins (rocket type for scuba only)
6. Long sleeved jersey shirt for protection against sun and coral
7. Gig or three prong pole spear
8. 18×18-in. small mesh net bag for shells
9. Diving flag
10. Diving float to hold flag or marker buoy
11. 6-ft. air mattress or swimming float
12. Small bottle ammonia for stings

Diving Tips:

1. Always display diving flag and be on the alert for small, fast power boats.
2. If you haven't snorkeled before, start on a beach or in shallow water where you can stand up to adjust equipment.
3. Tie 15 feet of very light line to a swimming float. Snorkel with float trailing behind. You are free to dive, but can still be securely out of the water in case of fatigue or danger.
4. Don't wear shiny objects which can attract unwanted or dangerous fish.
5. Don't dive in murky water or very early in the morning or late in the afternoon.

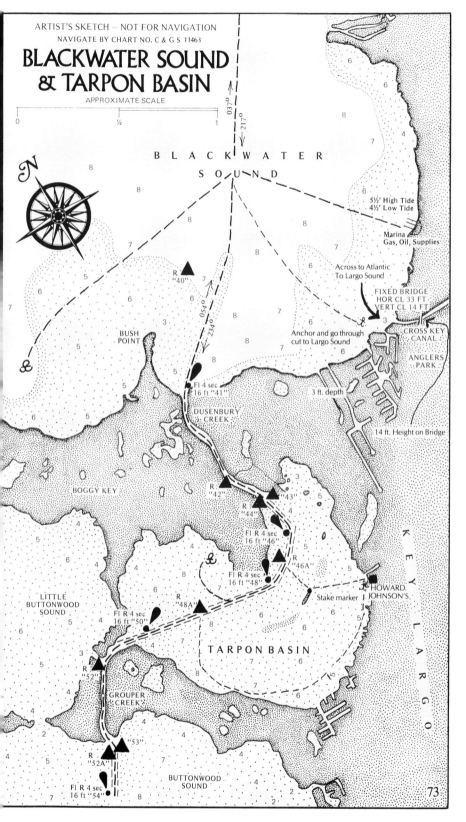

ARTIST'S SKETCH — NOT FOR NAVIGATION
NAVIGATE BY CHART NO. C & G S 11463

BLACKWATER SOUND
& TARPON BASIN

APPROXIMATE SCALE

B L A C K W A T E R

S O U N D

5½' High Tide
4½' Low Tide

Marina
Gas, Oil, Supplies

Across to Atlantic
To Largo Sound

FIXED BRIDGE
HOR CL 33 FT
VERT CL 14 FT

R
"40"

BUSH
POINT

Anchor and go through
cut to Largo Sound

CROSS KEY
CANAL

ANGLERS
PARK

3 ft. depth

Fl 4 sec
16 ft "41"

DUSENBURY
CREEK

14 ft. Height on Bridge

BOGGY KEY

R
"42"

"43"

R
"44"

Fl R 4 sec
16 ft "46"

R
"46A"

Fl R 4 sec
16 ft "48"

HOWARD
JOHNSON'S

Stake marker

LITTLE
BUTTONWOOD
SOUND

R
"48A"

Fl R 4 sec
16 ft "50"

K
E
Y

L
A
R
G
O

TARPON BASIN

R
"52"

GROUPER
CREEK

"53"

R
"52A"

BUTTONWOOD
SOUND

Fl R 4 sec
16 ft "54"

KEY LARGO

To reach the Atlantic side of Key Largo, you can come down from Miami through Government Cut or Biscayne Channel into Hawk Channel; or, if your draft is amenable, take the Inland Waterway and come out at Angelfish Creek. South of Angelfish Creek you pass the world famous Ocean Reef Yacht Club and the Garden Cove Marina just inside Rattlesnake Key. Their entance is kind of shallow, but they stand by on VHF 68.

From Broad Creek to Molasses Reef all the ocean floor under Hawk Channel is the John Pennekamp Coral Reef State Park and Key Largo Coral Reef Marine Sanctuary. Park headquarters are on Largo Sound, which is entered through South Sound Creek, south of El Radabob Key. See the following page for a detail chart of South Sound Creek and Largo Sound.

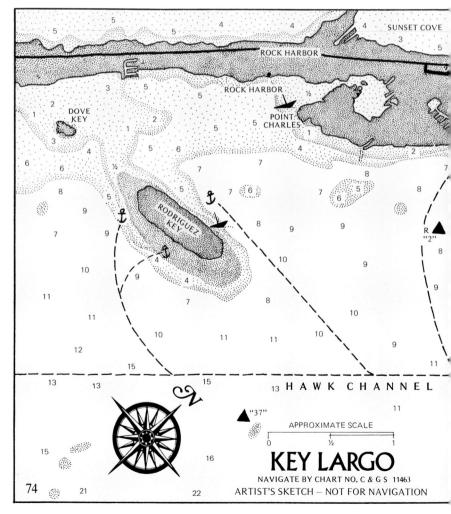

SUNSET COVE

ROCK HARBOR

ROCK HARBOR

DOVE KEY

POINT CHARLES

RODRIGUEZ KEY

R "2"

HAWK CHANNEL

"37"

APPROXIMATE SCALE

0 ½ 1

KEY LARGO

NAVIGATE BY CHART NO. C & G S 11463

ARTIST'S SKETCH – NOT FOR NAVIGATION

John Pennekamp State Park is a living coral reef. You're welcome to snorkel, scuba dive or fish off the reef, but you must observe park regulations, which are enforced strictly. Always display a diving flag. Don't take any samples of coral, rock or shells. If you want souveniers, go to park headquarters.

To explore the reef, use C&GS Chart No. 11462. Toward the north, at Carysfort Reef is a Sea Garden. South of the reef is a stag horn coral. Southwest of this is "Captain Tom's Wreck". There's a lot of heavy coral inshore.

Near The Elbow there are two wrecks, marked by the Elbow "K" marker. Just to the Southwest of the marker is "The Christ

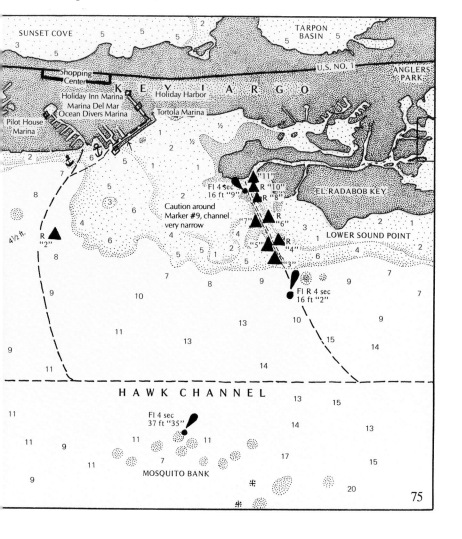

Shallow spot

Anchorage

Anchorage

RODRIGUE

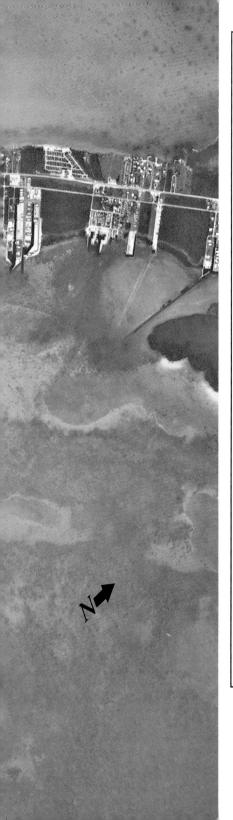

These are some of the diving equipment and service shops in the Key Largo area.

DIVE CHARTERS & SERVICES

ADMIRAL 1, MM 100, 451-1114
Capt. Bill Gordon, POB 0113, Key Largo, 33037

AMERICAN DIVING HEAD-QUARTERS, MM 106, 451-0037
Capt. Harry Keitz, Rt. 1, Box 274-C, Key Largo, 33037

ATLANTIS DIVE CENTER, MM 106.5, 451-3020
Capt. Spencer Slate, 51 Garden Cove, Key Largo, 33037

CORAL REEF PARK COMPANY, MM 102.5, 451-1621
Capt. Mike Bowman, POB 13-M, Key Largo, 33037

DIVER'S OUTLET, MM 105.9, 451-0815
105910 Overseas Hwy., Key Largo, 33037

DIVER'S WORLD, MM 100, MM 99.5, MM 96.5, 451-3200
Capt. Corky Toth, POB 1663, Key Largo, 33037

FINZ UNDERWATER PHOTO CENTER, MM 99.8, 451-3640
99850 Overseas Hwy., Key Largo, 33037

FLORIDA KEYS DIVE CENTER, MM 90.5, 852-4599
Capt. Tom Timmerman, POB 391, Tavernier, 33070

FRINK PHOTOGRAPHIC, MM 102.5, 451-3737
POB 2720, Key Largo, 33037

This aerial photo shows good anchorages on either side of Rodriguez Key. Note the shallow western end. Photo courtesy of N.O.A.A.

of the Deep", a 13 ft. bronze statue in 30 ft. of water. Here, as elsewhere in the park, there are small buoys marking shallow areas. When we cruise with a charter group, we generally anchor nearby and let the charterers discover the statue for themselves. It's a beautiful and awesome sight.

Mosquito Bank, where you'll find coral gardens and coral heads, has a big marker. At Molasses Reef, the most fascinating thing to me is the giant coral heads. They stand in 25 ft. of water, but some of them come up so high you can stand on them and have your head above water.

Some of the fish you'll see on the reef are white grunts, porkfish, sergeants majors, parrotfish, and queen, black and French angelfish. The four-eyed butterfly fish has a strange design on its tail which looks like an eye. There are numerous wrecks, such as the M.V. Brentwood, sunk in 40 to 50 ft. of water, which divers can explore. You'll see sea fans, pink tubular sponges, spotted eagle rays and leopard rays. It makes you realize that the Keys are unique: "out islands" and coral reefs, but still part of the continental United States.

Heading south down Hawk's Channel, leave Mosquito Bank Light to port, and start looking for a No. "2" red daymarker, using your chart as a guide. When the marker bears northwest, leave it to starboard and swing toward the north. You'll see a long, narrow bank on the starboard side of the

At low water you can carry 4.9" ft. into Best Western, Key Largo. There are several large fishing boats running out of this canal; be prepared to give them a wide berth. Holiday Inn Marina is at the end of the canal.

From these marinas you can walk over to a large shopping center where you can pick up supplies. Large shopping centers are not as expensive as marina shops, and have fresh meat and vegetables.

Many people on my character take advantage of the numerous commercial facilities offered at Key Largo. Guided diving or fishing trips, sail boat rentals and rides on the glass bottomed boat. This boat is called the "Key Largo Princess" and takes up the whole channel. Not to mention Gus Boulis's new gambling boat, "Paradise." She's 92 ft. long and 25 ft. wide. So it's wise to listen on the radio for their call when they're coming and going out of the canal. For reservations call Joel the dockmaster on Channel 16, at Key Largo Harbor, he can give you all the information you need. They have a nice boat yard there if you need hauling out. For some bargains, you can call "Strictly Marine" for new and used parts. Other things to see are the Treasure Museum and the Book Nook for reading material. You will see "Witt's End," a fine charter ketch tied up in front of Coconuts, a good spot for food and rum.

LARGO SOUND

Largo Sound is a delightful place to pull in after diving and snorkeling on John Pennekamp Reef. The first marker is No. "2," a 4-second red flashing light. The channel through is 6 ft. deep.

Red marker No. "2," at the mouth of South Sound Creek, looks as if you should leave it to port coming in. If you do, you may go aground. Leave it to starboard; the good water is on the port side.

Entrance into Largo Sound is through a spoil area; watch your markers carefully. Once you pass markers "22" and "23," you'll see the old Tahiti Village Marina which has been taken over by a private marine research institute called the Koblic Marine Center, where they study marine science, and the Jules Under Sea Lodge, where you can pay money and spend the night under 30 ft. of water.

Take a mooring in Largo Sound, go in the Dinghy just north of the marina. You can tie up and go to a real nice little seafood restaurant, the "Hideout," which features a food fish fry on Friday nights.

Just southwest of the marina is a nice beach for swimming, etc. Connected to the main land part of the John Pennekamp Park

Pictured above is the old Tahita Village Marina now taken over by a private research company, Koblic Marine Center.

where you can take your dinghy in for limited supplies.

Vessels ar no longer allowed to anchor in Largo Sound, but are required to take one of the State Park moorings located near the southwest end of the sound. The park reports tht these moorings are available to vessels of up to 4½ feet draft. Call on VHF 16 for payment of $11.38. This gives you use of Park Facilities including a pump out station.

Note for sizeable yachts: There is a large sightseeing vessel, The "SAN JOSE", which uses South Sound Creek. She takes up almost all the channel in the tight turns, and you want to stay out of her way. Her sailing times are 0900, 1200, 1500, and her return times are 1100, 1400 and 1700. If you need to get her position, the skipper is usually standing by on 16 VHF radio.

On the previous chart we've indicated marinas and anchorages southwest of Largo Sound.

There are several marinas with 5 ft. of water where you'll find restaurants and boat repairs. Also the Pilot House Marina and Restaurant. With a shallow draft you can go into the Mandalay Marinas.

In good weather you can anchor on either side of Rodriguez Key, where the holding ground is satisfactory. On the north side there is a wreck on the bottom. Be careful not to get you anchor snagged.

Marinas in the Keys

In the Keys, most marinas which accept transient boaters, do so on a first come, first serve basis. However, there are no set rules and it's safest to call ahead for reservations if you can. At the same time, you can ask the dockmaster whether there are any changes in the entrance or approaches to the marina. Privately maintained markers are subject to change without notice or often without indication on the charts.

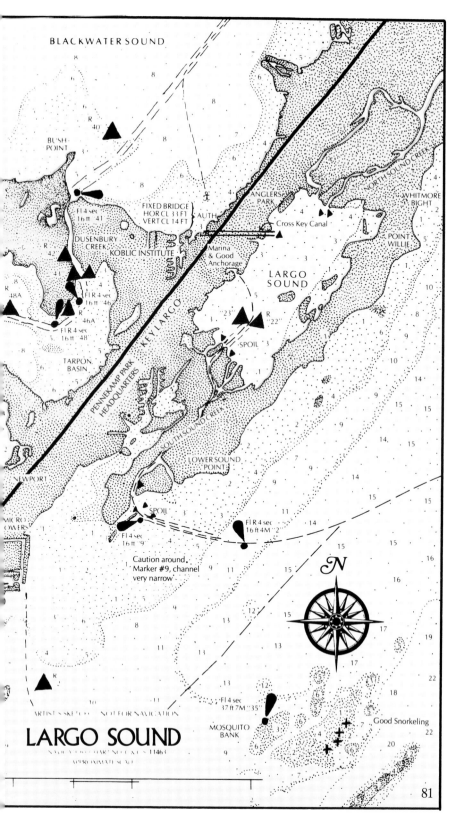

BLACKWATER SOUND

BUSH-
POINT

FIXED BRIDGE
HOR CL 33 FT
VERT CL 14 FT

ANGLERS
PARK

NORTH SOUND CREEK

WHITMORE
BIGHT

AUTH

Cross Key Canal

DUSENBURY
CREEK

KOBLIC INSTITUTE

Marina
& Good
Anchorage

POINT
WILLIE

LARGO
SOUND

Fl R 4 sec
16 ft 46

Fl R 4 sec
16 ft 48

TARPON
BASIN

KEY LARGO

R "22"

"23"

SPOIL

PENNEKAMP PARK
HEADQUARTERS

SOUTH SOUND CREEK

LOWER SOUND
POINT

NEWPORT

MICRO
TOWERS

SPOIL

Fl R 4 sec
16 ft 4M "2"

Fl 4 sec
16 ft "9"

Caution around
Marker #9, channel
very narrow

𝒩

R

Fl 4 sec
37 ft 7M "35"

Good Snorkeling

LARGO SOUND

MOSQUITO BANK

ARTIST'S SKETCH NOT FOR NAVIGATION

NAUTICAL CHART NO. U.S. 11463
APPROXIMATE SCALE

81

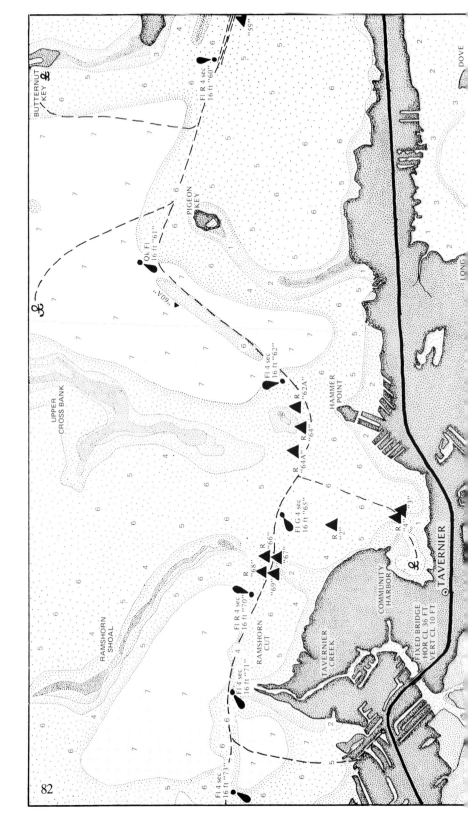

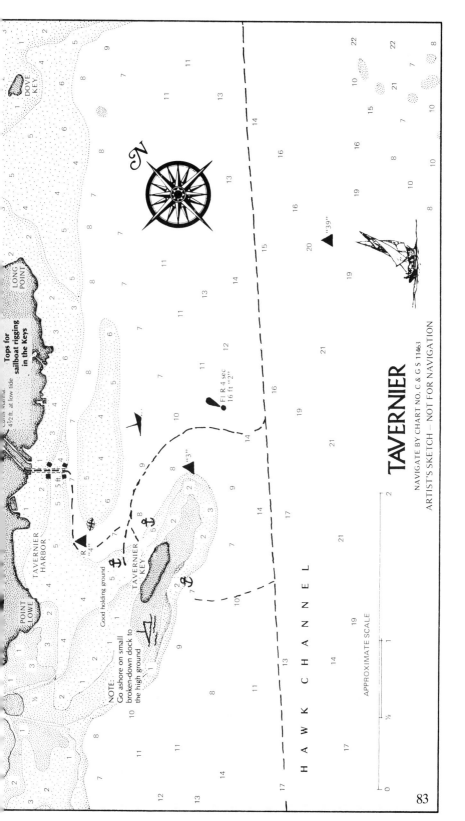

TAVERNIER

NAVIGATE BY CHART NO. C & G S 11463

ARTIST'S SKETCH — NOT FOR NAVIGATION

83

TAVERNIER

Tavernier is the name of both a small Key on the Atlantic side and a town on lower Key Largo. On the Inland Waterway, after rounding Pigeon Key, go through the channel off Hammer Point, watching your depth and your markers. If you draw about 3½ ft. you can swing into Tavernier at Community Harbor, where there's a small marina. The approach is tricky, but the harbor is protected from northerly winds.

A shallow draft boat can also go through Ramshorn Cut and get protection in Tavernier Creek, which separates Key Largo from Plantation Key. Boats with heavier drafts can go past the creek to the northern end of Plantation Key. As you come through these cuts, you may notice cormorants perched on the markers. After diving for fish, the birds must spread their wings to dry before they can fly again.

On the outside, coming down from Rodriguez Key in the Hawk Channel, you'll find anchorage and wrecks to explore off Tavernier Key. The water is fairly shallow on the northern side of Tavernier Key, especially between the Key and Point Lowe. Between Long Point and the entrance to the small channel, there's 6 ft. of water, so if you have a northwesterly wind, you can get some protection there.

Tavernier on the outside and Community Harbor on the inside offer shelter at Tavernier.

"Sailing the Mystic to the Dry Tortugas" by Millard Wells

SWIMMING WITH DOLPHINS

DOLPHINS PLUS

LOCATION:	RESERVATIONS:	SCHEDULE:	REQUIREMENTS:	FEES:
MM 100 Key Largo	(305) 451-1993	Daily: 9 & 11 am 2 & 4 pm	Max. 7 persons Min. age: 12-18 w/paying adult Good swimmer Mask, snorkel & fins optional	$5 observe only $30 per swimmer $150 for 2 scuba divers together

THEATER OF THE SEA

MM 84.5 Islamorada	(305) 664-2431	Sat. thru Thurs. 9:30 am, 12 & 2 pm	Max. 4 persons Min. age: 13 Able to swim Mask, snorkel opt. Fins required Flotation available	$40 per swimmer $11 adult observer $7 ages 4-12 obs. includes shows

HAWK'S CAY RESORT

MM 61 Duck Key	(305) 743-7000 Fla. (800) 432-2242 Nat. (800) 327-7775	Hawk's Cay guests only Daily: 10 am, 1 & 4 pm	Max. 5 persons Min. age: 2 w/parent Swimmer NO snorkel, mask or fins allowed Flotation supplied	$20 - over age 1 $15 - under age w/paying adult FREE observation

DOLPHIN RESEARCH CENTER

MM 59 Grassy Key	(305) 289-1121	Wed. thru Sun. 9:30 & 11 am, 1 & 3 pm	Min. 2/Max. 6 persons Min. age: 5-12 w/adult Confident swimmer Mask, snorkel opt. NO fins allowed Flotation required	$5 observe only $40 per swimmer (includes tour & dolphin lecture)

The Taking of a Florida Lobster:

Sports Fisherman's Lobster season takes place July 20 and 21 each year. The regular open season for lobster is July 26 through March 31.

The National Park Service will enforce the Florida State law for Lobstering. Check for appropriate date information. If you are planning to take lobster, please follow these guidelines:

1. The taking of lobster shall be accomplished by using hands, hand-held nets, bully nets, or in such a manner that individuals may be returned unharmed to the water if not legal length. NO SPEARING OR GIGGING OF LOBSTER PERMITTED.

2. Lobsters that are to be kept must have a carapace length (head, body or front section) of no less than 3 inches and/or a tail length of no less than 5½ inches. AT ALL TIMES LOBSTER MUST REMAIN IN A WHOLE CONDITION. Do not separate tail from body section.

3. The measurement of the carapace shall be determined by beginning at the front most edge of the groove on the boney part between the horns directly above the eyes, then proceeding along the middle of the back to the rear edge of the top part of the carapace. The tail (segmented portion) shall be measured lengthwise along the center of the entire tail until the rearmost extremity is reached: provided, the tail measurement shall be conducted with the tail in a flat, straight position with the tip of the tail closed. The tail measurement shall not include the meat showing from the forward portion of the tail.

4. Any egg-bearing females, regardless of size, shall be returned to the water. Eggs will be found on the underside of the tail portion appearing as opaque berry-like formations and ARE NOT TO BE REMOVED OR MOLESTED.

5. Limit of lobster allowed to be taken: During sportman season, a maximum of six (6) lobsters are allowed per person/per day and no more than twelve (12) lobsters for both days. During the regular season, a maximum of 24 lobsters per boat or vehicle/per day are allowed.

WHEN DIVING FOR LOBSTER..
LOOK FOR THE FEELERS.

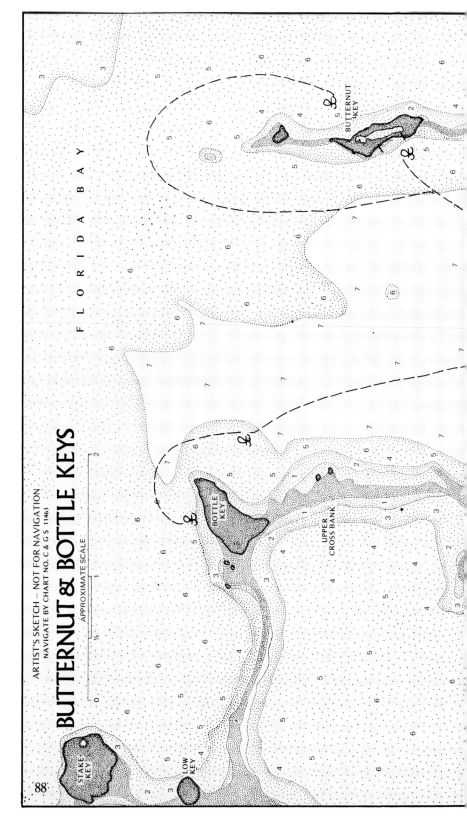

ARTIST'S SKETCH — NOT FOR NAVIGATION.
NAVIGATE BY CHART NO. C & G S 11463

BUTTERNUT & BOTTLE KEYS

APPROXIMATE SCALE

0   ½   1   2

FLORIDA BAY

BUTTERNUT KEY

BOTTLE KEY

UPPER CROSS BANK

STAKE KEY

LOW KEY

88

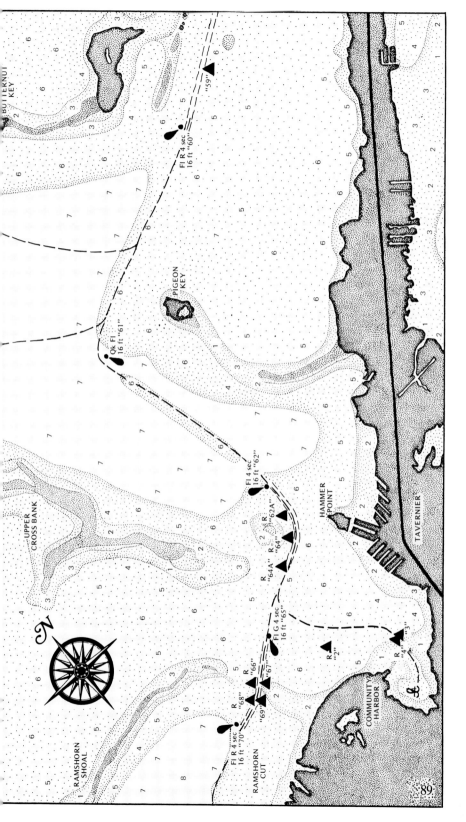

BUTTERNUT
&
BOTTLE KEYS

On the inside route, once you leave Buttonwood Sound, you're in Florida Bay. This is a great sailing area. If you get a good northerly or northeasterly wind, you can sail all of this area. Watch your markers and your draft.

Very seldom do we come through this part of the bay without seeing porpoise, the "sailors' friend", this is a favorite feeding area. Here the sailboat has a real advantage. The porpoise is attracted by the movement or shape of a sailboat hull, especially if it has a green or blue bottom. Porpoise follow the

boat and play about the bow. If porpoise appear while you're fishing, you may as well haul in your lines. The fish lose all interest in feeding and concentrate on escape.

As you approach Pigeon Key, you can swing northwest about halfway between marker No. "60" and Pigeon Key and anchor at Butternut Key.

If the wind blows from the opposite direction, you can go around to the other side, where there's good holding ground in southwesterly winds. If you do go across the western tip of Butternut Key, watch

The two marshy areas on Butternut Key are nesting grounds for birds, landing is prohibited during the nesting season.

carefully for shoaling in that area. Stay off Nest Key Bank to the north of Butternut Key.

In the grassy area around Butternut Key, you'll see small sharks. We call it "shark nursery". These babies are more scared of you than you are of them. They leave when they get to be 2 to 3 ft. long.

Pigeon Key has a lake on the inside which attracts birds and wildlife. Near marker No. "61", you can swing up along Upper Cross Bank to Bottle Key, where there are several protected anchorages. If you like privacy, they're really secluded, yet at night you can still see the lights of civilization. There's a pond on Bottle Key where mallard ducks winter, and the Key is a breeding area for the roseate spoonbill. If you're interested in wildlife you'll find it on small, out-of-the-way mangrove islands. We've seen pink ibis, seagulls, pelicans, several types of osprey and just about every kind of man of war bird. In the Keys you can observe and enjoy nature when you're only 80 miles away from the heart of Miami, with the horns beeping and the cars running and everybody pushing and shoving.

ATLANTIC OCEAN

This is a good aerial shot of both the Florida Bay side and the Atlantic Ocean side

FLORIDA BAY

N

of Tavernier Key. Photo courtesy of N.O.A.A.

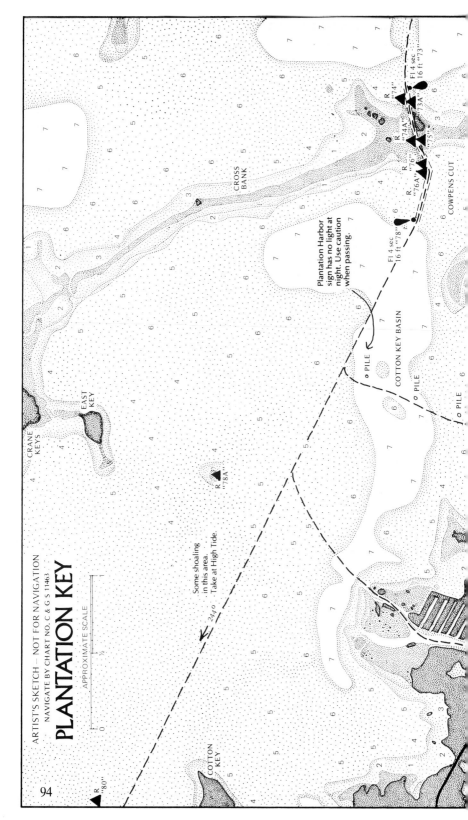

ARTIST'S SKETCH — NOT FOR NAVIGATION
NAVIGATE BY CHART NO. C & G S 11463

PLANTATION KEY

APPROXIMATE SCALE

CRANE KEYS

EAST KEY

R "8A"

COTTON KEY

Some shoaling in this area. Take at High tide.

240

R "80"

CROSS BANK

Plantation Harbor sign has no light at night. Use caution when passing.

COTTON KEY BASIN

PILE

PILE

PILE

COWPENS CUT

Fl 4 sec 16 ft "78"

R "76A"
R "76"
R "75"
R "74A"
R "4"
Fl 4 sec 16 ft "73"

94

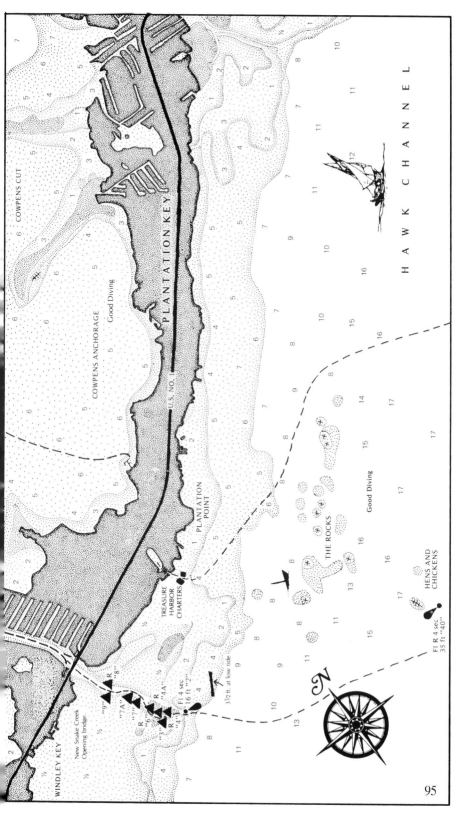

WINDLEY KEY

New Snake Creek
Opening bridge

R "8"
"9"
R "7A"
"6"
R "4"
R "3"
"4A"
Fl 4 sec
16 ft "2"

3½ ft at low tide

TREASURE HARBOR CHARTERS

PLANTATION POINT

COWPENS CUT

COWPENS ANCHORAGE

Good Diving

PLANTATION KEY

U.S. NO. 1

THE ROCKS

Good Diving

HENS AND CHICKENS

Fl R 4 sec.
35 ft "40"

HAWK CHANNEL

N

PLANTATION KEY

On the inside, as you come through the Cowpens Cut, you'll find a lot of small boats right on the edge of the channel. The Cut is fairly deep; you get 5 to 5½ ft. of water at about half tide. Go through with caution; fishermen let their boats drift into the channel to be ready for the mangrove snapper, which runs for the mangroves when it's hooked.

This area is a bird sanctuary. Use your binoculars and camera, but don't land. In addition to the familiar pelicans and seagulls, you'll see blue herons, egrets, white cranes, man-of-war birds and the rare pink ibis. National research headquarters for the Audubon Society are on Plantation Key.

After going through Cowpens Cut, steer 244°. If you want to swing into Cowpens Anchorage, don't cut too short. To the south of Cowpens Cut there's a bar and a submerged wreck. Cowpens Anchorage gets its name from the manatee or seacow. Early settlers used manatees for food, and kept them enclosed here until they were needed. Manatees are now a protected species. The singer Jimmy Buffett sponsors a drive to prevent them from being run over by power boats, their only unnatural enemy. So from Stewart on the intercoastal waterway, down through the keys, look out for these graceful creatures.

About halfway between markers No. "78" and "78A", you'll pick up the piles for Plantation Harbor Resort. I usually pass the first pile, and then follow them in on the port side. The resort has an

Plantation Marina's well-planned docks are protected by a breakwater.

easy 5½ ft. of water going in, and 6 to 7 ft. alongside the dock. Facilities at Plantation Harbor include a restaurant, dockside lounge with live entertainment and dancing, swimming pool, tennis courts, gift shop, laundromat and dock master Captain; **Bell** You can fish from the breakwater or docks. If you plan to stop here, it's best to call ahead.

Just off marker No. "78A", you can swing south into Snake Creek. Two small piles mark the creek entrance. There are two marinas in Snake Creek with 3½ to 4 ft. of water. The creek has a strong current, and there's an open bridge at the mouth, so it's necessary to make your turn properly when entering the canals where the marinas are located.

The new Snake Creek Bridge Channel has only 3½ ft. of water on the Atlantic Ocean at low tide, so proceed with caution.

Down from Plantation at Snake Creek is the Florida Keys House Boat Rentals and Florida Keys Sailing School. You can't go wrong with Capt. Zrett and his son; they know the Keys' waters very well. Call Geary at 305 664-4009.

If you want to overnight in the area, go on to Windley Key or Islamorada. The area between The Rocks and The Hens and Chickens Reef is a good place for diving and snorkeling. The wreck marked on the chart is difficult to find.

A GOLD
"DUBLOON"

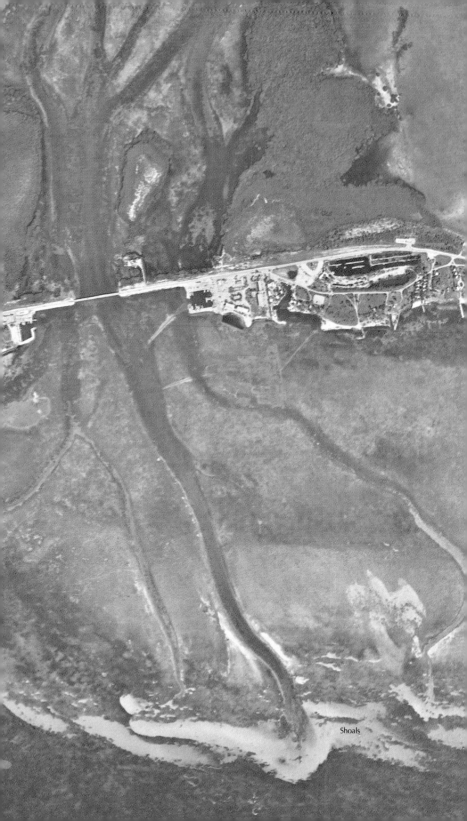

Shoals

Now that the Indian Key Bridge is closed, all traffic will have to pass through the new Snake Key Bridge, except small power boats. All sailboats going from the Gulf to the Atlantic side can take any of these 4 crossings: Angelfish Creek, Snake Creek, Channel #5 or Moser Channel.

Angelfish at Key Largo has no mast restriction, but there's a 5 ft. draft at high tide. Snake Creek has an open bridge but a shoaled depth of 3 ft. on the Atlantic side at low tide. Channel #5 at Lower Matecumbe has a 65 ft. mast limit and a 6 ft. draft. Moser Channel has a fixed bridge below and allows for a marathon mast height of 65 ft. and a draft of 6 ft.

In the Plantation area, if you are looking for a good charter boat, check in with Treasure Harbor Charters. Captain Pete and Pam run a nice little charter company and have a few transit slips. You can reach them on VHF 16 or 852-2458. It is also within walking distance of Jammers for rum and a fine little bakery in Treasure Village.

On page 100 is the Lorelei restaurant and marina. It's a good place to anchor and watch the sunset with the band Big Richard and the Extenders.

Shown here are the intricate shoals that lie southwest of Windley Key. Aerial photo courtesy of N.O.A.A.

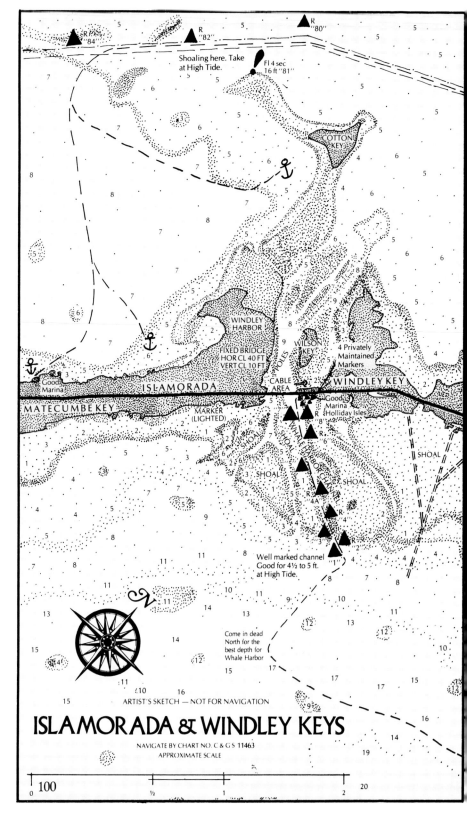

ISLAMORADA & WINDLEY KEYS

NAVIGATE BY CHART NO. C & G S 11463

APPROXIMATE SCALE

ISLAMORADA & WINDLEY KEYS

There are plenty of recreational facilities on either side of Whale Harbor, which separates Windley Key from Islamorada on Upper Matecumbe. The area is famous for bonefishing, and you can hire a guide, rent a boat or buy tackle. The reefs are worth seeing; you can view them from a glass bottom boat or rent diving equipment for an underwater look. On Windley Key is the Theater of the Sea, which has porpoise and sea lion shows, plus tanks of fish, including sharks. Islamorada is the third largest city in the Keys, and a good place to reprovision or take a shore break to visit art galleries, shop for resort wear or dine in one of the many excellent restaurants.

If you are coming from the northeast on the Inland Waterway, pass marker No. "84", and swing to the southeast. This is a fine, sheltered anchorage for boats up to 4½ ft. draft. Upper Matecumbe Key and Shell Key provide shelter from either north, northeast or south, southeast winds.

There are two marinas in this area. The Islamorada Yacht Basin offers facilities for yachts and small boats, while Max's provides marine repair and haul out service as well as dockage.

If you are traveling on the out-

Windley Key (pictured) and Islamorada are a center for land and water recreation with excellent marine facilities. More docks have been added on the eastern Bulkhead.

side, in Hawk Channel, Windley key is a good place to put in. A very strong current runs through Whale Harbor Channel. Be sure to allow for the set when entering Holiday Isle Marina on the northern side of Whale Harbor. The Marina has a 5-ft. channel and 8 ft. of water alongside. Facilities include beach, pool, several restaurants and an open air Tiki bar which serves the best Rum Runner Punch on the eastern shore. There's a great restaurant in the hotel called the Horizon. You can also fuel up your vessel with gas or diesel. It's wise to call for reservations ahead of time, because of the limited transient facilities. Ask for Kay Carter, dockmaster of the marina. She's very helpful.

Charter fishing boats tie up on the northwest side of the dock, where they sell the day's catch. If you've been trolling Hawk's Channel with no luck, walk over and pick up some fresh fish for supper.

For more island treats, visit the neat little tropical bakery in the holiday isle complex; for some mango bread, key lime pie, and banana cake. From here, if you throw a rock real hard, you will hit the mysterious beach of Kokomo, where everybody wants to go, mentioned in one of the latest pop songs. This marina is an excellent facility, owned by Mr. Joe Roth, famous Keys entrepreneur.

"Alligator Light off Islamorada" by Millard Wells

MATECUMBE KEY & STEAMBOAT CHANNEL

As you approach Steamboat Channel, keep the shoal areas well in view. The chart on pages 104 and 105 indicates two areas, just past marker No. "80", which are visible at high tide. The channel is 5 ft. deep, but the sand bars shift, so navigate carefully if you draw 4ft. or more.

Once you pass through Steamboat Channel, you're in Lignumvitae Basin, which is a fairly deep and broad expanse of water. During the lobster season, watch out for traps and floats in this area. Shell Key and Lignumvitae Key, both Government owned are an interesting contrast. Shell Key almost disappears at high water, while Lignumvitae is the highest elevation in the Keys. It also has the tallest trees, including the "tree of life" for which it's named. Wood of the Lignumvitae is so heavy that it sinks in water, but mahogany, once the most common tree in the Keys was popular with Bahamian ship builders. On the other keys, the hardwood forest have all been cut, but Lignumvitae gives you an idea of what the Keys were like when the Spaniards first sighted them.

On the northwest side of Lignumvitae Key there is an anchorage where you can get some shelter from northeasterly or easterly winds. A strong current runs through here, but if you should have a shallow draft, you get in close to shore near the point where the current splits. Another good anchorage is Matecumbe Bight, south of the Bowlegs Cut Channel. This offers good holding ground and shelter from east and southeast winds.

From the outside, north of Teatable Key is a marina with 4½ ft. of water on the approach. Indian Key, at the mouth of the channel, was once the home base for a gang of wreckers and salvagers who were notorious for trying to "rescue" boats which were not in need of help.

The chart on page 104 shows Indian Key, which was a notorious shipwrecker's colony in the mid 1800's. This colony was destroyed in an Indian attack in August of 1842, and all that now remains is scattered ruins.

For an underwater adventure, head south from Indian Key about 1¼ nautical miles, and you will spy the mooring buoys marking the final resting spot of the Spanish Galleon *SAN PEDRO* lying in 18 feet of water. On this site can be identified the typical characteristics of an ancient shipwreck; anchors, ballast stones and cannons. This will be excellent snorkeling for the entire family.

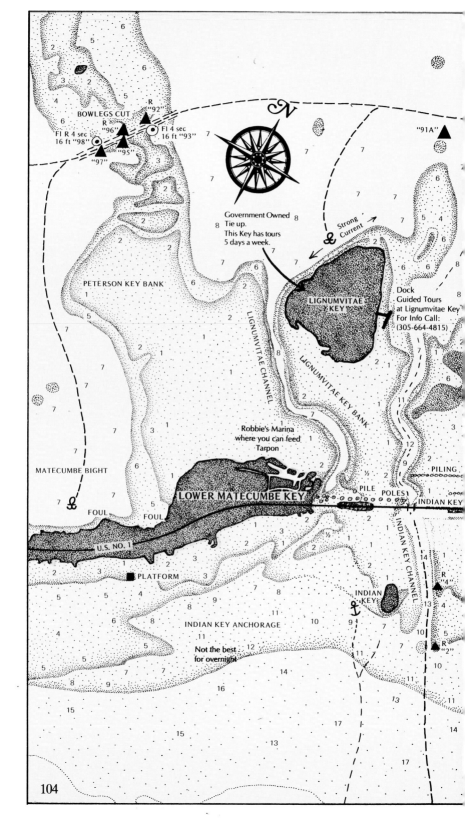

N

BOWLEGS CUT

R "92"

R "96"

Fl R 4 sec 16 ft "98"

Fl 4 sec 16 ft "93"

"95"

"97"

"91A"

Government Owned
Tie up.
This Key has tours
5 days a week.

Strong Current

PETERSON KEY BANK

LIGNUMVITAE KEY

Dock
Guided Tours
at Lignumvitae Key
For Info Call:
(305-664-4815)

LIGNUMVITAE CHANNEL

LIGNUMVITAE KEY BANK

MATECUMBE BIGHT

Robbie's Marina
where you can feed
Tarpon

PILING

PILE POLES

INDIAN KEY

LOWER MATECUMBE KEY

FOUL

FOUL

U.S. NO. 1

INDIAN KEY CHANNEL

PLATFORM

R "4"

INDIAN KEY ANCHORAGE

INDIAN KEY

R "2"

Not the best
for overnight

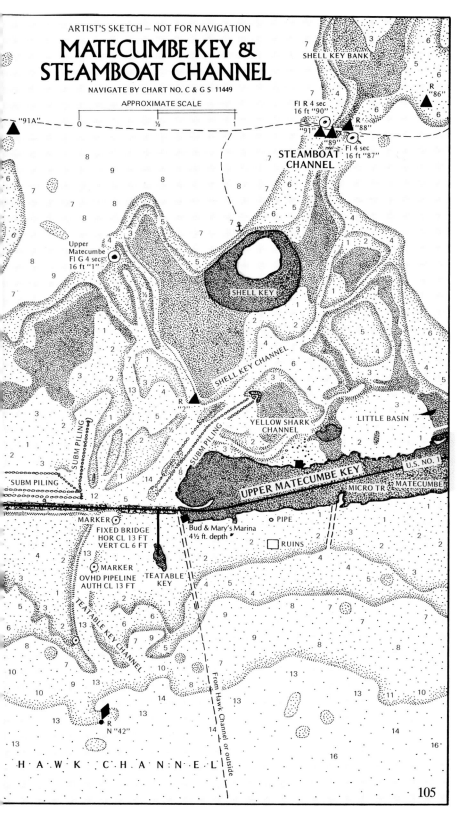

ARTIST'S SKETCH – NOT FOR NAVIGATION

MATECUMBE KEY &
STEAMBOAT CHANNEL

NAVIGATE BY CHART NO. C & G S 11449

APPROXIMATE SCALE

0   ½   1

"91A"

SHELL KEY BANK

R "86"

Fl R 4 sec
16 ft "90"

R "88"

"91"

"89"

Fl 4 sec
16 ft "87"

STEAMBOAT
CHANNEL

Upper
Matecumbe
Fl G 4 sec
16 ft "1"

SHELL KEY

SHELL KEY CHANNEL

R "2"

YELLOW SHARK
CHANNEL

LITTLE BASIN

SUBM PILING

SUBM PILING

"SUBM PILING

UPPER MATECUMBE KEY

U.S. NO. 1

MATECUMBE

MICRO TR

MARKER

FIXED BRIDGE
HOR CL 13 FT
VERT CL 6 FT

Bud & Mary's Marina
4½ ft. depth

PIPE

RUINS

MARKER

OVHD PIPELINE
AUTH CL 13 FT

TEATABLE
KEY

TEATABLE KEY CHANNEL

R
N "42"

Front Hawk Channel or outside

H A W K   C H A N N E L

105

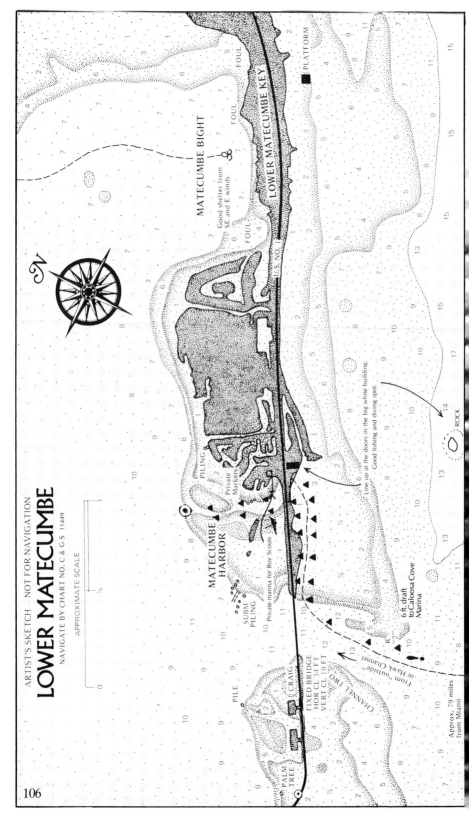

ARTIST'S SKETCH - NOT FOR NAVIGATION

LOWER MATECUMBE

NAVIGATE BY CHART NO. C & G S 11449

APPROXIMATE SCALE

MATECUMBE BIGHT

Good shelter from SE and E winds

LOWER MATECUMBE KEY

U.S. NO. 1

PLATFORM

FOUL
FOUL
FOUL

MATECUMBE HARBOR

PILING

Private Markers

SUBM PILING

Private marina for Boy Scouts

Line up at the doors in the big white building.

Good fishing and diving spot.

6 ft. draft to Caloosa Cove Marina

R

ROCK

CRAIG

FIXED BRIDGE
HOR CL 34 FT
VERT CL 10 FT

CHANNEL TWO

From "outside" or Hawk Channel

Approx. 79 miles from Miami

PILE

PALM TREE

106

LOWER MATECUMBE

To the southwest is a marina run by Sam Wampler called Florida's National High Adventure Sea Base, which is a subsidiary of the Boy Scouts of America. This marina is not open to the public.

However, Caloosa Cover Marina, which is open to the public, is located right across the highway on the outside. After you pass Alligator Reefs Light in Hawk Channel, start looking to starboard for the Channel 2 bridge. The approach to Caloosa Cove Marina is well marked, but you should watch the tide. There's a strong current through Channel 2 bridge, which

can set you over just as you turn the marks which run parallel to the highway. This marina offers boat repairs and has good charter fishing facilities.

To get to the diving spot off Lower Matecumbe, line up the doors so you can see through the big white building coming in from Hawk Channel. Keep going until you get near the dark rocks. It's a great spot.

On the Eastern head of Lower Matecumbe there's Robbie's marina where for 2 bucks you can feed fish to the wild tarpon. It's a land or small boat trip, but well worth it.

The picture above shows the easy entrance into Caloosa Cove Marina on the southwestern tip of Lower Matecumbe Key.

LONG KEY

Channel Five, just east of Long Key, is the first good cross-over for large sailboats between Florida Bay and Hawk Channel.

The Channel Five Bridge is fixed; overhead clearance is 65 ft. The old bridge is still there with its span open. Watch the strong current here. Use the radar domes, micro-tower and bridge on Long Key as navigational aids. Once inside, anchor in Jewfish Hole. Fishing here and off Jewfish Bush Banks is very good. To follow the waterway, swing past Old Dan Bank to the Outdoor Resorts of America Marina. The western entrance is 4 ft. deep; there is room for 40-footers on the eastern end of the gas dock. Facilities include tennis, pool, groceries and supplies.

On the outside, you can shelter in Long Key Bight. A saltwater creek, named for writer and sportsman Zane Grey, empties into the Bight and borders Long Key State Park, a 300-acre wilderness area with a sand beach, good campgrounds, tables and grills.

I've been told that when sailing offshore Long Key on a moonlit night, you can hear cries for help from some 100 railroad workers who were swept out to sea in a violent hurricane about 70 years ago. I suspect it takes a few drinks of rum before you can hear them.

"Oceanside, Plantation Key" by Millard Wells

Caloosa Cove
Marina Resort

- Tackle Shop
- Bait & Ice
- Ship's Store
- Restaurant
- Boat Rental
- Gas & Diesel Fuel

- Parts Department
- Motor Repairs
- Mechanic on Duty
- Sailboat Hardware
- Showers & Restrooms
- 32 Berths - 6 Ft. Draft

- 110/220V Electricity
- Overnight Dockage
- Charter Boats
- Back Country Guides
- In/Out Dry Storage for
  Boats to 24 ft.

Sales & Service - Mercury, Mercruiser, OMC Volvo
Exclusive Dealership for - Answer - Penn Yan - SeaCraft - Victoria 18 - Hydrasport

Located Between Mile Markers 73 & 74 • 6 Ft. Marked Channel from Channel Two Bridge

All Phases Open 7 Days - 8 AM to 7 PM

THE ONLY COMPLETE FULL-SERVICE MARINA/RESORT COMPLEX IN THE FLORIDA KEYS

Box 446, Islamorada, Florida 33036
Phone: (305) 664-4455

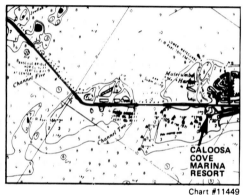

Chart #11449

109

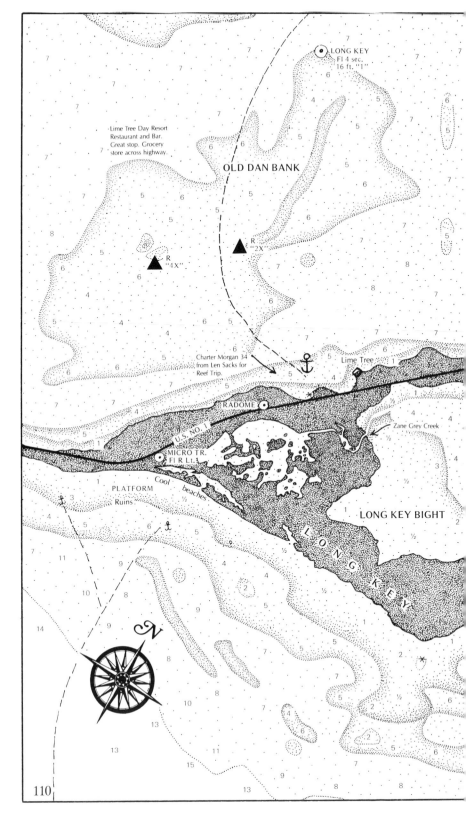

LONG KEY
Fl 4 sec.
16 ft. "1"

Lime Tree Day Resort
Restaurant and Bar.
Great stop. Grocery
store across highway.

OLD DAN BANK

R "2X"

R "4X"

Charter Morgan 34
from Len Sacks for
Reef Trip.

Lime Tree

RADOME

Zane Grey Creek

U.S. NO. 1

MICRO TR.
Fl R Lt.

LONG KEY BIGHT

PLATFORM
Ruins

Cool beaches

LONG KEY

N

110

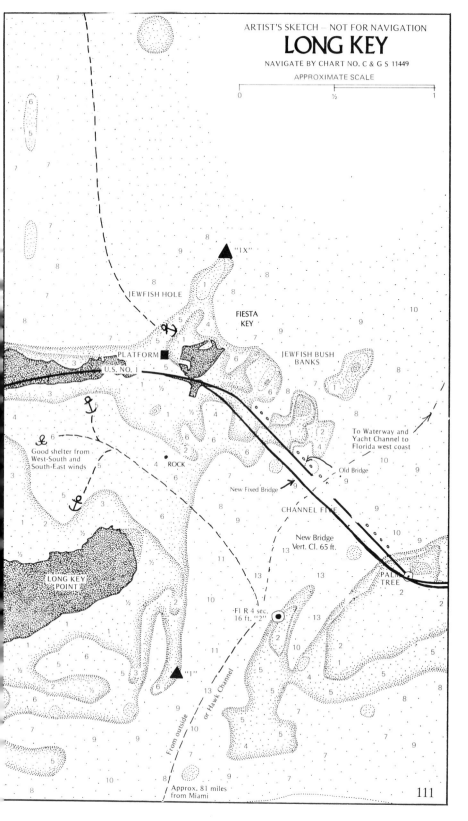

ARTIST'S SKETCH — NOT FOR NAVIGATION
LONG KEY
NAVIGATE BY CHART NO. C & G S 11449

APPROXIMATE SCALE

0 ½ 1

"1X"

JEWFISH HOLE

FIESTA KEY

JEWFISH BUSH BANKS

PLATFORM

U.S. NO. 1

Good shelter from West-South and South-East winds

ROCK

To Waterway and Yacht Channel to Florida west coast

Old Bridge

New Fixed Bridge

CHANNEL FIVE

New Bridge Vert. Cl. 65 ft.

PALM TREE

LONG KEY POINT

Fl R 4 sec. 16 ft. "2"

"1"

From outside or Hawk Channel

Approx. 81 miles from Miami

111

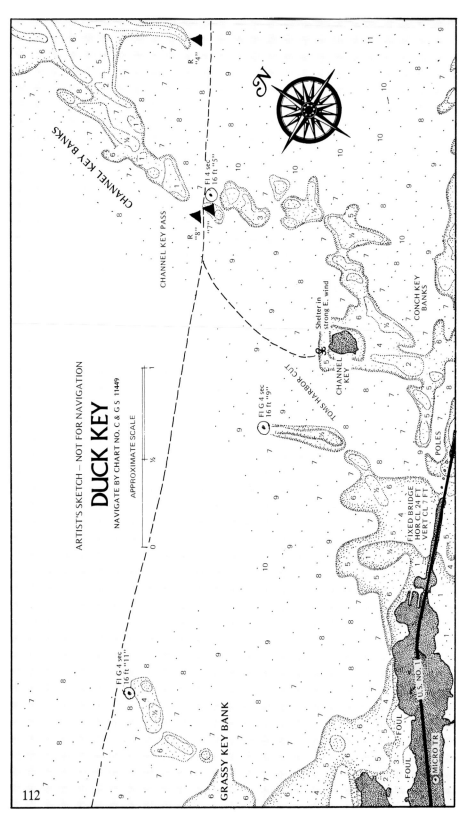

ARTIST'S SKETCH – NOT FOR NAVIGATION

DUCK KEY

NAVIGATE BY CHART NO. C & G S 11449

APPROXIMATE SCALE

CHANNEL KEY BANKS

CHANNEL KEY PASS

R "4"

Fl 4 sec 16 ft "5"

R "8" "7"

N

Shelter in strong E. wind

CONCH KEY BANKS

CHANNEL KEY

TOMS HARBOR CUT

Fl 4 sec 16 ft "9"

POLES

FIXED BRIDGE HOR CL 24 FT VERT CL 7 FT

U.S. NO. 1

Fl 4 sec 16 ft "11"

GRASSY KEY BANK

FOUL

FOUL

FOUL

MICRO TR

112

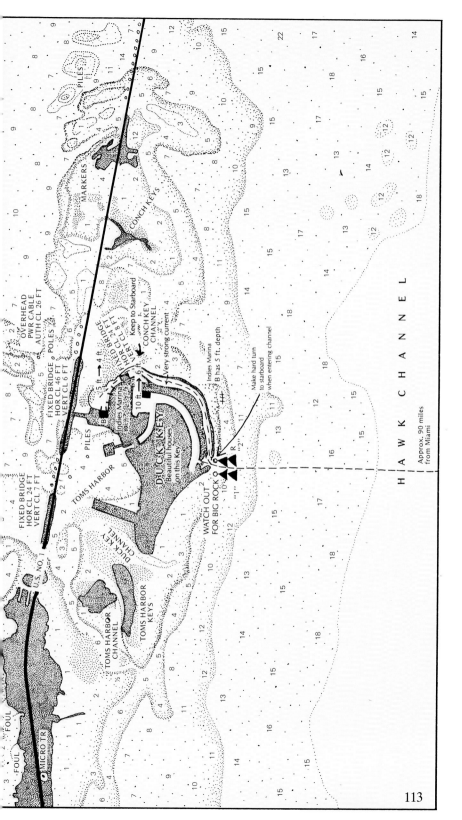

FIXED BRIDGE
HOR CL 24 FT
VERT CL 7 FT

U.S. NO. 1

MICRO TR

FOUL

TOMS HARBOR CHANNEL

TOMS HARBOR KEYS

DUCK KEY CHANNEL

TOMS HARBOR

PILES

FIXED BRIDGE
HOR CL 46 FT
VERT CL 6 FT

OVERHEAD
PWR CABLE
AUTH CL 26 FT

FIXED BRIDGE – POLES

MARKERS

PILES

CONCH KEYS

5 ft. → 4 ft.

FIXED BRIDGE
HOR CL 28 FT
VERT CL 8 FT

Indies Marina

Indies Marina

10 ft → 6 ft

DUCK KEY

Beautiful houses
on this Key.

Keep to Starboard

CONCH KEY
CHANNEL

Very strong current

Indies Marina
B has 5 ft. depth

Make hard turn
to starboard
when entering channel

R "2"

WATCH OUT
FOR BIG ROCK

"1"

HAWK CHANNEL

Approx. 90 miles
from Miami

113

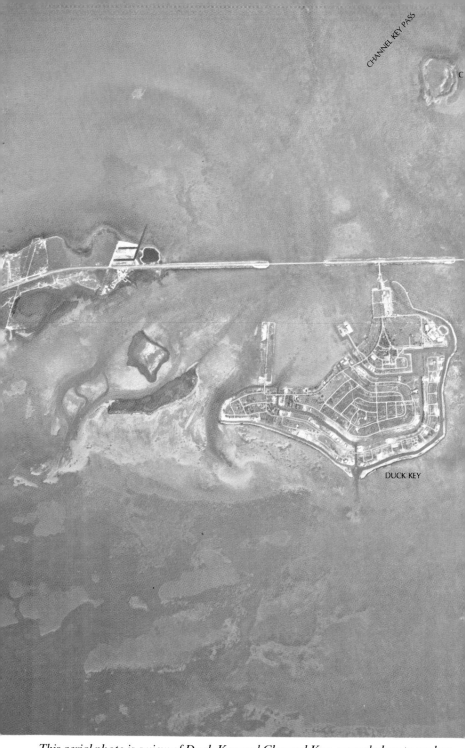

This aerial photo is a view of Duck Key and Channel Key, a good place to anchor N.O.A.A.

when following the waterway through Channel Key Pass. Photo courtesy of

DUCK KEY

If you are coming down on the inside, you can follow the waterway through Channel Key Pass, then swing south and anchor off Channel Key.

Duck Key lies to the seaward of the Overseas Highway, so if you have a sailboat or large powerboat, you'll have to go outside through Channel 5, east of Long Key, and into Hawk's Channel for the nine mile run down to Duck Key.

If you're traveling on the outside, Duck Key is a good place to stop, whether you're heading down to Marathon or coming back up to Miami. It's close to good diving areas, and entrance to its facilities is well-marked. They include the Hawk's Cay Marina, with a fine restaurant, featuring fresh fish, a bar, ships' store and showers, and the Hawk's Cay Inn, a luxury resort which provides swimming pools, tennis courts and bonefishing guides.

As you enter the mouth of the channel and approach the large rock in the center, turn hard up the channel to the east. A strong tidal rip of about 2½ knots runs through this channel. Follow the channel around to the Hawk's Cay Marina. You'll want to call ahead on VHF Channel 16 and talk to Tony or Mary for directions.

Just to the southwest of of Duck Key, you can pull up into Tom's Harbor, which is close to the highway and offers good holding ground. Watch the current running through the bridge over Tom's Harbor Cut.

With a boat drawing from 2 to 3 ft., you can thread your way through the shallows at Tom's Harbor Key. This must be done in calm weather with good light, but you'll find a sheltered anchorage away from the annoying city lights.

FAT DEER KEY &
GRASSY KEY

Just south of Duck Key lies Grassy Key, where Flipper, the porpoise star, was trained. The Sea School here holds porpoise shows several times a day. A new and interesting service has been added at Grassy Key. If you haven't time to cruise all the way to the Dry Tortugas, call the sea plane base (305) 289-0050. They'll fly you to the Dry Tortugas and supply the equipment, so you can "sight-sea" and snorkel, then fly back the same afternoon. The fare is about $50 per person and ½ price for kids. Crawl Key, to the west, is named for the "corrals" or "kraals," where sea turtles were penned. Sea turtles are rare in the Keys now, but they once formed an important part of the settlers' diet.

Fat Deer is the next large Key. You may see an occasional Key deer on Fat Deer Key, but the wildlife sanctuary for these miniature deer is farther west, on Big Pine and Howe Keys.

If you're cruising on the inside and want a take-it-easy type of life, this is a good area in which to stop for a little out-of-the-way quiet. Once through Grassy Key Bank, you can swing to the south and anchor behind Burnt Point, where boats drawing 3 to 4 ft. can take shelter from east and southeasterly winds on average holding ground.

Further to the west, Bamboo Key is another good place for shelter and anchorage. The eastern side carries about 5 ft. of water, and the western side about 4½ ft.

On the outside, Grassy Key has some excellent beaches on the southern side. If you pass Grassy Key in clear weather, use the micro-tower as a navigational aid.

Fat Deer Key boasts two famous resort areas, Coco Plum Beach and Key Colony Beach. Bone Fish Towers, a tall white building, is a good landmark and navigational aid. There's a marina just to the starboard as you enter the channel. But, unfortunately it is now a private condominium.

For the visiting yachtsman, there are two nice marinas here. Marathon Inn will take boats with a draft up to 4 ft. and Fantasy Harbour, with a fairly easy entrance, will take boats with a draft up to 6 ft. Both marinas are close to the Marathon airstrip, with daily flights to Key West and Miami. It's a convenient spot to begin or end a cruise when you can't make the full trip. It's a good place to pick up groceries and supplies; just catch a short ride into Marathon.

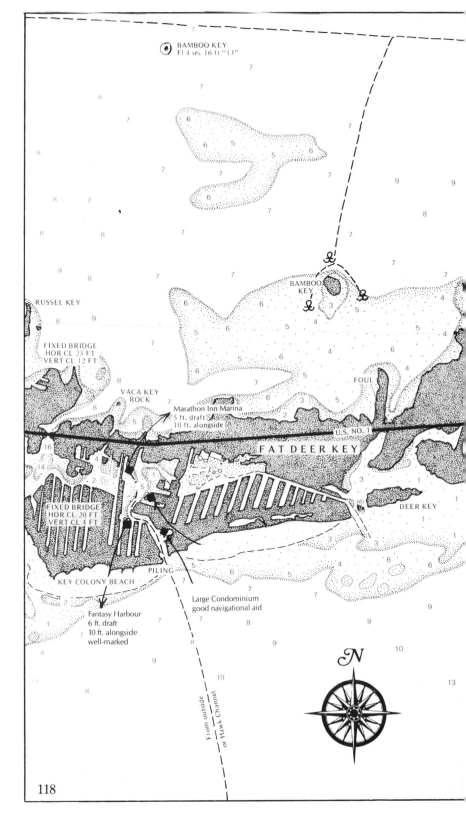

BAMBOO KEY
Fl 4 sec 16 ft "13"

BAMBOO KEY

RUSSEL KEY

FIXED BRIDGE
HOR CL 23 FT
VERT CL 12 FT

VACA KEY
ROCK

Marathon Inn Marina
5 ft. draft
10 ft. alongside

FOUL

U.S. NO. 1

FAT DEER KEY

DEER KEY

FIXED BRIDGE
HOR CL 20 FT
VERT CL 4 FT

KEY COLONY BEACH

PILING

Fantasy Harbour
6 ft. draft
10 ft. alongside
well-marked

Large Condominium
good navigational aid

From outside
of Hawk Channel

𝒩

ARTIST'S SKETCH — NOT FOR NAVIGATION
FAT DEER KEY & GRASSY KEY
NAVIGATE BY CHART NO. C & G S 11449

APPROXIMATE SCALE

0   ½   1

MARATHON & VACA KEY

Marathon is the city; Vaca Key is the place, with a population of about 8,000. Marathon has a library, hospital, an airport and rental car facilities, as well as numerous good restaurants, shops and markets. It's an important center for both sport and commercial fishing, and a good place to purchase fresh seafood, reasonably priced, right from the boats.

For the yachtsman there are marine supplies and several boat yards for hauling and repairs. Sombrero Reef and Washerwoman Shoal provide interest for divers. The microtowers make good aids for navigation.

On the Florida Bay side, after you pass Rachel Bank, you'll find several marinas which can accom-

moderate boats up to 50 or 100 ft. in length. All of them contain restaurants, and some offer shore accommodations and resort facilities.

Hurricane Motor Lodge has 8 ft. of water on the approach and 12 ft. alongside. Tarpon Lodge (now Banana Bay) has 6 ft. on both the approach and dockside. Faro Blanco Marine Resort just east of the Coast Guard Station, has a 7 ft. channel and 12 ft. alongside. Dockmaster John Bauchman monitors VHF Channel 16. At Marathon Yacht Basin, the approach is 5 ft., the depth alongside is 7 ft.

Coming in from Hawk Channel, use the East Washerwoman Shoal light as a reference point, then the western tip of Kinght Key, to pick up markers leading into Boot Key Harbor.

Enter here on the Atlantic side for Key Colony Beach Marina and Holiday Inn.

Large yachts ply the waters of the Keys.

Boot Key Harbor is well protected, and if you don't care to tie up at a marina, you can anchor there; check your depth carefully.

Marathon is the beginning of the Seven Mile bridge, and west of Boot Key, Moser Channel and Bahia Honda Channel (20 ft. clearance) are the last cross-over spots in the Keys. If you intend to continue to Key West, you must decide at Marathon whether you want to travel on the Atlantic or Gulf side. Moser Channel has a new fixed span with a mast height clearance of 65 ft.

If you haven't time to cruise all the way to Key West and back, rent a car or take the bus from Marathon. It's a short drive which will leave you plenty of time to see this exciting, historic city, enjoy a leisurely lunch, and be back in Marathon before dark.

There are two entrances into Boot Key Harbor. The Sister Creek entranct has a 4 ft. draft limit at low water. The western entrance near the start of the 7 Mile Bridge is the one we use the most. It's well marked and has about 7 ft. of water at low tide.

When you come in this way, on your port side you will pass Marathon Seafood and Marina and Faro Blanco ocean side and houseboat docks. Both have good grog and grub.

If you want to anchor, keep going through the bridge. This will lead you into the best spot to anchor. Here also are two nice marinas, the Sombrero Resort and Lighthouse Marina, with its sophisticated atmosphere and tennis courts. At Carolyn Voit's Sombrero Marina and Dockside Bar she charges 3 bucks to tie up your dinghy, and 1.50 to shower. At the anchorage on Sunday you will see the Saved By Grace, a big ketch; preacher Frank does church on board. For food you've got Kelsey's, Shuckers, Crocodile's and I like Herbie's for lunch. For dancing and partying you've got Frankie's Silverado.

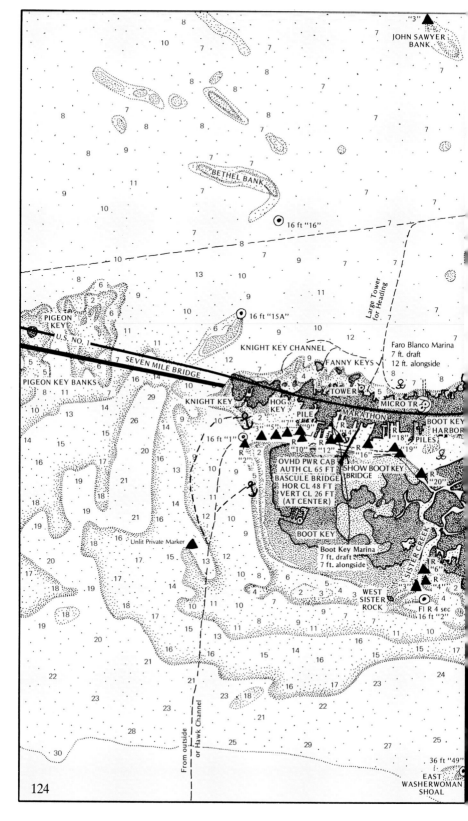

"3"
JOHN SAWYER BANK

BETHEL BANK
16 ft "16"

PIGEON KEY
U.S. NO. 1
SEVEN MILE BRIDGE
PIGEON KEY BANKS

16 ft "15A"

KNIGHT KEY CHANNEL

Large Tower for Heading

Faro Blanco Marina
7 ft. draft
12 ft. alongside

FANNY KEYS

KNIGHT KEY
HOG KEY
PILE
TOWER
MICRO TR
MARATHON
BOOT KEY HARBOR
PILES

16 ft "1"
R "5"
R "7"
R "9"
R "4"
R "18"
R "19"
R "2"
R "10"
R "12"
R "16"

OVHD PWR CAB
AUTH CL 65 FT
BASCULE BRIDGE
HOR CL 48 FT
VERT CL 26 FT
(AT CENTER)

SHOW BOOT KEY
BRIDGE
R "20"

BOOT KEY

Boot Key Marina
7 ft. draft
7 ft. alongside

SISTER CREEK

R

Unlit Private Marker

WEST SISTER ROCK

R "3"
R "4"
R "6"

Fl R 4 sec
16 ft "2"

From outside or Hawk Channel

36 ft "49"

124

EAST WASHERWOMAN SHOAL

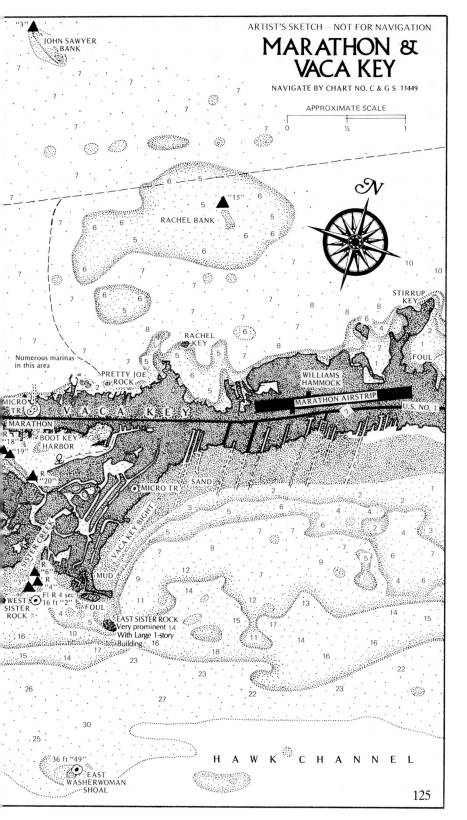

MARATHON &
VACA KEY

NAVIGATE BY CHART NO. C & G S 11449

APPROXIMATE SCALE

"3"

JOHN SAWYER
BANK

7

7

7

7

7

7

6   5

7

5   "15"

7   6   RACHEL BANK

5   6   6

7   6   5

6   6

7   5

7   8   8   STIRRUP KEY

8   6   6

Numerous marinas
in this area

5   RACHEL
KEY   6

7   5   5   8   FOUL

7   5   6   WILLIAMS HAMMOCK   1

PRETTY JOE
ROCK   5   2

2   MARATHON AIRSTRIP

MICRO TR   VACA KEY   7   U.S. NO. 1

MARATHON
R "18"   BOOT KEY
"19"   HARBOR

R "20"

MICRO TR   SAND   1

3   5   1

3   4   3

VACA KEY BIGHT   5   7   7   6   2   7

SISTER CREEK   7   8   9   2   5   7

12   7

R "6"   14   9   1

"3"   R "4"   MUD   7

FI R 4 sec   11   12   13   14   15

WEST   16 ft "2"   FOUL   15   17

SISTER   4   EAST SISTER ROCK   11   14   15

ROCK   5   Very prominent 14   16

16   10   With Large 1-story   16

15   14   17   Building 16   18   16   22

23   23

26   23

27   22   23

30

25

36 ft "49"

EAST
WASHERWOMAN   H A W K   C H A N N E L
SHOAL

125

PIGEON KEY

KN

BOOT KEY

This aerial photo shows Boot Key and Knight Key Channel. Sister Creek is a N.O.A.A.

SISTER CREEK

N

good route into Boot Key Harbor from Hawk Channel. Photo courtesy of

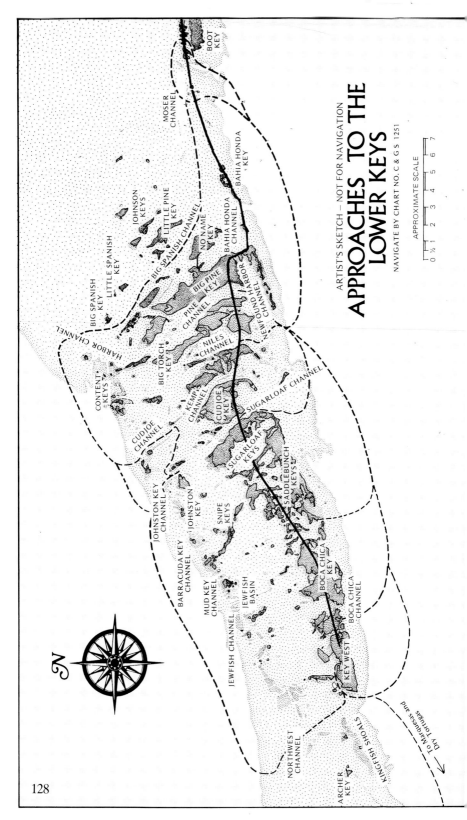

ARTIST'S SKETCH — NOT FOR NAVIGATION

APPROACHES TO THE LOWER KEYS

NAVIGATE BY CHART NO. C & G S 1251

APPROXIMATE SCALE

0 ½ 1   2   3   4   5   6   7

BOOT KEY

MOSER CHANNEL

BAHIA HONDA KEY

BAHIA HONDA CHANNEL

NO NAME KEY

BIG SPANISH CHANNEL

LITTLE PINE KEY

JOHNSON KEYS

BIG PINE KEY

PINE CHANNEL

LITTLE SPANISH KEY

BIG SPANISH KEY

HARBOR CHANNEL

NILES CHANNEL

NEW FOUND HARBOR

NEW FOUND CHANNEL

BIG TORCH KEY

CONTENT KEYS

KEMP CHANNEL

SUGARLOAF CHANNEL

CUDJOE KEY

CUDJOE CHANNEL

SUGARLOAF KEYS

JOHNSTON KEY CHANNEL

JOHNSTON KEY

SNIPE KEYS

SADDLEBUNCH KEYS

BARRACUDA KEY CHANNEL

MUD KEY CHANNEL

JEWFISH BASIN

BOCA CHICA KEY

BOCA CHICA CHANNEL

JEWFISH CHANNEL

KEY WEST

NORTHWEST CHANNEL

KINGFISH SHOALS

ARCHER KEY

To Marquesas and
Dry Tortugas

𝒩

128

APPROACHES TO THE LOWER KEYS

Both routes from Marathon to Key West have advantages, depending upon the speed, draft and type of your vessel, and the season of the year. Get a good weather report and choose the most comfortable route. During the summer, when the winds are east and southeast, sailboats will get more breeze on the Atlantic side. In the winter, when the Northers are blowing north and northwest, the Gulf side gives sailors a screaming fast run. Your other option is to take the Atlantic route, staying on the northern side of Hawk's Channel, and let the Keys give your craft some natural protection from north and northeasters.

In Hawk Channel you may get a bit of counter current from the Gulf Stream, but you're in deep water, there are buoys and lights every few miles, and for boats up to 5½ ft. draft there are several marked channels where you can put in: Newfound Harbor, Sugar Loaf Channel and Saddle Bunch Key anchorage. At 6½ knots you can make the run from Marathon to Stock Island, where you can put in with as much as a 6 ft. draft.

On the Gulf side, you go through Big Spanish Channel, which has a shoal area 5 ft. deep at the northern end. From there you enter the Gulf, and once you make the commitment out into the Gulf, there are not many places where you can stop. After Cudjoe Channel and Johnson Key Channel, the next stop is Key West. This is not a heavily traveled area, and is interesting to visit. We go through with a 4½ ft. draft, usually from Marathon to Big Spanish, then from Big Spanish to the Northwest Channel into Key West, with a little swimming, fishing and exploring along the way.

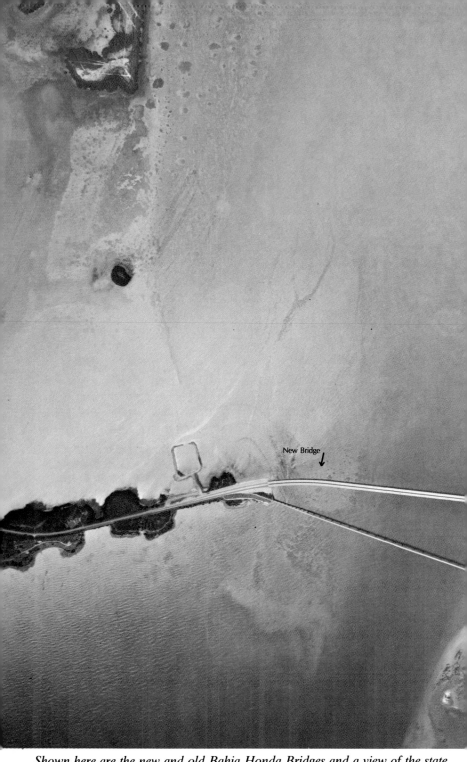

Shown here are the new and old Bahia Honda Bridges and a view of the state

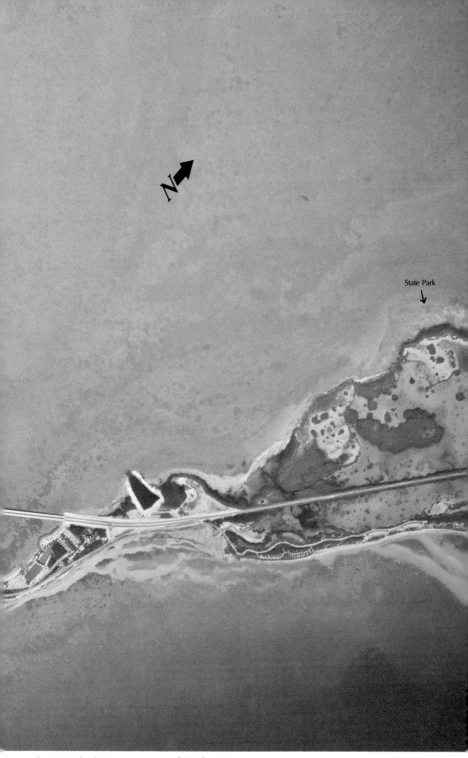

park. Aerial photo courtesy of N.O.A.A.

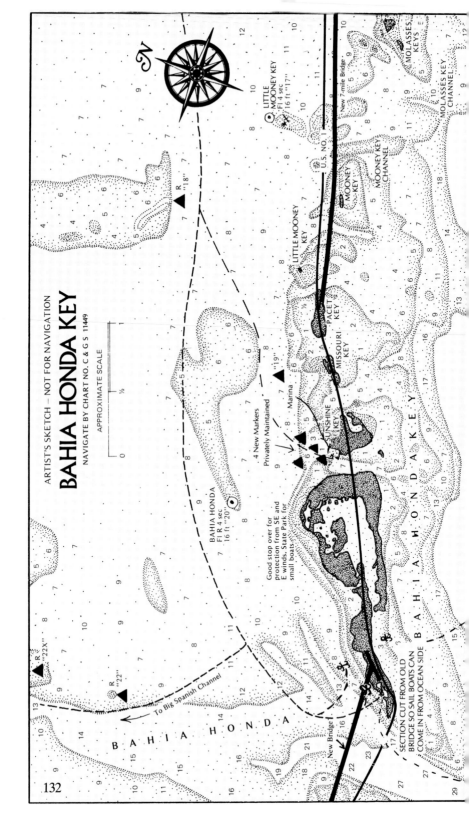

ARTIST'S SKETCH – NOT FOR NAVIGATION

BAHIA HONDA KEY

NAVIGATE BY CHART NO. C & G S 11449

APPROXIMATE SCALE

0   ½   1

BAHIA HONDA
Fl R 4 sec
16 ft "20"

R "18"

R "19"

Marina

4 New Markers
Privately Maintained

Good stop over for
protection from SE and
E winds, State Park for
small boats

SUNSHINE KEY

LITTLE MOONEY
KEY

LITTLE MOONEY KEY

MOONEY KEY

MOONEY KEY
CHANNEL

PACET KEY

MISSOURI
KEY

U.S. NO. 1

New 7 mile Bridge

MOLASSES
KEYS

MOLASSES KEY
CHANNEL

R "22X"

R "22"

To Big Spanish Channel

B A H I A   H O N D A

New Bridge

SECTION CUT FROM OLD
BRIDGE SO SAIL BOATS CAN
COME IN FROM OCEAN SIDE

B A H I A   H O N D A   K E Y

132

BAHIA HONDA KEY

If you are taking the Gulf of Mexico route from Marathon to Key West, this is a good place to stop before heading into Big Spanish Channel. The marina at Sunshine Key is the last Gulfside marina from here to Key West. Keep daymarker No. 19 on your port side, and then follow their well-marked channel on in.

There is a strong setting current through the entrance to Sunshine Channel, with 4 to 4½ ft. of water, depending on the tide. You can get propane gas and marina supplies here while your kids take advantage of the children's playground and teenage recreation room. Power boats can go further west, under the fixed bridge to Bahia Honda Park Marina. The state recreational area on Bahia Honda rents out bicycles, skiffs and canoes for sightseeing. This is where the waters of the Florida Keys take on tropical colors and variations. It's a great help for navigation and provides interesting skin diving and snorkeling. In these clear waters we have seen green turtles, pilot whales and hundreds of porpoises feeding and playing in their natural environment.

Through a cut in the old bridge, Bahia Honda State Park is accessible to sailboats only from the ocean side with a 3 ft. draft.

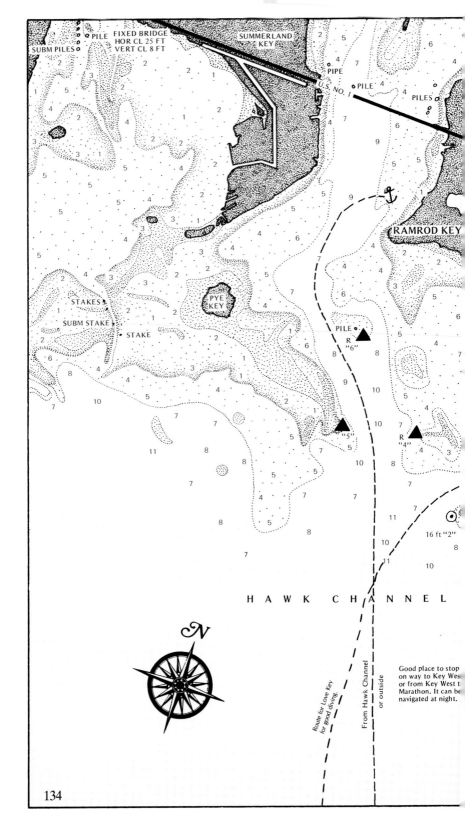

PILE
FIXED BRIDGE
HOR CL 25 FT
VERT CL 8 FT
SUMMERLAND
KEY
SUBM PILES
PIPE
U.S. NO. 1
PILE
PILES

RAMROD KEY

STAKES
SUBM STAKE
STAKE
PYE
KEY

PILE
R
"6"

"5"

R
"4"

16 ft "2"

H A W K   C H A N N E L

𝒩

Route for Love Key
for good diving.

From Hawk Channel

or outside

Good place to stop
on way to Key West
or from Key West to
Marathon. It can be
navigated at night.

134

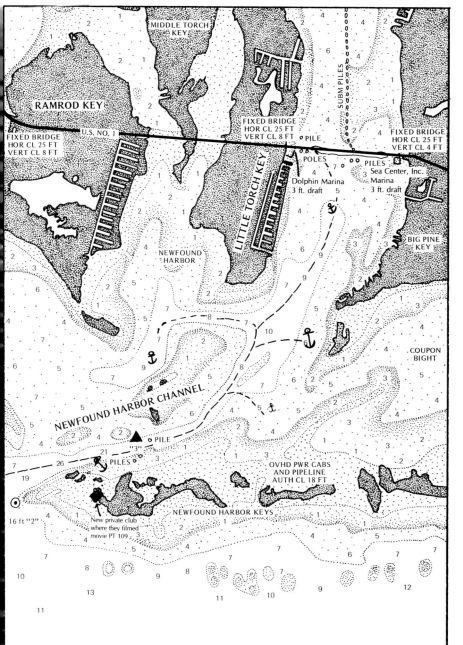

RAMROD KEY

MIDDLE TORCH KEY

FIXED BRIDGE
HOR CL 25 FT
VERT CL 8 FT

U.S. NO. 1

FIXED BRIDGE
HOR CL 25 FT
VERT CL 8 FT

FIXED BRIDGE
HOR CL 25 FT
VERT CL 8 FT

LITTLE TORCH KEY

SUBM PILES

PILE

POLES

PILES

FIXED BRIDGE
HOR CL 25 FT
VERT CL 4 FT

Sea Center, Inc.
Marina
3 ft. draft

Dolphin Marina
3 ft. draft

BIG PINE KEY

NEWFOUND HARBOR

COUPON BIGHT

NEWFOUND HARBOR CHANNEL

PILE

"3"

PILES

OVHD PWR CABS
AND PIPELINE
AUTH CL 18 FT

16 ft "2"

NEWFOUND HARBOR KEYS

New private club
where they filmed
movie PT 109

ARTIST'S SKETCH — NOT FOR NAVIGATION

NEWFOUND HARBOR

NAVIGATE BY CHART NO. C & G S 11445

APPROXIMATE SCALE

0   ½   1

NEWFOUND HARBOR

The gin clear waters of Looe Key

If you choose the Hawk's Channel route from Marathon to Key West, Newfound Harbor is a good stopping point for an overnight anchorage or a retreat from bad weather. The entrance is fairly easy, and with a few time's experience, could even be navigated at night. The northeast channel passes north of Newfound Harbor Keys and shallows up to about one fathom. The first key is the Little Palm Island Club on Munson Island. This is where they filmed PT 109, the movie about John Kennedy. We always stop here on the way to Key West to get the gals out of the galley. The food and the amenities compensate for their slightly higher dockage rate.

Speaking of higher, up in the sky over the Newfound Harbor area, you will see Fat Albert, the nickname for the large white radar blimp you can use as a landmark.

Newfound Harbor is an excellent stopping place on the way down from Marathon in Key West. The island with the dock is the Little Palm Island Club. Don't forget the diving on Looe Key.

Farther up in Newfound Harbor Channel there are several spots to anchor west of Big Pine Key or just south of Little Torch Key.

As you head north up Newfound Harbor Channel, you'll find a marker west of the bridge for the Dolphin Marina. You can carry 3 ft. in, depending on the tide. They stand by on VHF Channel 6 and Charlie & Ronie provide showers, supplies, charter boats and rentals. Also to the east is the Sea Center Marina.

On Big Pine Key, largest of the lower keys, is the headquarters for the National Key Deer Refuge. These miniature deer measure between 20 to 30 inches at the shoulder, and live on pinenuts and mangrove leaves. When the refuge was established the Key

deer were almost extinct, but with protection the population is increasing. If you anchor here, you can dinghy ashore and see some of these small creatures at the Ranger Station.

If you beat northwest after passing the lighted marker off Newfound Harbor Key, there are several anchorages between Summerland and Ramrod Keys. Even though the holding ground is good, two anchors should be put out because there is some strong tidal action. Be careful when swimming in this tidal rip. Snorkeling in 3 to 4 ft. of water is interesting in the Newfound Harbor area. Up in Coupon Bight we've found lobster, stone crabs, and good fishing.

LITTLE TORCH KEY

Here is an excellent view of Newfound Harbor Keys and Little Torch Key. This is courtesy of N.O.A.A.

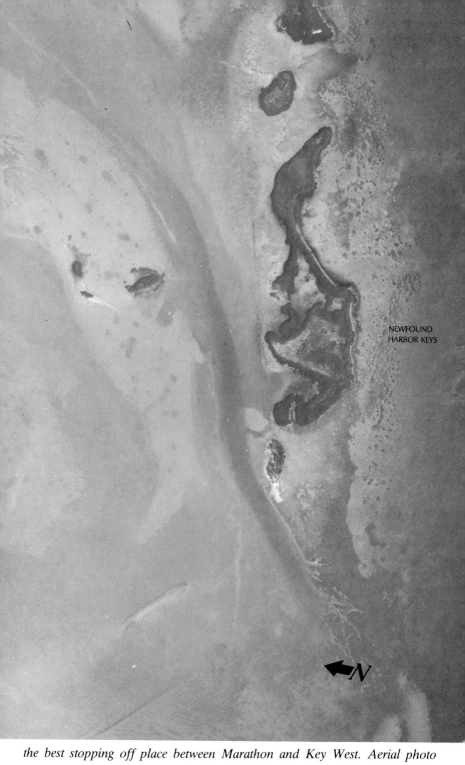

NEWFOUND
HARBOR KEYS

N

the best stopping off place between Marathon and Key West. Aerial photo

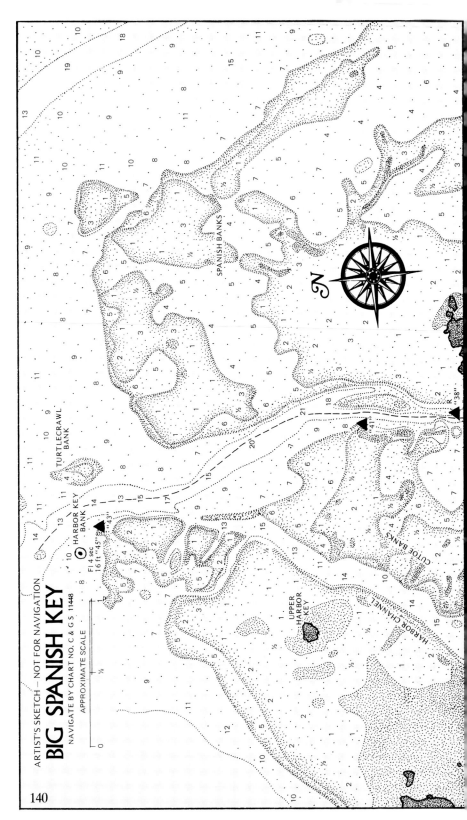

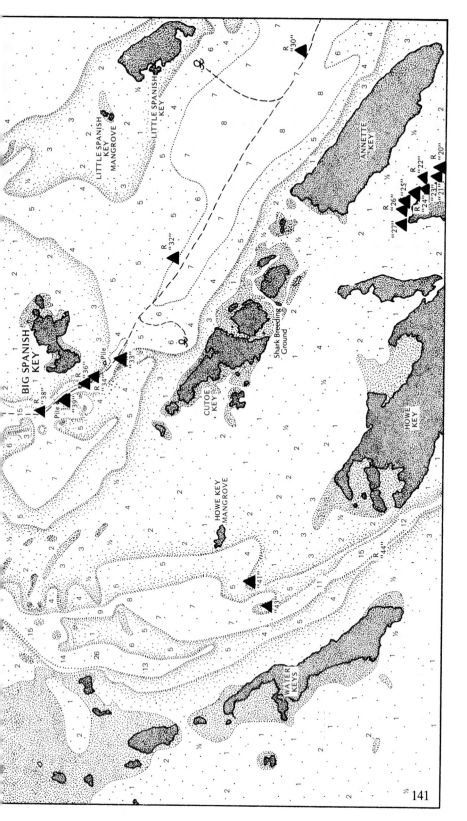

141

What to Wear

What you wear depends upon the season and your own cruising style. We like layered dressing, because even in warm weather you can get a cool night, and in winter you can have a tropical day. We start with several layers in the morning, peel as the day goes on, then add as the sun goes down.

You'll want a swimsuit or shorts and sleeveless shirt, and a pair of lightweight, long trousers and long-sleeved shirt to keep cool but be protected from the sun. When the breeze freshens, add a windbreaker. Take a sweater which can be worn alone or under the windbreaker.

During the winter season, you may need a heavier pair of pants and a warm jacket. If you are chartering, make sure the boat has foul weather gear aboard, or bring your own.

Dress ashore in the Keys is casual, but private clubs and luxury marinas call for a jacket and possibly a tie for men. For these places, women will want a dress, long skirt, or dressy pant suit.

Never go to a boat with hard luggage or too much stuff. The following gear will all fit in one large duffle bag and keep you 7 days. If you need dress clothes, carry them on a hangar.

2 pair jeans
2 pair sneakers or boat shoes
2 lightweight, long-sleeved shirts
2 sweat shirts
2 windbreakers
1 long-sleeved jersey shirt for snorkeling
3 bathing suits
Sleeping attire
3 or 4 pair cutoffs or shorts
5 sets underwear and sox
2 hats with chin straps
2 sun glasses with strings to keep you from losing them, especially if they're prescription.
Foul weather gear
Rubber or canvas gloves
Suntan lotion
2 packs of antiacid tablets
Books
Camera and film
Underwater camera (rental available)
Any medication you need
Scopolamine band-aid, fits on skin behind your ear. (Check with your doctor.)
Matches in a watertight container
Pocket knife
Flashlight
Plastic bag for dirty clothes
For winter:
Long johns
Rubber boots
Pocket flask of rum

BIG SPANISH KEY

After leaving Marathon or Bahia Honda, proceed about one mile past marker No. "20" and start your swing to the Northwest into the entrance for Big Spanish Channel, which is well marked. Depending upon the direction of the wind, there are several good anchorages in here. After you pass marker No. "30", you can hold up behind Little Spanish Key, or, if the wind is from the south, continue past marker No. "32" and head off to the southwest.

Exploring this area with a dinghy or small boat is enjoyable. There are a lot of turtle and porpoise; the water is clear; and up in the mangroves or out on the flats, the fishing is very good. While pulling around in the mangroves or on the edges of the flats, we have seen numerous schools of small sharks which look black with bright green eyes. Just north of Big Spanish Key there are several deep holes where we find good bottom fishing at slack tide.

When navigating through Big Spanish Channel, keep a lookout posted for shoaling areas, especially toward the northern end. Once you pass Harbor Key Bank Light, you are home free into the Gulf. Stay well off shore, beyond 18 ft. depth, to avoid the small keys and reefs. We find the depth finder a good navigational aid in the Gulf of Mexico. Trolling with a 2 to 3-in. spoon or a yellow jig will usually pick up some mackerel and grouper.

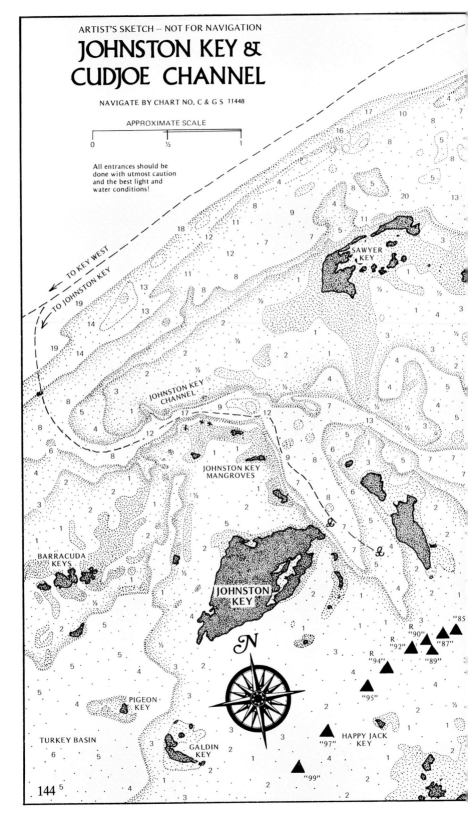

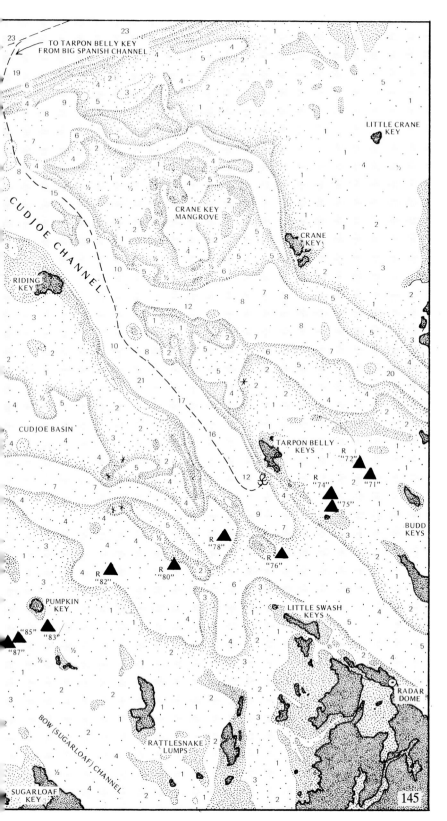

145

JOHNSTON KEY & CUDJOE CHANNEL

When coming from Big Spanish Channel southwestward there are numerous mangrove keys for exploration. The first group can be seen by bearing northeast into Cudjoe Channel watching the 4 ft. spots passing Riding Key to starboard and ending up at Tarpon Belly Key. All of this is in 8 to 10 ft. of water. If your draft permits you can go on down to little Swash Key using a radar dome for a navigational aid. On the way out of Cudjoe Channel you pass Sawyer's Key to the southwest. The bone and snapper fishing and small panfish in this area is excellent.

Further on to the southwest is the entrance to Johnston Key Channel. Using the southwestern end of Johnston Key, coming on a slightly northwesterly course, 5 ft. of water can cautiously be taken over the bar. Then bearings to the east and anchoring in the pocket in 5 to 6 ft. of water in between the two keys. The holding ground here is fairly good but I wouldn't recommend large boats anchoring overnight in these areas in the winter months.

Chartering

Before you charter a boat, there are several things you'll want to decide. The first is how much you can afford to spend. Check sailing, yachting and cruising magazines for available boats, then write or phone the various companies about their services and rates.

Your yachting experience and the number of people in your party will determine the size and type of boat you'll need. You don't want to be crowded, but a party of friends can share expenses.

A third question is whether you want a bareboat charter or a captain charter. A good skipper will cost from $75 to $90 a day, plus expenses, which usually means food, drink and travel. On a business entertainment trip, having a captain gives you more time to spend with your guests and relieves you of the responsibility for the vessel.

Hiring a captain can be a wise investment if the boat you're handling is larger than you're accustomed to.

The average deposit is $600 to $700, and with yard bills the way they are now, a very small amount of damage can use up your deposit.

You may also have more

SUGARLOAF KEY

As you come down Hawk's Channel on the outside you can pick up Loggerhead Key, which lies just northeast of Sugarloaf Beach. It has an interesting anchorage on the southern side, but soundings should be made on the way in because of the shoaling area. It gives good protection from a sudden northern which might catch you in Hawk's Channel. To the west is Sugarloaf Beach, which is a good anchorage when the weather is right. It is dead north of Ninefoot Shoal.

West of Loggerhead Key there are the remains of an old wreck which should be given a wide berth. Beyond that is the entrance to Cudjoe Bay, which is a well-marked, easy entrance for boats with up to 3½ to 4 ft. draft. Watching your draft, you can go on up as far as Pirate's Cove, or you can anchor inside Cudjoe Bay. Either spot offers good protection from north or northwest winds. Use your judgement to get on the lee shore if the draft and size of your boat permit.

fun with a captain aboard, due to his knowledge of the area.

Always tell him what you prefer: diving, sailing, touring ashore, so he can take you to the best places. "One of a skipper's hardest jobs is to get a group to decide what they want to do and then stick to that decision." His plans must also allow for wind, weather, draft and speed of the boat, and the number of daylight hours. Discuss all of this with your captain so he can help you plan the cruise.

Once you're decided on a boat, try to check it out as well as you can. If you have a friend in the area, even if he is not a sailor, he can give you some opinion. Ask for the name and address of a local captain, who can give you some cruising tips. Some captains are available for one or two days on a check-out cruise. Read up on the area, plan your itinerary, and book well in advance, as much as six months, to assure getting a good yacht. This will also give you time to correspond or talk with the captain, if you are using one. Ask the charter company for an inventory of the equipment on the boat, so you will know exactly what to bring.

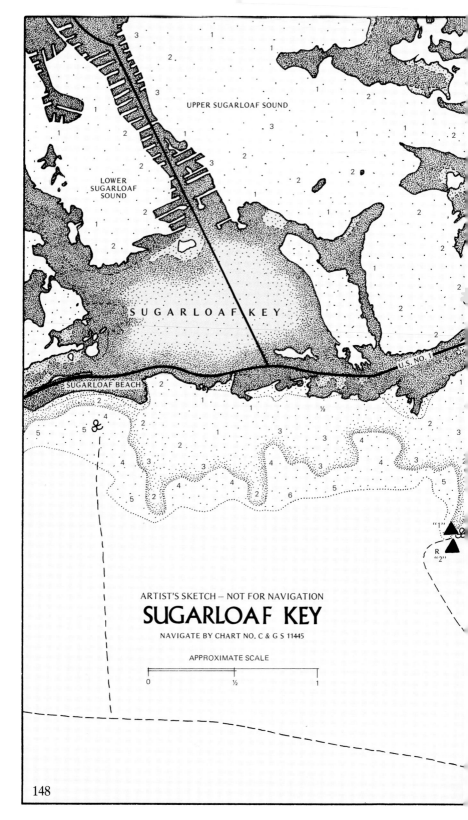

ARTIST'S SKETCH – NOT FOR NAVIGATION
SUGARLOAF KEY
NAVIGATE BY CHART NO. C & G S 11445

APPROXIMATE SCALE

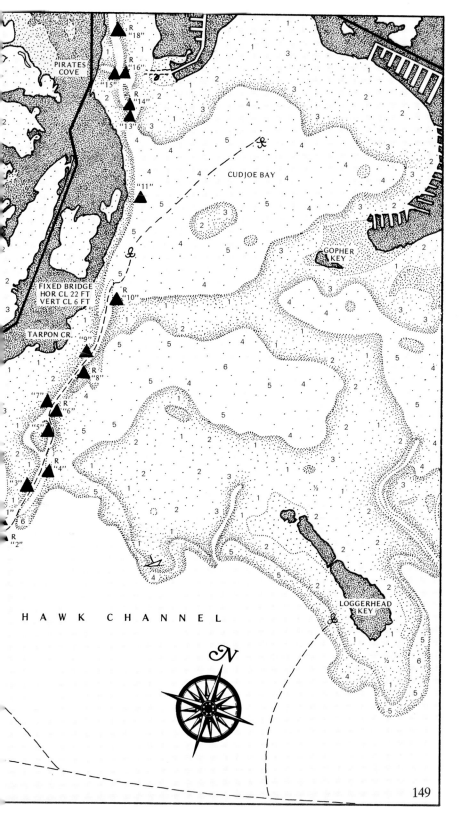

PIRATES
COVE

R "18"
R "16"
"15"
R "14"
"13"

CUDJOE BAY

GOPHER
KEY

"11"

FIXED BRIDGE
HOR CL 22 FT
VERT CL 6 FT

R "10"

TARPON CR.

"9"

R "8"

"7"
R "6"

"5"

R "4"

3'

R "2"

LOGGERHEAD
KEY

H A W K   C H A N N E L

N

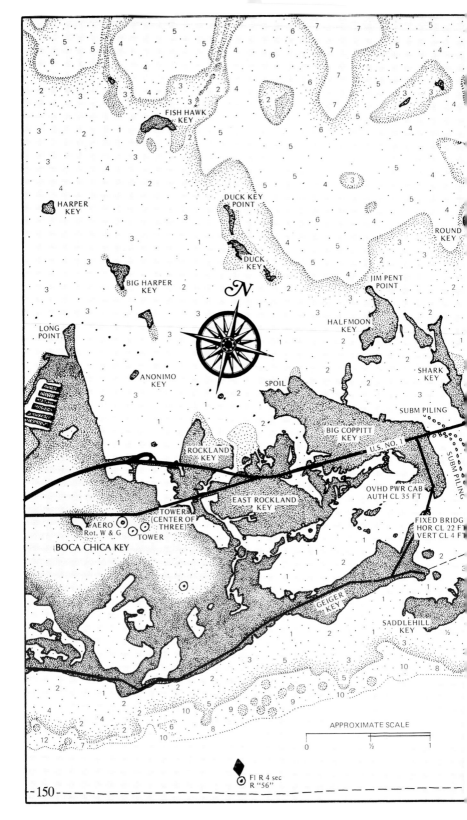

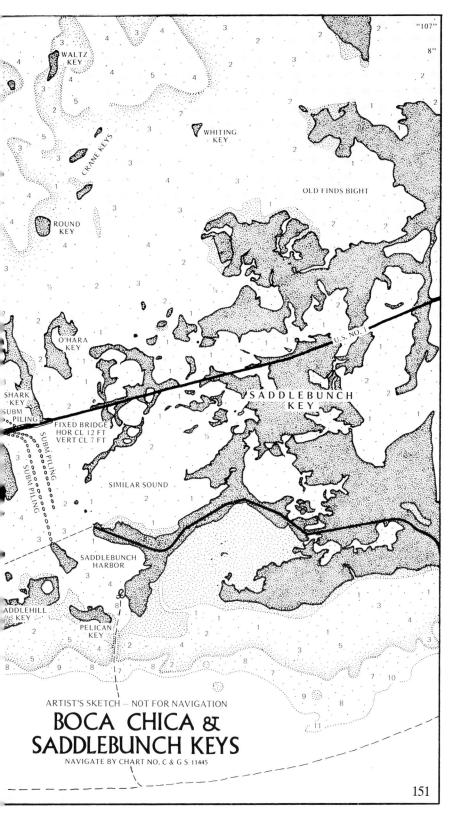

ARTIST'S SKETCH — NOT FOR NAVIGATION

BOCA CHICA &
SADDLEBUNCH KEYS
NAVIGATE BY CHART NO. C & G S 11445

151

BOCA CHICA &
SADDLEBUNCH KEYS

Just before you reach Key West on the outside, you pass Saddlebunch and Boca Chica Keys. Between Saddlebunch and Saddlehill Keys lies Pelican Key. Just off the eastern tip of Pelican Key is a channel where smaller craft, with a draft up to 3 to 3½ ft., can duck into to avoid bad weather.

South of Saddlebunch is Boca Chica, site of a naval air station. Towers and jet planes make good landmarks for boats coming from Hawk Channel, since Stock Island, first of Key West's dockage areas, lies just beyond.

This aerial photo shows typical vegetation on an island found in this vicinity (on the Atlantic side).

This aerial photo shows typical vegetation on a gulf side island.

KEY WEST

Historic old Key West is one of the high points in any cruise of the Florida Keys. It's a charming city with a colorful, if rowdy, past, popular with artists, writers and sport fishermen. Boating facilities are excellent and the restaurants of Key West are famous, especially for seafood, Conch and Spanish cooking. Since this is a commercial fishing area, shrimp and seafood purchased directly from the fishermen are delicious and very reasonably priced.

In good weather you can anchor off the northwest tip of Key West.

If you come down from Marathon on the outside, the first group of marinas are on Stock Island. Safe Harbor has an easy entrance with plenty of water for vessels up to 10 to 12 ft. in draft, as you head into Safe Harbor Channel. To reach Oceanside Marina, dogleg to the east halfway up the channel. They stand by on VHF Channel 16. Caution should be taken here; the rest is well-marked. The Dockmaster's office is at the northernmost pier. The marinas offer full facilities, including repairs, and welcome transient yachtsmen. There is bus service from Stock Island to the center of the city, but you have to walk about ½ a mile to the bus stop.

Unique tropical architecture and famous homes, such as the Audubon House above and Ernest Hemingway's home below, attract sightseers in old Key West.

In the main entrance to Key West Harbor there are several areas where you can anchor in calm weather and be within walking distance of the old city. This area is exposed to both weather and fishing traffic. When you come into the main channel, the old navy base is just to the starboard. The base is open to transient sailors. There is a heavy surge in the basin so put out an anchor and plenty of fenders. Call on VHF 16 for Lary Christoffel.

If you follow the harbor channel on up behind the rock jetty you will see the convenient floating docks of The World Famous Galleon A and B marinas all within walking distance of grub and grog, shops, Key West Marine Hard-ware and Perkins Chandlery if you need any stuff for your boat. To the south is Lands End Marina, Home of Florida Yacht Charters, Key West Base. For yacht club fans, you'll have to sail around Fleming Key to Garrison Bright. Watch out for overhead power lines and favor the starboard side of the channel and you can take 57 ft. under them with no trouble. The Key West Municipal Marina is dead head or head on over to the Key West Yacht Club. Give them a call on VHF 16 if you need any further information.

The south side of Stock Island has become an important boating center. Marinas like Oceanside, pictured above, are easily reached just off Hawk Channel. The island offers many marinas and facilities, and bus service is available to the city center.

Garrison Bight is close to the center of town and the nearest anchorage for boats coming from Florida Bay, but the height of overhead power cables limits its use. We usually hit Sloppy Joe's Bar and then the El Cacique for some real reasonable Cuban food. By this time you are ready for the sunset.

Many newcomers to Key West begin their visit with a ride on the Conch Train. This open-air sightseeing tram will give you an overall view of the island and its history, after which you can return at leisure to special points of interest.

The Conch Train Depot is near Mallory Dock, a restored area which is a focal point for Key Westers. Here you'll find the Aquarium, the Waterfront Play-

Power lines span the entrance to Garrison Bight.

A ride on the famous Conch Train is a good way to get your first view of the city.

house and the ticket office of the old Mallory Steamship Line. The Old Island Restoration Foundation has turned this building into a Hospitality House, where you can get information about Key West's history, attractions and artisans (handmade fabrics, jewelry, palm hats, leatherwork, musical instruments and cigars). Get a map of The Pelican Path, a selfguided walking tour of the Old Town. One of the most convenient places to tie up was the Key West Development Agency Dock.

As you walk out on Mallory Dock, you may be puzzled by a sign announcing the precise time of sunset for the day. In Key West sunset watching is a daily ritual. I don't know any other place in the world where this phenomenon occurs. If you try walking east on

Stroll the streets of Old Key west for a closer look at characteristic Conch architecture.

An Old Key Wester displays his talking iguana.

Leisurely citizens congregate on the wharf.

Duval Street at the end of the day, you may be stampeded by the crowds heading west. They start gathering on Mallory Dock about 2 hours before sundown, and the celebration really rocks the dock. If you like music in a less frantic atmosphere and have enough coins for a drink of rum, head downtown. Many singers get their start in the bars, restaurants and streets of Key West. You never know who you'll see at Captain Tony's or Margaritaville. Lately, Jimmy Buffet, who plays some mighty fine music about sailing and the Keys, performed in some of these places.

Part of Key West's charm comes from the unique Conch architecture. The city has res-

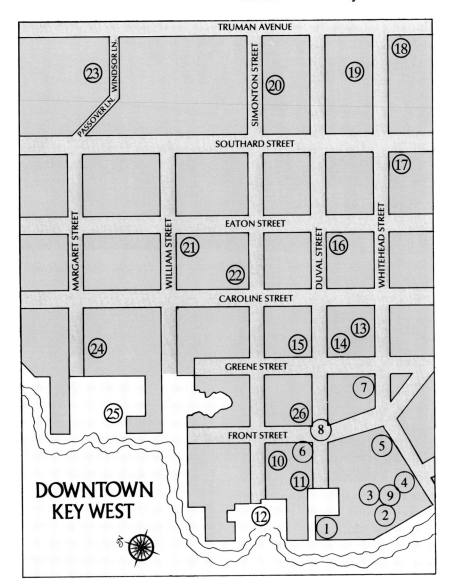

toration fever, so you'll find these old places in every condition from collapsed to brandnew. Most of them are clustered in the Old Town; stroll around and admire. A few are open to the public, so you can see them from the inside.

The Audubon House, where the naturalist stayed while working in the Keys, is a beautiful example of Conch architecture, and gives you an idea of what life was like during Key West's golden era.

The Hemingway House is another memorial to Key West's exciting past. If you need a ship's cat, you may be able to provide a home for one of the 6-toed Hemingway kittens which have the run

Downtown Key West

1. Mallory Dock - site of the sunset watching ritual.
2. Hospitality House - Information Center for Key West.
3. Mallory Square - restored Civic Center of Old Key West.
4. Municipal Aquarium - the local marine life and shark feeding.
5. Key West Art Center - exibitions by resident artists.
6. Conch Tour Train - 14-mile sightseeing tour.
7. Pirates Alley - shopping area for local crafts and imports.
8. Old Town - renovated shopping area.
9. The Mole Hole Gift Shop - distinctive gifts.
10. Key West Handprint Fabrics-factory and salesroom of silk-screened fabrics.
11. Pier House Motel & Restaurant-sunset watching from a fine waterfront restaurant.
12. Haul your dinghy here, if you anchor out. (Lock up.)
13. Audubon House and Gardens - *Elephant Folio* by Audubon in Wrecker's House from 1830's when Key West was the wealthiest city in U.S.
14. Captain Tony's Saloon-

historic and colorful landmark.
15. Sloopy Joes Bar-made famous by Hemingway.
16. Oldest House - typical Key West house with 18th century garden.
17. U.S. Naval Station - the site of Truman's "Little White House."
18. Lighthouse Museum - display of naval history in Key West
19. Ernest Hemingway's House - Hemingway's first permanent home in the U.S.
20. Peggy Mills Garden - tropical plants which can't grow outdoors anywhere else in North America.
21. Conch Houses - fine examples of Conch & Bahamian architecture between Caroline & Southard Streets.
22. U.S. Post Office.
23. Key West Cemetery - memorial to victims of USS Maine disaster.
24. Turtle Kraals - pens for giant sea turtles.
25. Shrimp Boat Dock - home base for Key West's major fishing fleet.
26. Jere Cavanagh's - imports and gifts.

161

of the old place.

While you're studying the architecture, keep an eye out for Key West's exotic plants. Some of them have blown in on the trade winds from as far away as Africa, and can't be found anywhere else in continental U.S.

Numerous gardens and museums point up the climate and character of Key West . . . a blend of New England, Caribbean and Spanish influences, spiced with seafaring, piracy and rum-running.

Now if your cruising schedule is getting tight for time, and you still want to see and snorkel the Dry Tortugas give a call to the Key West Sea Plane Service, 305-294-6978. They will take you down for some of the finest snorkeling and lunch, for a nominal fee of course!

This Nasa aerial photograph was obtained from Eros Data Center, Sioux Falls, South Dakota. It shows downtown Key West, noted for its tropical vegetation and historic landmarks.

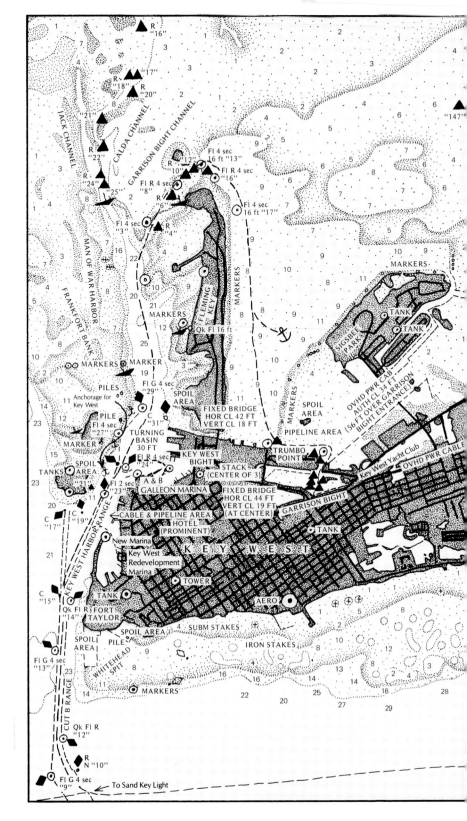

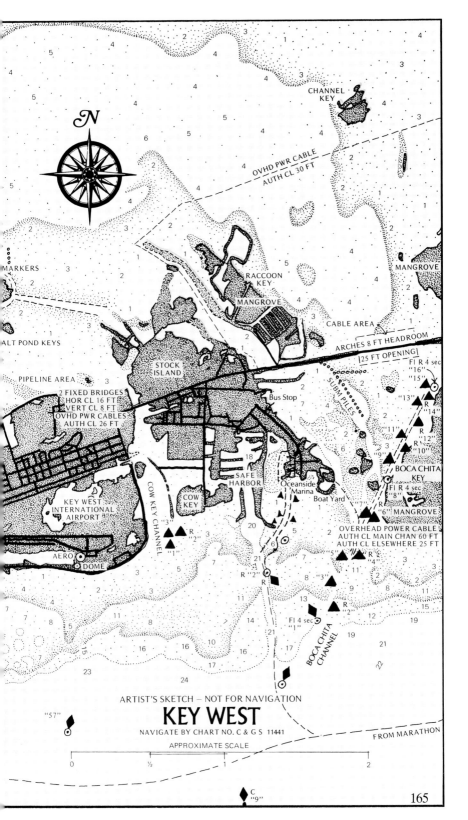

ARTIST'S SKETCH – NOT FOR NAVIGATION

KEY WEST

NAVIGATE BY CHART NO. C & G S 11441

APPROXIMATE SCALE

"Key West House" by Millard Wells

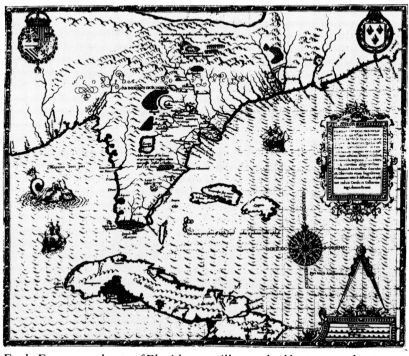

Early European charts of Florida are still consulted by treasure hunters.

Treasure Hunting in the Keys

In the days of the Spanish gold fleet, galleons and merchant ships set sail from Spain to the New World to gather gold, silver, tobacco, copper and weapons from Spanish colonies in South and Central America. The ships traveled along the northern coast of South America, stopping to pick up gold from Peru and then Mexico. From there the treasure-laden galleons sailed through the Gulf of Mexico to Cuba, 90 miles south of present day Key West. There, at Havana, they formed a convoy for the dangerous trip home to Spain.

The chief dangers to these ships as they traveled north to the Keys and southern Florida were the weather, with the possibility of hurricanes, the un-marked, jagged coral reefs of the Keys, and the presence of the many pirates who were based in Florida and, to the east, in the Bahama Islands.

Many of the galleons never made it past the Keys. Hurricanes sometimes wrecked entire fleets on the reefs, killing hundreds of people and spilling tons of precious cargo to the bottom of the ocean. Almost every Key, from Biscayne Bay to the Dry Tortugas, has seen a gold ship wrecked on the reefs.

Today, people strolling the beaches of the Florida Keys still find gold coins and small objects or jewelry washed up on shore. In fact, this is often one of the clues that leads to the location of a shipwreck. Some of the Keys' most famous treasure-hunters began exactly this way. When a beach yielded a sizable number of gold or silver coins, they looked for the treasure ship on the offshore reef.

While you may not want to take time to comb the beaches for silver coins or gold rings or swords and muskets, you will probably enjoy a visit to one of the several treasure and pirate museums located in the Keys. These museums display treasures salvaged from the sea and relics of buccaneering days on the Spanish Main.

Old Spanish Treasure Routes

How To Plan Your Cruise

In planning your cruise, major considerations are the draft, clearance and speed of your vessel, the type of activities you enjoy, and how much time you have. A 3-day cruise on Biscayne Bay can introduce you to both sides of the Keys. Anchor off uninhabited Elliott Key for swimming and snorkeling; get a yachtsman's view of Miami with a concert or marine circus and dinner at a marina.

A week's cruise on the outside should include the beautiful coral reefs of John Pennekamp Park.

We always recommend at least a week and a half for a cruise to Marathon because there are so many interesting things to see and do on the way, including a day's land trip to old Key West.

A cruise to Key West will take two to two and a half weeks; three or more if you make the entire trip to Fort Jefferson.

An alternative is to make the trip one way. There are marinas in Key West or Marathon which will take care of your boat until you return to complete the cruise. If you have a charter vessel, many charterers will allow you to leave the boat in either city. For a reasonable charge they will bring it back to Miami while you fly or drive back.

Don't plan to do too much. If you are running ahead of schedule, you can always take an interesting side trip; but nothing is worse than a crowded itinerary or a tight schedule which won't permit you to fish if the fishing is good, or explore an interesting spot, or enjoy some of the on-land attractions. If you plan to live on fresh provisions, consult the cook, and include a stop every 3 or 4 days at some spot where you can buy fresh food. (The most important part of a cruise is to keep everybody comfortable and to have a good time.)

Equipment To Check On Your Own Boat Or Charter:

Anchor, plow
Anchor, Danforth
Batteries, 12V double bank,
Bell
Bilge pump, electric
Bilge pump, manual
Binoculars 7×50
Blankets & pillows
Boat hook
Brushes
Brushes, long, whisk, scrub
Buckets
Charts
Clothes hangers, pins
Compass, hand bearing
Dinghy, outboard, oars
Dinnerware, flatware, glasses
Dock lines (4)
Emergency Tiller
Engine spare parts
Fenders
Fire extinguishers
First aid kit

Flares, emergency
Flashlight, extra batteries
Horn
Ice Bag
Insect repellent
Lead line
Life lines
Life preservers
Life ring, horseshoe
Light bulbs, extra
Linen & towels
Parallel rulers, dividers
Plastic bags
Pots, pans & utensils
Radio, AM broadcast
Radio telephone
Reefing main
Safety Harness
Snorkeling gear
Swim ladder
Tool kit
Trash container

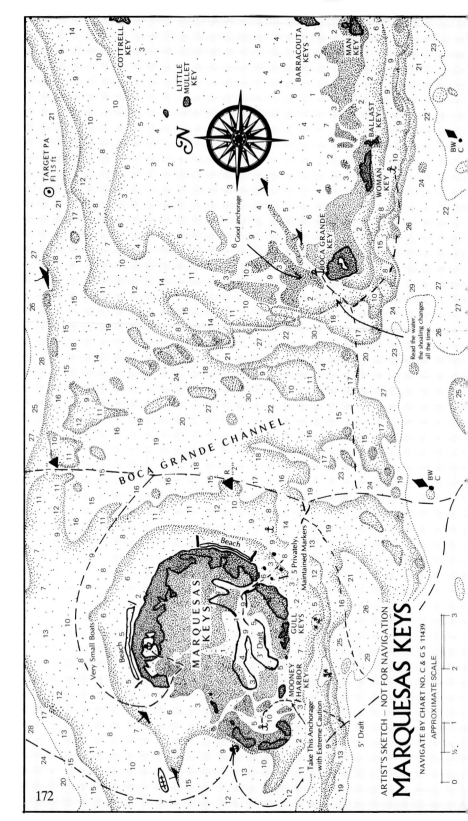

ARTIST'S SKETCH — NOT FOR NAVIGATION

MARQUESAS KEYS

NAVIGATE BY CHART NO. C & G S 11439

APPROXIMATE SCALE

172

MARQUESAS KEYS

The Marquesas Keys lie about 24 miles to the west of Key West. This low lying group of islands and Boca Grande Key to the east are excellent places to stop and anchor on the way to the Dry Tortugas.

After you leave Key West, pick up the 109 ft. tall Sand Key Light and leave it well to starboard. The southwestern side of Sand Key Light is a great spot for snorkeling and diving. You can go ashore on the beach under the light. A narrow trench, which will give you 18 fathoms of water, runs behind the outer reef. You can plot it on the chart. The Satan Shoal and Vestal Shoal buoys are right on the edge of this trench. We troll as we sail through the trench and catch dolphin, bonita and mackerel. It's a 17 nautical mile sail, but well worth it.

Run on down to Cosgrove Light, which is 29 ft. tall. Make a wide turn between Cosgrove Light and Marquesas Rock and pick up a heading of about 30^0. This will bring you to the landfall of the first of the Marquesas, Mooney Harbor Key. Watch your depth, as there are some coral heads about 1100 yards off Mooney Harbor Key.

The advantage of coming in from this direction is that you can see the openings of the harbors and identify each of the islands. The eastern entrance of Mooney Harbor is marked with privately maintained stakes and tree limbs. You can take a draft of 3 to 3 $^1/_2$ ft. into the harbor, which offers a good, protected anchorage.

With a deeper draft, anchor off shore and dinghy in to go ashore or explore the mangrove creeks. There are several good diving spots in this area, particularly the rocks off Mooney Harbor and Gull Key.

On the eastern side of the Marquesas there's an old wreck about halfway between markers "1" and "2". Four more wrecks lie north of Boca Grande Key. One of them is the destroyer Alexander. She is in about 30 ft. of water and some of her superstructure is still exposed.

The Marquesas are in a wild life refuge. John Andrew, the manager, does a fine job with buoys marking idle speed and no entry zones. Call them at 305-872-2239 for information and a chart of the Great White Heron and Key West refuge.

How To Anchor "Bahama Style"

When cruising the Keys, you'll meet several situations where we recommend anchoring "Bahama Style". For example, to limit swinging in a crowded anchorage, or to insure against drifting after a shift in wind or tide. Be provided with two anchors made fast forward.

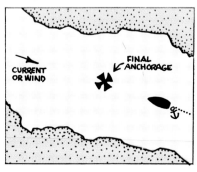

1. Approach headed into the tide or with the wind off the bow. Drop the leeward or downstream anchor the normal distance from the spot where you intend to anchor. Let the rope run free.

2. Continue up tide or wind until double the amount of scope is out. Set first anchor and immediately drop the windward or upstream one.

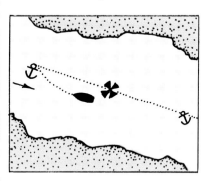

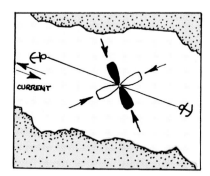

3. Fall back on tide or wind until both scopes are equal, and set the second anchor.

4. Pull up tight on both anchors. When the tide or wind shifts, the bow will remain where you want it while the stern swings free.

"ggerhead Light, Dry Tortugas" by Millard Wells

DRY TORTUGAS

The Dry Tortugas are the southernmost waters on the eastern coast of the United States. This is a place where you don't want to go without plenty of water, fuel, ice and supplies. It's a good idea to carry extra supplies in case of delay due to weather or a mechanical breakdown.

The first navigational aid you pick up is Loggerhead Key Light, then Pulaski Shoal Light, then East Key, where you will see that the diving is really beautiful. Southwest of East Key you'll find the entrance to Southeast Channel. Head up it, then come around Iowa Rock and into Garden Key, the site of Fort Jefferson. There are several anchorages around Garden Key. Which one you choose depends upon the wind. We usually stop on the eastern side, between Bush Key and Fort

Anchor off Garden Key and dinghy ashore to explore Fort Jefferson, "the Gibralter of the West".

Jefferson, and ask the ranger which anchorage is best for current weather. There is a strong tidal set across southeast channel.

Once you establish your base, you can work your way around, fishing and diving the entire area. You'll want to sightsee in the old fort, snorkel through the underwater nature trail, observe the birds on Bush Key from your boat (land-ing is prohibited), and explore Loggerhead Key and Hospital Key. If you go ashore for a cook-out, make sure you're in a place where it's permitted. Clean up the area properly so as to stay on the good side of the rangers at the fort. Allow plenty of time to return to Key West, and pick your weather carefully.

Loggerhead Key, with its lighthouse, is the farthest point south in the United States.

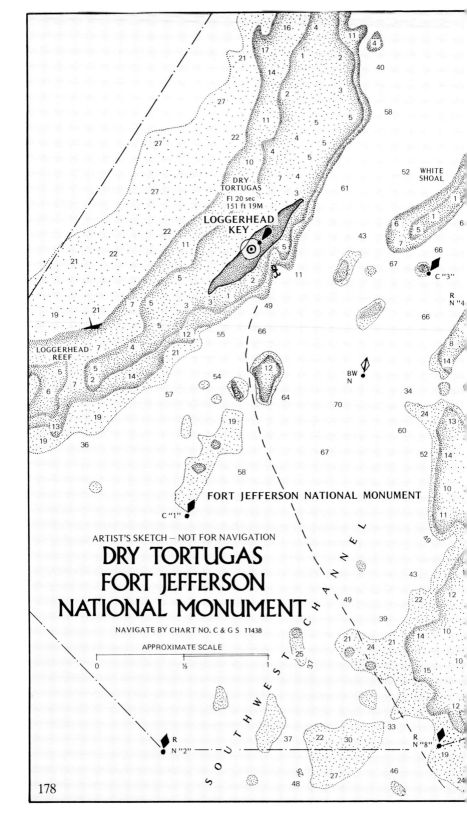

ARTIST'S SKETCH – NOT FOR NAVIGATION

DRY TORTUGAS
FORT JEFFERSON
NATIONAL MONUMENT

NAVIGATE BY CHART NO. C & G S 11438

APPROXIMATE SCALE

FORT JEFFERSON NATIONAL MONUMENT

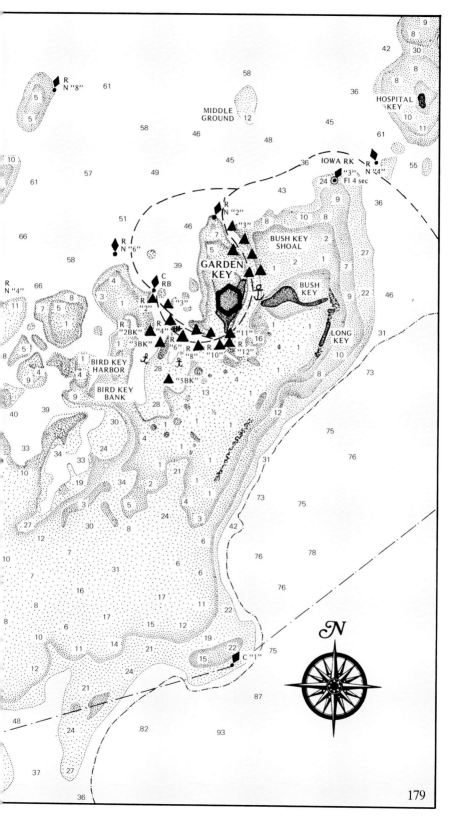

179

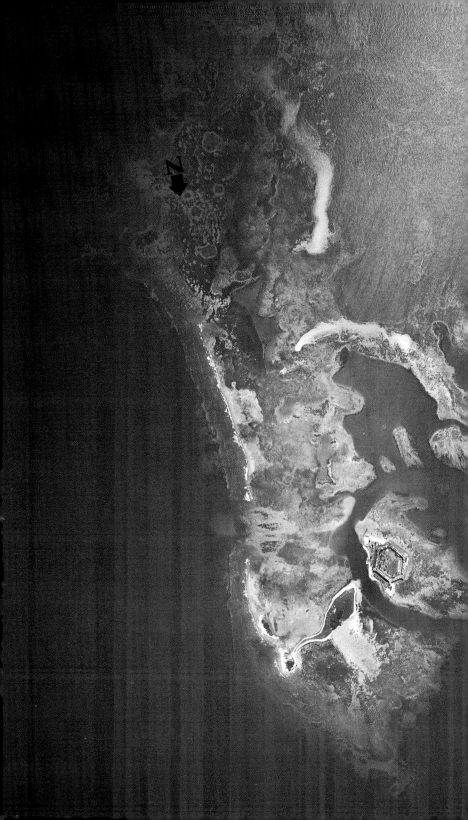

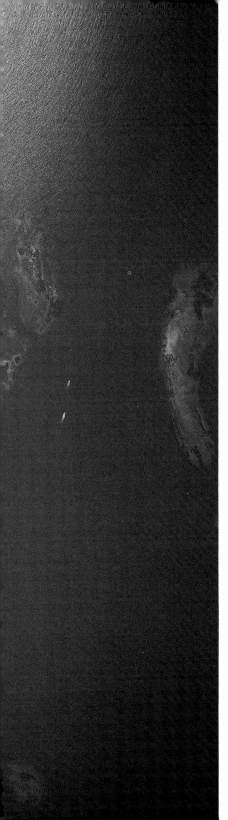

Tortuga Archipelago

No cruise is complete without a trip to the Dry Tortugas archipelago. If you have made it as far as Key West and are running out of cruising time, gather up a few spare dollars and call one of the sea plane services. They will fly you there and back for about $85.00. You will see a most spectacular aerial view of the Keys, and have a tour of the fort, picnic lunch and snorkeling. Gear is provided, but I suggest you take your own. Some added attractions are a helicopter pad at Fort Jefferson and restrooms (toilets that you don't have to pump), grill, and picnic tables at the campgrounds.

When we were down there last time, there was a limit on the time you could stay camping out. I guess that's to keep people from moving in.

Another interesting note is the moat around the fort, filled with small sea turtles, some kind of project by the rangers.

Speaking of rangers, we always give them our old reading material, books, magazines, etc. I guess they are tired of seeing the fifteen minute show of the fort's history that's available.

The Tortugas are known to Keys charter captains as the Gibraltar of the west. This picture shows the beauty caused by the contrast of colors in the water and reef.

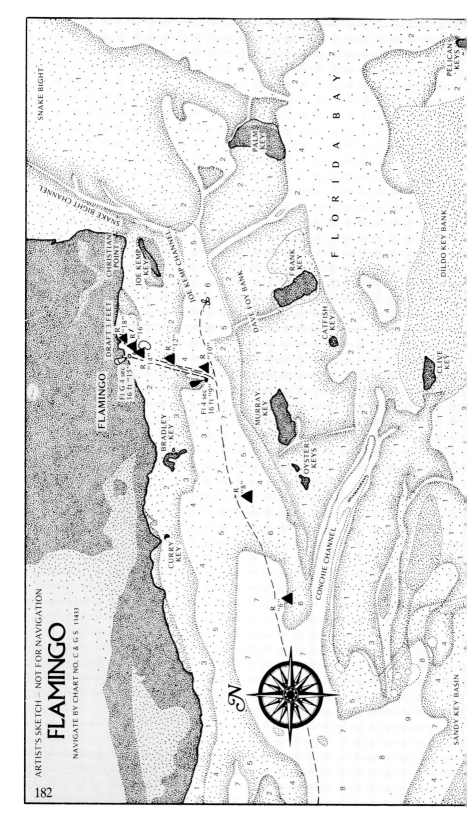

ARTIST'S SKETCH — NOT FOR NAVIGATION

FLAMINGO

NAVIGATE BY CHART NO. C & G S 11433

182

FLAMINGO & CAPE SABLE

Flamingo, an old fishing village, is a very interesting place to stop. Now a lot of people come to Flamingo from Miami, so it's developed into a nice place to stay, with motels, swimming pools and supplies. When coming up from the south to the entrance of Flamingo, stay close to Marker #3, avoiding a 5-foot shoal area between East Cape and the First National Bank. Between Marker #2 and middle ground, there's a setting current, southeasterly on an outgoing tide and northwesterly on an incoming tide. There's excellent fishing and trolling in the winter months in this area.

After passing Marker #5, use Oyster Key and Murray Key for bearings, as Marker #6 is hard to see. There's a setting current at about a 45° angle across the channel entrance into Flamingo, so watch your markers astern and stay in the middle of the channel at all times. The entrance directly into Flamingo Harbor is a sharp turn to port coming in. It's not easy to see until you're right on top of it, but it's very well marked. They accommodate boats up to 50 feet with 4½- to 5-foot drafts.

Sandy Key and Carl Ross Key are good places to stop on the way to Flamingo. When heading through the yacht channel to this area, make sure you line up the markers correctly. This is a diffi-cult navigational area. I've seen a lot of boats aground here.

When coming around East Cape, there's a small campground on the beautiful beaches as you travel toward the entrance of Lake Ingraham. There are several spots to anchor off the beach and go ashore. You'll enjoy very good fishing at these Middle Cape canals and the entrance to Lake Ingraham. We don't usually like to stay here overnight in case the weather blows up. You may end up with a rough, bouncy night or a west wind on a lee shore.

We take a dinghy into Lake Ingraham for exploring and fishing. This is an area for snapper, snook, trout and red fish. Bait is readily available. For freshwater fishing, you'll need a Florida State fishing license. You can check into purchasing one from your state office before you go on your cruise. There's also some good birdwatching in this area. A bird book will help you recognize the interesting species in this area.

There are a few scattered areas where you'll see "No Fishing" signs. This is due to some technicality in a small area. We found the beauty of the Everglades to be the best deterrent for man abusing his own backyard, so it's appreciated to follow the simple rules like no fishing to preserve these parks.

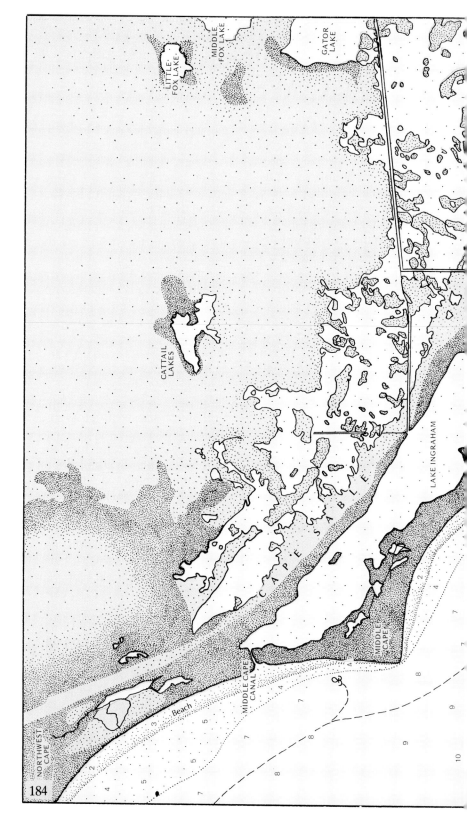

NORTHWEST CAPE

LITTLE-
FOX LAKE

MIDDLE
FOX LAKE

GATOR
LAKE

CATTAIL
LAKES

LAKE INGRAHAM

C A P E   S A B L E

MIDDLE
CAPE

MIDDLE CAPE CANAL

Beach

184

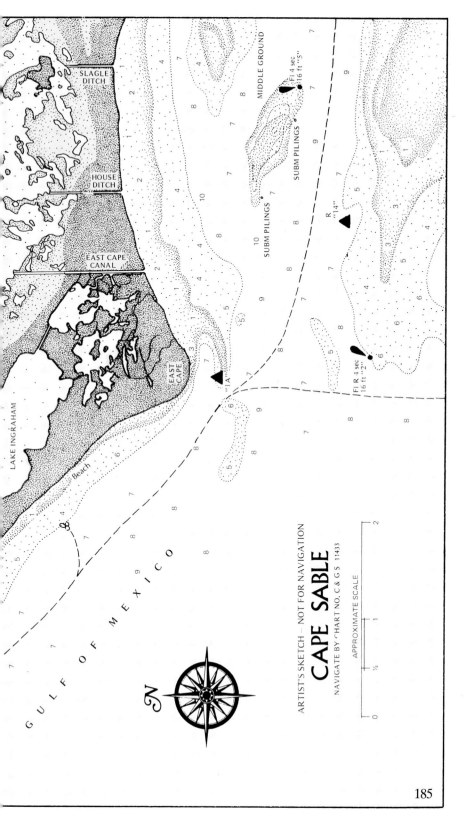

ARTIST'S SKETCH — NOT FOR NAVIGATION

CAPE SABLE

NAVIGATE BY CHART NO. C & G S 11433

APPROXIMATE SCALE

0   ½   1   2

N

GULF OF MEXICO

LAKE INGRAHAM

Beach

EAST CAPE

EAST CAPE CANAL

HOUSE DITCH

SLAGLE DITCH

MIDDLE GROUND

SUBM PILINGS

SUBM PILINGS

Fl 4 sec
16 ft "5"

R "14"

Fl R 4 sec
16 ft "2"

185

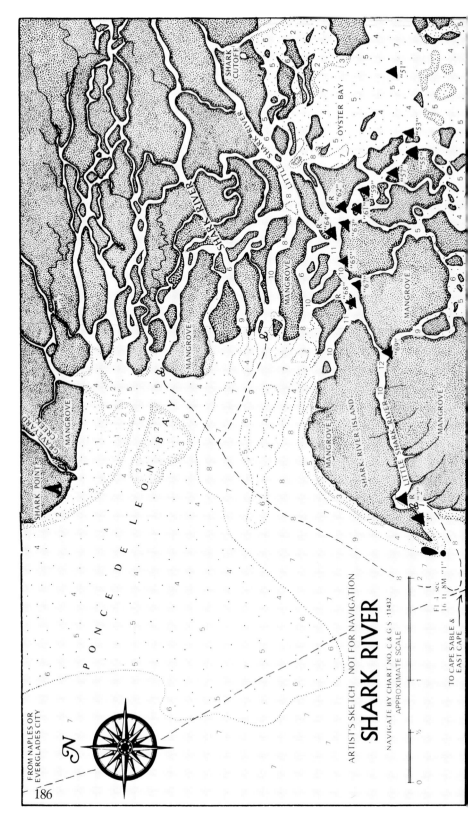

186

ARTIST'S SKETCH NOT FOR NAVIGATION
SHARK RIVER
NAVIGATE BY CHART NO. C. & G.'S 11432
APPROXIMATE SCALE

FROM NAPLES OR
EVERGLADES CITY

PONCE DE LEON BAY

SHARK POINT

GRAVEYARD CREEK

MANGROVE

SHARK RIVER

SHARK CUTOFF

LITTLE SHARK RIVER

OYSTER BAY

MANGROVE

SHARK RIVER ISLAND

LITTLE SHARK RIVER

MANGROVE

"51"
"53"
"55"
"57"
"59"
R "62"
"61"
"63"
"64"
"65"
"67"
"68"
"69"

R

Fl 4 sec.
16 ft 8M "1"

TO CAPE SABLE &
EAST CAPE

SHARK RIVER

The Little Shark River is a good anchorage point for getting out of bad weather when coming up from Cape Sable and when you're going up to cross over to the west coast. The markers are difficult to see in the daytime unless you really line them up against the mangroves. Then you'll find a day Marker #1. We usually alter our course in and out a little bit to eventually pick up the sun glancing off the marker. Once you find it, there are several good anchorages, both at the mouth and further into the river. Fishing is very good here, although it varies with the time of year. In winter months, you may find a few boats crossing here; sometimes fishermen from further down the keys.

There are many lobster and crab pots further out into the bay. You really have to be careful so they don't damage your prop. This is a very nice area.

Coming up from Flamingo, there's a waterway called Wilderness Waterway in between Flamingo and the Little Shark River and further up. You can enjoy several types of cruising in this area. For example, we once sent two boys off our Morgan 41 at Flamingo to take a canoe trip while the rest of us cruised around, enjoying the beaches.

The Marina at Flamingo is shown with Joe Kemp Key in the background.

FISH of the FLORIDA KEYS

Long before the Florida Keys became known as a cruising ground, they were famous for their number and variety of fish. Visitors who come to the Keys especially for the fishing will have the greatest pleasure and success if they hire a fishing guide or charter-boat captain. These experts know where to find the fish and how to land them. There are also several books available which provide de-

MACKEREL

Mackerel migrate through the Keys during the winter months. Both Spanish and King mackerel are slender and sleek-looking with deeply forked tails and iridescent coloring. Spanish mackerel have spots above the lateral line.

Trolling is the usual method of fishing mackerel, which are excellent eating.

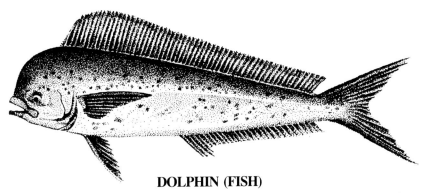

DOLPHIN (FISH)

Not to be confused with the dolphin (porpoise), which is a warm blooded mammal, the dolphin (fish) is famous for its dazzling and rapid changes of color when hooked.

Large dolphin travel in pairs along the Gulf Stream from early spring to late summer. The male has a large square forehead. Dolphin are a table delicacy.

tailed information on bait, tackle and technique, notably "Florida's Game Fish and How to Land Them", by Captain Hal Scharp of Marathon.

This section is intended to help snorkelers, divers and casual fishermen identify the fish they encounter while cruising. Some of the Keys' most famous blue water game fish are omitted because they require special equipment.

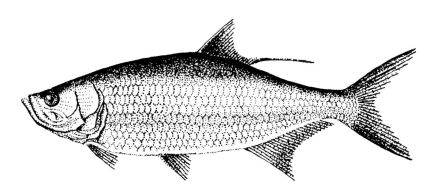

TARPON

Tarpon are identified by a featherlike extension of the last dorsal fin. They are inedible, and should be released if not desired for mounting.

Hooking and landing this great game fish is a specialized art. Tarpon leap, run or sound with great stamina. Boating one which is not played out can be dangerous.

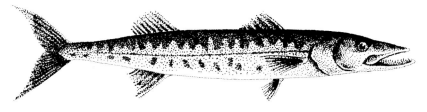

BARRACUDA

The barracuda's most prominent feature is its large mouth with jutting lower jaw and ferocious teeth. They are curious, and will often follow a swimmer, observing him with a large, staring eye.

They rarely attack swimmers, but will strike a hooked fish aggressively. Wading fishermen should be careful.

DOLPHIN (PORPOISE)

In the Keys, playful schools of dolphin put on a natural water circus. These intelligent mammals are easily trained to perform complicated tricks. Sailors believe they bring good luck, and they are known to have rescued swimmers and guided them to shore.

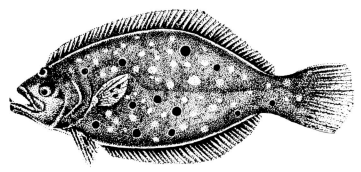

FLOUNDER

An occasional flounder can be observed in shallow waters. They begin life like ordinary fish and become flat as they mature. The eye from the under side drifts to the upper, which takes on the color of the bottom over which the flounder swims on its side.

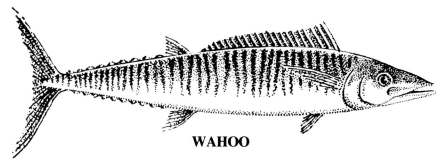

WAHOO

Wahoo are related to the mackerel, but do not run in schools. During winter and spring you may hook one while fishing the deep water for other game. Keys fishermen consider them the fastest of all fighting fish. After the battle, if you win, the light meat is excellent eating.

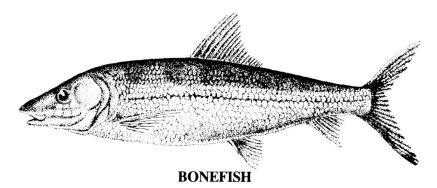

BONEFISH

Bonefish are one of the Key's famous fighting game fish, and provide a swift, running battle. They live in deep water and move onto the flats to feed. A novice bonefisherman should employ an expert guide, as the fish are extremely wary and easily spooked.

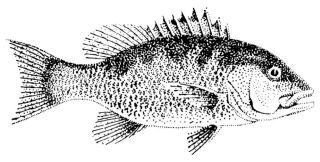

SNAPPERS

Several varieties of snapper are found in the Keys. They make excellent eating and challenge the sportsman. Snappers have large mouths and eyes, strong teeth and flattened snouts. They feed on the bottom, and are frequently found with grunts and groupers.

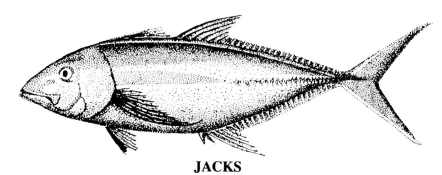

JACKS

Amberjack cruise the outer reefs, and are respected by sportsmen for their tenacious underwater battle. The smaller crevalle jacks school in channels and bays. They are memorable fighters, but fishermen anxious for other game may find voracious jacks a nuisance.

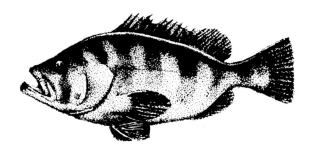

GROUPER

The grouper species range from 2 to 100 lbs. They have broad heads, square tails and change color when hooked. Groupers are bottom fish, favoring holes or caves in rocky bottoms. The best way to catch them is still fishing with cut or live bait.

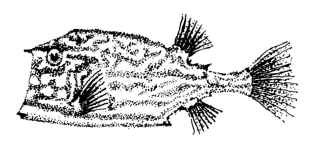

TRUNKFISH

The trunkfish is distinguished by its triangular, box-like shape. Its six-sided scales are fused together to form an inflexible shell, from which the eyes, mouth and fins protrude. It is found over grassy flats and in brackish water. Sometimes baked in the shell.

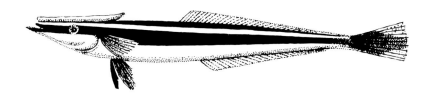

REMORA (SHARKSUCKER)

Remoras have no value for food or sport, but interest fish-watchers. The remora attaches itself to larger fish by a ribbed sucking dish on the top of its head. When the host fish feeds, the remora drops off to feed on the scraps. Its most common host is the shark.

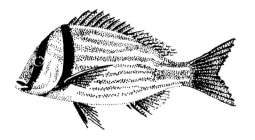

PORKFISH

A member of the grunt family, which makes excellent eating, the porkfish is easily identified by two black stripes. The body is bright yellow with blue stripes.

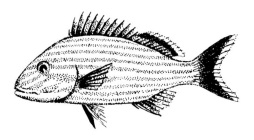

BLUESTRIPE GRUNT

The grunt is an excellent pan fish with sweet meat. "Grunts and grits" is a staple Keys diet. They are bright yellow with blue stripes running the length of the body. The name grunt derives from the sound they make by grinding their teeth together.

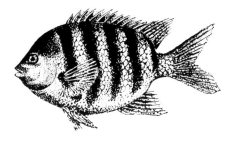

SERGEANT MAJOR

Large schools of diminutive sergeant major may be observed around docks and pilings or over rocks and coral. The deep yellow and white body is boldly striped with black. A good pan fish.

STONE CRAB   **BLUE CRAB**

Stone crabs are difficult to catch because they bury deep in the sand. They are distinguished by a flat, oval shell and black-tipped claws. Body meat is negligible, so Florida sportsmen take one claw, and return the crab to water. It will use the remaining claw to feed while it grows a second claw. NEVER TAKE TWO CLAWS.

Blue crabs favor warm, shallow water. They look smaller than Stone crabs because of their shape. Like Stone crabs, the best meat is in the claw, but the body meat is good, too.

SPINY LOBSTER

Like its California cousin, the Florida lobster lacks the claws which distinguish the Maine variety. They look like giant shrimp and favor holes in rocky or coral shores. When roused they swim rapidly with backward thrusts of their strong tails. Use a poking stick (to avoid Moray eels) and wear rubber gloves. Catching a lobster with bare hands can be painful. Spearing is forbidden.

FISH TO AVOID

In any tropic waters you will find creatures which are either dangerous or unpleasant. Usually they can be avoided with reasonable precaution.

Moray Eels lurk in caves or holes. Use a poking stick, not your hand, to investigate a hole. Fishermen who hook a moray should cut the line. Never handle them.

Sting Rays hover over the bottom, and can inflict painful wounds on waders or swimmers in shallow water. They have wing-like fins and a lashing barbed tail. Cut the line if you catch one. The large surface manta ray is harmless.

Sea Urchins look like spiny black balls. Barbs are painful and can be serious. Use protective footwear.

Portugese Man-of-War are jellyfish which look like balloons floating on the water and have stinging purple streamers below. If stung by a Portuese Man-of-War, wash affected areas with ammonia.

Sharks are attracted by blood and thrashing movement. Don't swim from twilight to dawn in shallow areas adjacent to deep water.

Fire Coral. Try to avoid contact with this reddish-brown coral. It can cause bad cuts.

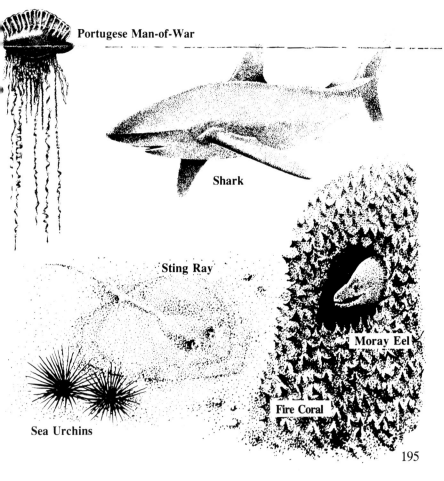

Portugese Man-of-War

Shark

Sting Ray

Moray Eel

Fire Coral

Sea Urchins

195

GALLEY GUIDE & PROVISIONING

Provisioning is one of the most important parts of the trip. You need the right amount and type of food to satisfy everyone, yet it should be fast and easy to cook and clean up. A lot depends on your personal tastes and cruising style. You can cruise "Bahama Style", by relying on canned and dried foods with occasional stops for water, ice and fuel. Or you can cruise by day and dine ashore every night. Restaurants in the Keys offer everything from American hamburgers and steaks to international cuisine, local specialties and, of course, fresh seafood.

Most people choose a middle course, living aboard with stops every 3 or 4 days for fresh meat and produce. Even though food is readily available in the Keys, it's wise to provision as completely as possible before you start your cruise. Bring aboard any heavy or bulky items, such as canned goods or paper products, so that on future stops you can take a short walk to a supermarket and carry back whatever fresh provisions you need.

The initial marketing list should include everything you'll need for the cruise. Don't forget staples, such as salt and sugar, or paper products and cleaning supplies. Many of these items may already be aboard, even on charter boats.

A pre-marketing check of the storage lockers will tell you what items can be crossed off the list. Rather than buy a supply of herbs and spices, bring a tablespoon or two of your favorites in plastic medicine bottles. They can be carried aboard with your luggage to add variety to your meals.

Refrigeration plays a big part in provisioning. Ice is readily available in the Keys, but many yachts do not have large ice boxes. We use a separate cooler for cold drinks and beer, so that the main ice box, which is used for storage of meats and perishables, will be opened as few times as possible.

When you first board the boat, bring along 200 to 300 pounds of block ice to "prime" the cooler. By the time gear is stowed and the shopping done, the cooler will be cold enough for perishables and additional ice. Block ice keeps better and can be chipped with an ice pick, but a bag or two of ice cubes at the top of the cooler is very convenient for cold drinks.

Most galley stoves have limited burner space and operate on alcohol, which is expensive. The best meals are those which cook quickly on one or two burners. Once lit, a galley stove should not be left unattended, so a long-simmering stew would not only consume a lot of fuel but make the cook a "galley slave". This doesn't mean that meals on board have to be dull casseroles. Some of the world's greatest dishes have been invented in countries where cooking fuel is scarce and refrigeration non-existent. Chinese, Japanese, Italian and country-style French cooking are all good choices for the floating gourmet.

Some boats have charcoal grills, which are a real advantage if you watch the flames. We find fresh fish especially good cooked on the barbecue. As the fire cools, you can make toast, which can be cubed as a garnish for soups and salads, or mixed with chopped bacon and scrambled eggs for a one-dish breakfast the next day.

Storing & Using Fresh Foods

Some meats, fruits and vegetables keep better than others. A lot depends upon the weather, the amount of ice you can carry and still have room for food, and how cold the cooler is when you add the food. Careful planning can help you avoid spoilage and waste.

Following are some guidelines to help you in shopping for, storing and using meats, dairy products, vegetables and fruits.

Papy's Fish & Cocktail Sauce

10 tablespoons mayonnaise
4 tablespoons soy sauce
2 teaspoons rum
½ teaspoon white pepper (or black pepper)

Stir all ingredients together and chill. Serve on conch lobster, shrimp or fish. It also makes a good salad dressing.

Meat Marinades

WINE MARINADE
1½ to 2 cups red or white wine
¼ cup wine vinegar
2 tablespoons oil
3 cloves garlic, halved, unpeeled
1 onion, sliced
1 carrot, sliced
1 to 2 teaspoons salt
2 bay leaves
1 teaspoon mixed herbs (fennel, oregano, thyme or marjoram)
⅛ teaspoon pepper

Marinates 3 pounds of beef or lamb. This marinade will keep at least 3 days. If you plan to marinate the meat longer, omit the garlic, onion and carrot. Substitute 2 teaspoons garlic salt for the salt and double the bay leaves.

LEMON MARINADE
½ cup lemon juice
½ cup olive oil
2 cloves garlic, mashed
1 to 2 teaspoons salt
¼ teaspoon pepper
½ teaspoon rosemary OR 2 bay leaves and ½ teaspoon thyme

Marinates 3 pounds of lamb or pork chops.

SOY MARINADE
1 cup soy sauce
¼ cup Worcestershire sauce
¼ cup lemon juice
½ teaspoon pepper

Marinates 3 pounds of beef, lamb or pork.

Perishable Meats

• **Ground beef** should be cooked within 24 hours of purchase. If you want to serve hamburgers, plan them for the first day out. Ground beef can be kept at least an extra day if it is cooked for spaghetti sauce, chili or other ground beef dishes. The meat should be covered with sauce or fat to seal out bacteria and air, cooled to room temperature, and stored in a plastic container directly on ice.

• **Chicken** should be washed in salted water and cooked within 24 hours. If you don't want to serve it the first day, poach or steam it until it is thoroughly cooked and cool it to room temperature. Then skin, bone, dice and store it for use the next day in salad, á la King, curry, or any other recipe calling for cooked chicken.

• **Fresh pork chops** should be cooked within 24 hours. They will keep a little longer if marinated from the start in lemon juice and olive oil. (See marinades.) Cooked pork, such as barbecued spareribs, will keep until the second day.

Less Perishable Meats

• **Beef and lamb (unground)** should keep three days on ice. Marinated, they should keep several days longer. Since marinade flavors as well as preserves, you may want to make several marinades to vary your menus.

Trimmed, boneless meat is easier to store in the cooler and takes less space in the cooking pan. A solid piece of meat keeps longer than meat which is sliced or cut up because there are fewer surfaces exposed to bacteria and air. If your budget is unlimited, tenderloin steaks are a good choice for a boat because they are solid meat and several can be cooked at one time. Less tender cuts of boneless meat, such as flank steak, round steak or sirloin tip, can be marinated in one piece, then sliced thinly and used for Chinese stir-fried, Japanese sukiyaki, French stroganoff or Italian steak a la pizzaiola. Cooked in this way, one pound of boneless meat can serve four, and can be as economical as hamburgers.

• **Cured meats,** such as ham and bacon, are now available in cans which need no refrigeration. Before purchasing, check the label to make sure it reads 'needs no refrigeration'. These meats are a boon to the yachtsman, especially on a long cruise or during delays due to bad weather or an unplanned layover in a remote spot. Some stores sell dry sausage and beef jerky which need no refrigeration, but most 'lunch meats' should be stored directly on ice and used within a few days.

Dairy Products

• **Fresh milk** should be stored directly on ice. When possible, buy 'dated' milk. It will keep several days beyond the last date of sale.

• **Sour cream** keeps well, and can be used for snack dips, stroganoff or casseroles.

• **Fresh cheeses,** such as cottage or ricotta, should be stored on ice and used within two days.

• **Harder cheeses,** such as Swiss, Monterey Jack or Cheddar, keep well, especially when they are not sliced or shredded.

• **Dry cheeses,** like Parmesan, add flavor and variety to foods and keep a long time.

• **Eggs, butter or margarine** keep in the cooler as they do in the refrigerator. To test an egg's freshness, fill a glass with water and slip the egg in gently. If it sinks, it's good, if it floats, throw it out.

Vegetables

The keeping quality of fresh vegetables is similar to the home refrigerator, although some vegetables actually keep better in the boat cooler. Ever since sailors discovered the cure for scurvy, fresh vegetables have been traditional in the yachtsman's diet.

• **The basic three: onions, carrots and celery** are used to flavor and give natural moisture to almost any meat or fish. They can be used as vegetable side dishes or served raw as snacks. Onions and carrots will keep well outside the cooler.

• **Green peppers** keep better in the ship's cooler than the home refrigerator, since it likes cool but not cold temperatures.

• **Tomatoes** keep well in the cooler. Partially ripened tomatoes from the home garden or a roadside stand will ripen at room temperature as you cruise. Tomatoes which have been refrigerated will never ripen.

• **Potatoes and winter squash** keep well outside the cooler, but take a long time to cook. You may prefer to buy instant mashed potatoes in foil packets (to keep out the humidity), or canned potatoes, sweet potatoes or pumpkin.

• **Asparagus, beans, broccoli, peas, summer squash and sweet corn** taste most flavorful when cooked shortly after picking. Use them as you would at home.

• **Lettuce** keeps in the boat cooler as well as it does in the refrigerator crisper. Wash just before using, as excess moisture causes leaves to rot, or turn limp or brown.

• **Fresh bean sprouts** are as easy to grow on a boat as they are at home. They're a good choice for extended cruises with few stops for fresh provisions.

Fruit

• **Apples** are traditional boat fare. They need no refrigeration, but most people prefer them chilled.

• **Avocados** ripen at room temperature. If you're lucky enough to be cruising the Keys while this plentiful and inexpensive fruit-vegetable is in season, it will give a Caribbean flavor to your meals.

• **Bananas** ripen at room temperature. Try sautéed green bananas for a tropical vegetable.

• **Berries,** such as strawberries or raspberries do not keep well, and should be used immediately.

• **Citrus fruits** keep well in the cooler, or even at room temperature. They are usually picked green for out-state shipment, but in the Keys you can sometimes find tree-ripened fruit, which will be sweeter and juicier tasting.

• **Peaches, pears and pineapples** can be kept in the cooler or ripened at room temperature. Pineapple is native to the area, and can double as a vegetable in Caribbean or Oriental dishes.

Sample Menu

The following menu is for a 7-day cruise for four persons. It starts with fresh foods, then uses canned goods to finish the trip. If you plan a provisioning stop after the third or fourth day, you can substitute fresh foods for these items.

For the second dinner, buy a frozen chicken and let it defrost in the cooler. Put the lamb chops into the lemon marinade before storing them in the cooler directly on the ice. Remember to turn them once or twice a day.

Departure Day Dinner
Crackers and cheese appetizer
Hamburgers in buns,
  garnished with sliced onion,
  tomatoes and pickles
Fresh green vegetable
  (in season)
Lettuce wedges with crumbed
  bleu cheese
Fresh fruit
Coffee or tea

1st Day
Breakfast
Fresh grapefruit
Bacon and eggs
Toast with jam or jelly
Dry cereal with fresh milk
Coffee

Lunch
Sandwiches with cold cuts,
  sliced cheese, lettuce, pickles
Fresh fruit
Iced tea, coffee or lemonade

Dinner
Sour cream and onion soup
  dip with chips, appetizer
Sautéed chicken
Instant mashed potatoes
Sliced carrots, cooked in
  butter and rum
Tossed salad with chopped
  onion, tomato, green pepper
Fresh fruit

2nd Day
Breakfast
Fresh oranges
Ranch-style eggs with bacon,
  onion, green pepper, tomato
Toast and jelly
Dry cereal with fresh milk
Coffee

Lunch
Soup and sandwiches
Carrot sticks
Fruit
Coffee, iced tea or lemonade

Dinner
Mixed nuts appetizer
Steaks with mushrooms
Pan-browned (canned)
  potatoes
Green beans (canned)
Tossed salad
Fresh fruit

3rd Day
Breakfast
Fresh grapefruit
Cheese omelet with canned
  luncheon loaf
Toast with jam or jelly
Coffee

Lunch
Bacon, lettuce and tomato
  sandwiches
Potato chips
Fruit
Iced tea, coffee or juice

Dinner
Crackers, pâté and sardines
Greek lamb chops (lemon
  juice marinade)
Rice with sliced stuffed olives
  or black olives
Three bean salad (canned)
Sliced oranges and bananas
Cookies

4th Day

Breakfast
Juice
Scrambled eggs with Vienna
  sausage (canned)
Toast with jam or jelly
Cereal with powdered milk
Coffee

Lunch
Grilled cheese sandwiches
Sliced tomatoes or stewed
  tomatoes
Pickles
Fruit

Dinner
Pan-fried ham slices (canned)
  glazed with marmalade
Macaroni and cheese (canned)
Tossed salad
Canned peaches
Cookies

5th Day

Breakfast
Juice
Omelet with chopped ham
Toast with jam or marmalade
Dry cereal with powdered milk

Lunch
Tuna salad sandwiches
Pickles
Potato chips
Fruit
Iced tea, coffee, juice or
  lemonade

Dinner
Peanuts, shrimp cocktail
Chicken chow mein (canned)
Rice
Canned pineapple slices
Fortune cookies

6th Day

Breakfast
Scrambled eggs with chopped
  beef
Toast with jam or jelly
Dry cereal with powdered milk
Coffee

Lunch
Chopped ham and egg salad
  sandwiches
Pickles, olives
Fruit
Coffee, iced tea or juice

Dinner
Assorted appetizers (use
  remaining nuts, crackers,
  spreads, sardines)
Beef stew (canned; sauté
  remaining onions or carrots
  and add to stew)
Buttered corn (canned)
Sliced tomatoes (canned) or
  stewed tomatoes
Canned pears

7th Day

Breakfast
Juice
French toast with jelly or jam
  (use the leftover bread
  and eggs)
Dry cereal with powdered milk
Coffee

Lunch
Hot dogs (canned) with baked
  beans (canned)
Canned green vegetable
Iced tea, coffee or juice

Provisioning List

Starred items are canned goods for which fresh food may be substituted if you plan to make a provisioning stop midway through your cruise. Some amounts are unspecified because they depend upon your tastes.

Fresh meats
Lean ground beef (hamburgers for 4)
1 broiler-fryer chicken, frozen
4 small steaks (tenderloin, strip or rib eye)
4 lamb chops
5 pkgs. cold cuts
2 pounds bacon

Fresh fruit and vegetables (in season)
1 bag oranges
1 bag apples
4 grapefruit
1 pineapple
Bananas (some green to ripen)
Limes
4 heads lettuce
1 pkg. fresh green vegetables
3 large onions
1 small bag carrots
10 tomatoes
1 green pepper

Dairy products
4 dozen eggs
2 pounds butter or margarine
2 pounds Cheddar cheese
Small pkg. bleu cheese
2 quarts milk

Canned meats
*1 canned ham
1 can Vienna sausage
*2 cans wieners
*1 jar chipped beef
*2 cans beef stew
2 cans pork and beans

*1 large can tuna fish
2 cans sardines
2 cans luncheon loaf
*1 can shrimp
2 cans pâté
* Large can chicken chow mein
*2 cans macaroni and cheese

Juices and beverages
4 cans tomato juice
4 cans orange juice
4 cans grapefruit juice
1 can ground coffee or 1 jar instant coffee
1 jar non-dairy creamer
Instant tea
1 box tea bags
6 pkgs. lemonade mix
Soft drinks and other beverages

Canned and packaged fruit and vegetables
1 jar reconstituted lemon juice
*1 large can pears
1 large can peaches
*1 can sliced pineapple
*1 can sliced tomato for salad
1 can stewed tomatoes
2 cans boiled potatoes
2 cans mushrooms
1 can green beans
2 cans three bean salad
*1 can corn
1 large can shoestring potatoes
1 pound rice
Instant mashed potatoes
*1 can peas or mixed vegetables

Snacks and sweets
2 cans peanuts
2 cans mixed nuts
3 boxes crackers
3 bags potato or corn chips
2 boxes cookies
1 box fortune cookies
2 bags candy

Staples
5 loaves of bread

202

1 pkg. hamburger buns
Sugar
Salt
Pepper
Seasoned salt
Cooking oil
Vinegar
1 bottle ketchup
1 bottle mustard
1 small shrimp cocktail sauce
2 jars mayonnaise
1 bottle salad dressing
1 jar dill pickles
1 jar sweet pickles
1 jar stuffed olives
1 jar plain olives
1 bottle Worcestershire sauce
1 bottle soy sauce
1 jar sandwich spread
1 jar peanut butter
1 jar marmalade
1 jar grape jelly
1 jar strawberry jam

2 boxes cereal
1 small box powdered milk

Miscellaneous
Dishwashing liquid
Scouring powder
Disinfectant
1 pkg. sponges
1 pkg. scouring pads
5 bars hand soap
2 pkgs. paper napkins
2 pkgs. paper plates
2 rolls paper towels
2 boxes facial tissue
4 rolls toilet paper
1 box aluminum foil
Plastic food storage bags
Plastic garbage bags
1 box kitchen matches
1 can insect repellent
1 can roach spray
Charcoal and starter if boat is
equipped with grill

Yacht Jacking

This is an unpleasant subject to talk about when everyone is having a good time cruising, but it's best to be prepared. As a skipper licensed in the U.S. and Panama to 1000 tons, I take precautions.

1. Keep a good flare pistol available.
2. Be cautious about giving assistance to a vessel in distress. Check it out with your binoculars and look for a larger vessel in the area. Call the Coast Guard with the vessels identification and location. Never go near a boat which doesn't have a name and number.
3. When you hire temporary help, check their references.
4. Before you shove off on a long open water sail, check all spaces where someone could hide; the engine room, hanging lockers, heads or covered dinghy.
5. Bring the swimming ladder aboard when you anchor for the night.
6. When leaving your boat for long periods of time, pull the coil wire on the engine or use a fuel cutoff switch. This might cause just enough trouble to deter yacht jackers.

How to Go Through Bridges With Style

Some of the most hair-raisin', vocabulary-exercisin' experiences can occur while going through draw bridges.

The following routine procedures make things easier for both the boat captain and bridge tender.

Know the height above the water line of your mast, antenna, flying bridge or tuna tower. Lower outriggers and motor boat's radio antenna to prevent unnecessary bridge openings. You should also know the depth of your boat below the water line (draft), since maneuvers required while waiting for a bridge opening may take you into shoal waters.

The most reliable signalling device is a hand held compressed gas-powered horn. This type of horn can be aimed at the bridge tender's shack to give him the full benefit of your signal. It's disadvantage is that the supply of gas is not endless; it's a good idea to have at least one extra can of compressed horn gas on board.

Before nearing a bridge which requires opening, consult your charts to determine the width of the bridge opening and the vertical clearance below the closed span at high tide. Some bridges have restricted opening schedules; when in doubt consult the latest "Notices to Mariners" and the latest edition of the "Coast Pilot". Further study of the chart will reveal the likelihood of current tables) and whether or not there is deep water near the bridge to maneuver.

When you come in sight of the bridge, train your binoculars on the bridge tender's shack to see if he is visible, this check will give you a clue as you know how difficult it may be to get his attention. As you near the bridge, listen for the sirens of emergency vehicles since the bridge will not open for boaters until any emergency vehicles have exercised their right of way.

As you near the bridge, check the vertical clearance gauges which are usually located on the bridge pilings or dolphins. These gauges show the actual vertical clearance at any stage of the tide. You may find that at low tides you will not need to open the bridge. While examining the vertical clearance gauges, look at the center of the span. A red flag flying there indicates that the bridge is out of operation; further information may be obtained by contacting the Coast Guard or bridge tender on your VHF radio. If you see a sign at the center of the span, it usually means that the bridge is restricted in its opening; this sign will inform you of the schedule. If you find that the bridge is restricted, wait to one side of the channel to allow the passage of boats which don't require opening of the bridge. Consult chart to find out how much maneuvering room you have!

Before sounding your horn, try contacting the bridge tender by VHF Channels 16 or 13, since many bridges are now equipped with VHF radios. If the VHF contact doesn't work, warn your passengers to "cover yer ears", point the horn toward the bridge tender's shack and give him 1 long horn blast and 1 short. I know of one bridge that requires 4 short blasts, but such exceptions are usually indicated by large signs located near the approaches to these bridges.

After sounding your horn, check the bridge tender's shack with your binoculars for any signs of life. When signalling a bridge at night, it helps to flash your spreader lights or to flash a spot light on your sails or deck. If you feel that the situation warrants flashing your spot light onto the bridge tender's shack, choose a moment when there are no vehicles crossing the bridge. During the daytime, a mirror might also be used to attract the attention of the bridge tender. If, after all of your signalling, you feel that the bridge tender has not been sufficiently alerted, suppress your desire to turn the atmosphere blue with an exercise of profanity-...many of today's bridge tenders are attractive ladies!!

As we all know, there are books of "Rules of the Road" governing passing situations between vessels at a bridge. If you're like me, you can't recite these rules verbatim; I try to let common sense and courtesy determine my actions.

Don't always crowd up near the bridge in an attempt to be the first boat through. All this does is raise your blood pressure and that of other skippers trying to get through the bridge.

To a sailor, nothing is more discourteous than some wise guy sailor trying to get through a bridge under sail, when he has auxiliary power available. These "salts"

may think that this sort of maneuver sets them apart as real sailors, but those who are experienced consider it nothing but an exercise in poor seamanship. Of course, some vessels are truly restricted in their ability to maneuver while going through a bridge; this would include commercial tugs with tows, boats with high masts that are trying to get through the bridge without raising it, etc. You should alway stay clear of these vessels.

A bimini top on a sailboat often restricts the helmsman's view of the boat's mast. For this reason, I alway lower my bimini top while going through a bridge. This allows me to have an unobstructed sight of the clearance between the mast and the opening bridge spans. Sometimes a bridge span may hang up and not open all the way and your bimini top might block your view of this situation.

When the bridge has been raised and you are going through, keep that horn handy to sound the danger signal (four or more short blasts) if the bridge starts to close too soon. I have had the tar scared out of me by a bridge tender closing the bridge too soon. The only thing that saved my rig was being able to sound the danger signal quickly.

One thing that will make friends among fellow yachtsmen (bridge tenders too) is slowing down to await boats close astern so that you can all go through the bridge at one opening. Slowing down or waiting 4 to 5 minutes to allow such boats to catch up will brand you as a "real pro".

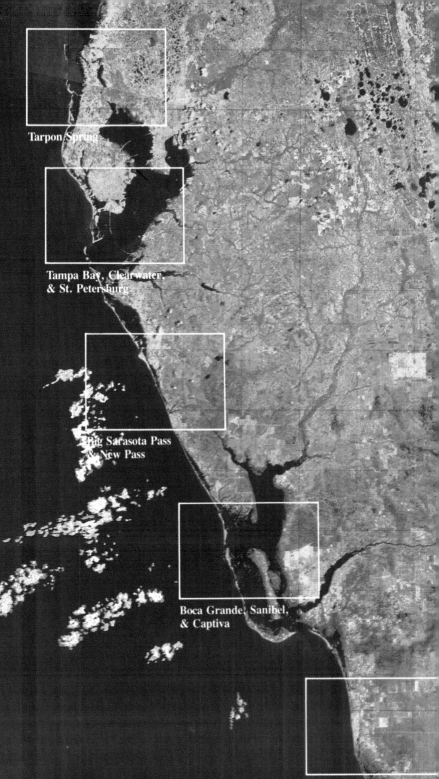

Tarpon Spring

Tampa Bay, Clearwater,
& St. Petersburg

Big Sarasota Pass
& New Pass

Boca Grande, Sanibel,
& Captiva

Naples

New Florida West Coast Supplement

Cruising in south Florida waters on the west coast has become increasingly popular. This section has been expanded to address the numerous requests we've had to extend our coverage of this area.

The reason for the west coast's popularity becomes clear as you travel from the lower Florida keys north to Tarpon Springs. This area offers 280 miles of incredible cruising areas. There's the beauty and solitude of the Everglades. Then famous shelling beaches of Sanibel and Captiva Islands, dotted with quaint little towns. Boca Grande, the tarpon fishing capital of the world, leads to Charlotte Harbor, a beautiful inland sailing area.

Venice and Sarasota lead up to the Tampa Bay area, a sailor's haven with a number of yacht clubs and marinas.

As you continue, you'll discover Tarpon Springs, with its sponge fishing fleet, fantastic Greek food and atmosphere.

So little accurate information about this area has been reported, that the author is presently compiling a complete guide to the west coast. Until it is published, this supplement will serve as an introduction to expand your interest and knowledge of this beautiful cruising area.

207

TARPON SPRINGS

I usually leave from Clearwater Pass and go on the outside, sailing up past Clearwater Beach. Then I travel down Eden Pass, by Hurricane Pass and pick up Anclote Key. Just to the southwest of Anclote Key is a 4-second flashing #1, visible from about 5 miles. I leave that to port and head on course about 89° to the east. Then you'll pick up a green flashing 4-second #7. Leave it to port, turn and take a course about 28° into the pass toward Anclote River.

The Anclote River leads into Tarpon Springs, pictured here. Note the excellent navigational aid — the stack in the upper left.

At Anclote Key, which is to the north, there are two anchorages (marked on the chart). One is by Dutchman Key and the other is about ¼ of the way up Anclote Key. I've also anchored on the front side of Anclote Key with a strong easterly and southeasterly wind, pulling fairly close to the land. It's a very pleasant spot in calm weather. There are several spots to anchor in this area to get out of the wind.

As you come into the Anclote River and pass through the channel into Tarpon Springs, you'll come upon a stack for the power plant that serves as a very good landmark with a good range light. There are also a couple of good range lights and range markers as you come in through the channel, alongside of Bird Key and Brandy Island. The first marina you'll come to on the northern side as you head into the channel is Port Tarpon Marina. It's a nice little spot with a small, pleasant restaurant. I didn't have any problem going in there with 5½ feet. They have a railway there, so it's like a boat yard and a marina.

Further into Tarpon Springs, where the city was originally settled by Greek sponge fishermen, you'll find J. Reis' and Louis Papass' Greek Restaurants. They serve delicious Greek food and play traditional Greek music. I found 5½ to 6 feet of water there, and a dock to tie up at. The Tarpon Springs Municipal Marina is just next to the restaurant. I've also been there with 5½ to 6 feet of water without any problem. They have a few slips and an accommodating dockmaster. It's very nice.

There's also a yacht club with facilities — the Tarpon Springs Yacht Club. I haven't been in there with a boat because they told us there were only 3 feet of water. We were there on January 6th, while they celebrated their spactacular Blessing of the Fleet. The people get all dressed up and are joined by a Greek Orthodox priest to parade around in their boats. It's really something to see.

One of the highlights as you travel around Tarpon Springs along the west coast is the number of state parks in the area. Caladesa Islands in particular are very pleasant. They're not accessible by car, which makes it especially nice. All in all, Tarpon Springs is a fantastic place to visit.

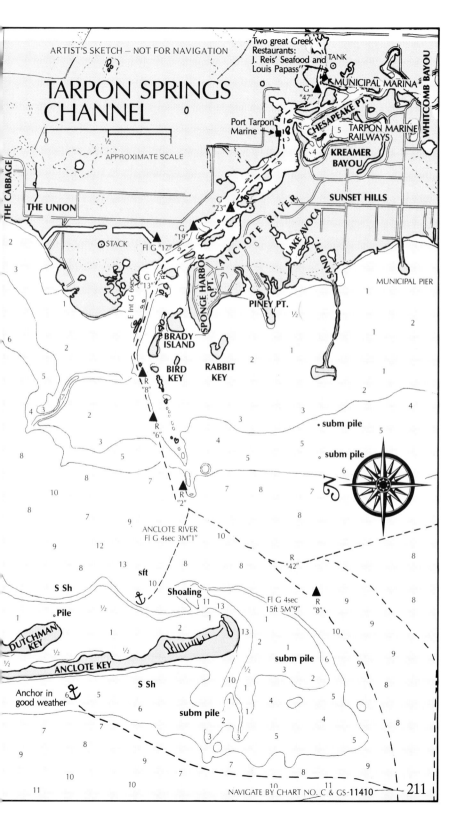

TARPON SPRINGS CHANNEL

ARTIST'S SKETCH – NOT FOR NAVIGATION

Two great Greek Restaurants: J. Reis' Seafood and Louis Papass"

TANK

MUNICIPAL MARINA

G "47"

CHESAPEAKE PT.

TARPON MARINE RAILWAYS

Port Tarpon Marine

5

KREAMER BAYOU

4

WHITCOMB BAYOU

0   ½   1

APPROXIMATE SCALE

THE CABBAGE

THE UNION

STACK

Fl G "17"

SUNSET HILLS

G "23"

G "19"

ANCLOTE RIVER

LAKE AVOCA

SAND PT.

MUNICIPAL PIER

G "13"

E Int G 6sec

SPONGE HARBOR PT.

PINEY PT.

BRADY ISLAND

BIRD KEY

RABBIT KEY

R "8"

R "6"

subm pile

subm pile

R "2"

ANCLOTE RIVER
Fl G 4sec 3M"1"

R "42"

Fl G 4sec
15ft 5M"9"

R "8"

sft

Shoaling

S Sh

Pile

DUTCHMAN KEY

ANCLOTE KEY

subm pile

S Sh

subm pile

Anchor in good weather

Your First Bahamas Voyage

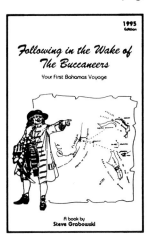
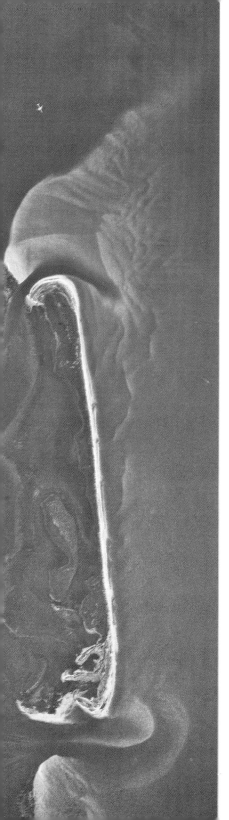

This is an aerial view of the Tarpon Springs area with the sandy beaches of Anclote Key on the right. If you like scallops you can find them by snorkeling in this area. Check the season. It varies with the summer months.

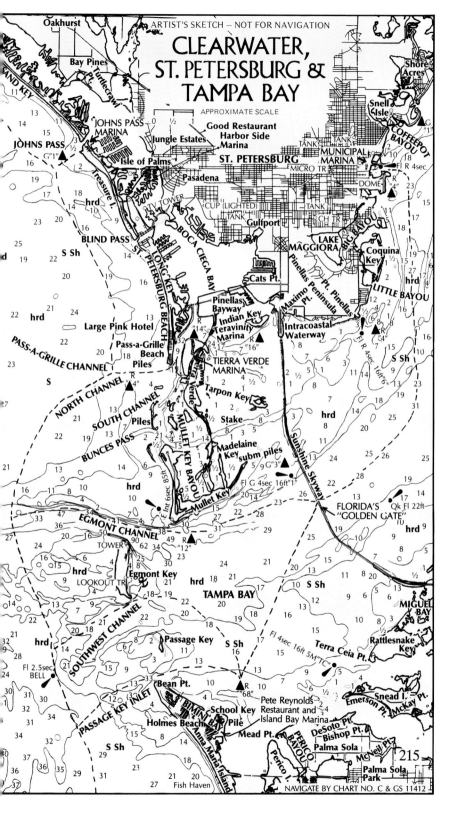

ARTIST'S SKETCH — NOT FOR NAVIGATION

CLEARWATER,
ST. PETERSBURG &
TAMPA BAY

APPROXIMATE SCALE

NAVIGATE BY CHART NO. C & GS 11412

215

CLEARWATER, ST. PETERSBURG & TAMPA BAY

Going south from Tarpon Springs and Anclote Key into Clearwater, we usually take Clearwater Pass. Pick up the No. 1 bell buoy and take the channel in. The channel doglegs to starboard with a strong tidal rip. Watch the tide and allow plenty of time for the bridge to open.

Once inside if you need fuel or supplies head north to the Clearwater Municipal Marina. We usually call ahead for a slip there. The Municipal Marina has numerous shops as well as good restaurants and a beach for swimming (and sunsets) within walking distance. If you want to stop

The beach at Clearwater Pass with the Intercoastal Waterway above to the east.

at a club, call ahead to the Clearwater Yacht Club to check on available slips and draft. Their docks, with a nice marina, are on the way to the Clearwater Municipal Marina.

For yacht repairs, you can't do much better than Clearwater. I've found that parts and labor prices are more reasonable on the West Coast, with many skilled craftsmen from the boat factories in the area. Head north on the Intercoastal Waterway to Ross Yachts. They are dealers and service representatives for many lines of boating equipment. Ross does lots of work on the S.O.R.C. boats, so January and February are very busy months for them. Clearwater Marine Ways is another good stop for haul out and repairs. They're also north on the Intercoastal Waterway.

If you prefer to anchor out, head down the Waterway south and pull in behind Sand Key. The holding ground here is fair.

As you head south down the coast toward St. Petersburg, the next place you can go in is John's Pass. We go down to North Channel Pass, which leads into Pass-A-Grille Channel. The landmark we use is a large pink hotel on the beach a little north of North Channel Pass.

Once inside you can head south and anchor just past the spoil bank in about 16 ft. of water. We usually take the opening to the east and go up into Tierra Verde. There's a great marina there with a hotel and restaurant. Go into St. Petersburg Beach to the Um-pa-pa Bar for some dancing and singing. If you like large marinas, go eastward to the St. Petersburg Municipal Marina. One of the highlights of cruising in the St. Petersburg area, the Marina has 600 slips, shops, restaurants, museums and

John's Pass. Be careful of this bridge, it opens very slowly.

This aerial photo shows Mullet Key and the main ship channel into Tampa Bay.

the Marina Point Ship Store.

The Sunshine Skyway Bridge, Golden Gate of the South, dominates the view as you near the Tampa Bay area. Coming in Egmont Key Channel, we often duck in the east side of Egmont Key and anchor. Another good spot is behind Mullet Key, a favorite anchorage with the locals. Once under the bridge, there is another route into the St. Petersburg Munical Marina, or up into old Tampa Bay or Hilsborough Bay for some exploring.

Tampa's Latin quarter, called Ybor City, has some great restaurants and cigar factories where you can watch the excellent local product being made.

In the Bay, watch out for the ship traffic. There have been many accidents involving ships lately; one struck a bridge piling, and another cut a Coast Guard cutter in half.

Check out the anchorage (4 ft. draft) in the Manatee River, near Desota Point. The river's mouth is at the southwest end of Tampa Bay, near Anna Maria Island. The Anna Maria Yacht Club, just northwest of the Key Royale Bar, is another nice spot in the area to overnight.

Egmont Key with "The Golden Gate of The South" in the background.

221

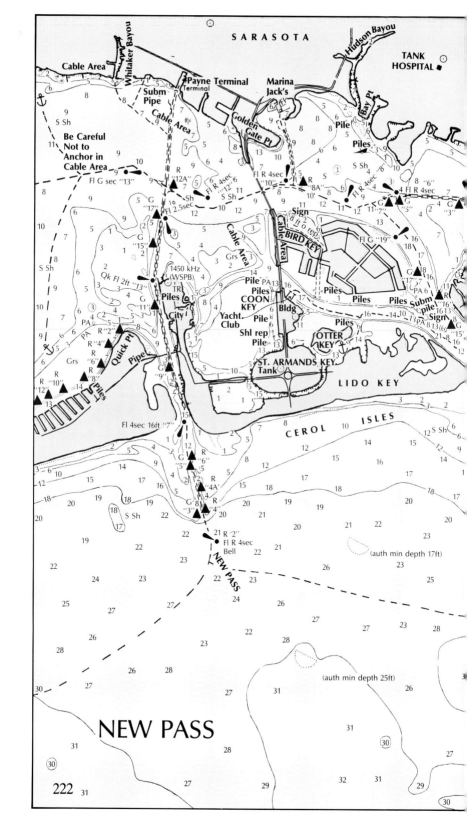

NEW PASS

222

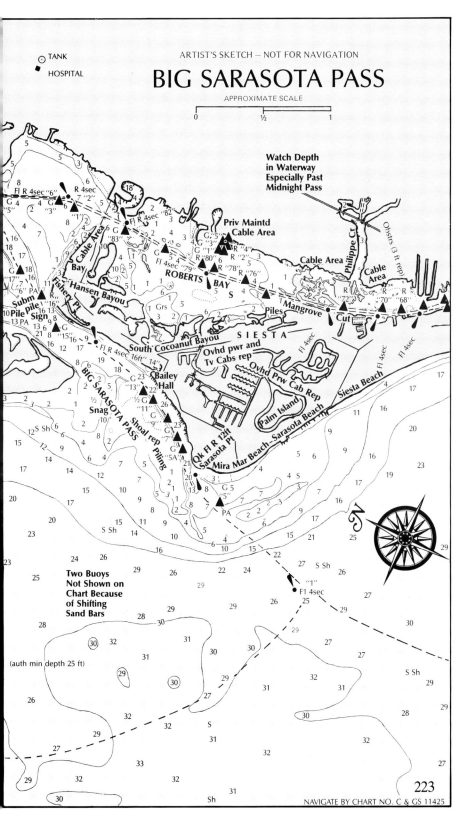

ARTIST'S SKETCH – NOT FOR NAVIGATION

BIG SARASOTA PASS

APPROXIMATE SCALE

⊙ TANK

■ HOSPITAL

Watch Depth in Waterway Especially Past Midnight Pass

Two Buoys Not Shown on Chart Because of Shifting Sand Bars

(auth min depth 25 ft)

NAVIGATE BY CHART NO. C & GS 11425

BIG SARASOTA PASS & NEW PASS

The next port of interest south of Tampa Bay is Sarasota. Enter at New Pass or Big Sarasota Pass, being careful of shoaling on both. New Pass, with a 4' 2" draft is no problem in fair to moderate weather; its our usual route. For a quick fuel stop once inside New Pass, there's a fuel dock on the south side just east of the bridge. For a longer stay, go east to the Intercoastal Waterway and head south through the next bridge to Marina Jack's. There are good restaurants at the marina and others within walking distance.

Within 2½ miles of Marina Jack's are the Van Wensel and

This shows Big Sarasota Pass with the Sarasota skyline in the background.

Ringling House Museums, as well as an excellent public library. On Saturdays at the intersection of Lime Ave. and Main Street local farmers set up a produce market with very reasonable prices. Check this out with the dockmaster.

Local yacht clubs include the Bird Key Club, across from Marina Jack's, and numerous others in the area. Good anchorages can be found in Sarasota Bay, either on the mainland side or near Longboat Key, depending on the weather.

The bridge and sand bar of New Pass are pictured above.

GOURMET

ODYSSEY

GOURMET ODYSSEY
by
CAPT. AL & JULIE PLANT

Captain Al and Julie lived a GOURMET ODYSSEY from Michigan to Molokai. This true life adventure was based on incidents recorded in the log book of the Motor Vessel Black Sheep and the experience of ten years cooking gourmet food in a yacht galley or compact kitchen. You join them when they cruised aboard their Chris Craft Aquahome™ on the rivers, lakes, ocean and Intra Coastal Waterway from Detroit to Fort Lauderdale, Florida. Then when the couple changed course, follow them to Honolulu and on to the tropical Hawaiian Island of Molokai.

Your cruising guide for cooking healthy meals in a Yacht Galley

ORDER SEND $16.95 (U.S.) plus $2.00 each shipping to:

Gourmet Odyssey
Capt. Al & Julie Plant
Box 61751, Honolulu, HI 96839, USA.

NAME _____

Address _____

City _____ State ____ Zip _____

Pay by Money Order or use your Visa/MC

MC __ VISA__ EXP DATE _ _ / _ _ / _ _

No: _ _ __ __ __ __ __ __ __ __ __ __ __ __ __ __ __

Quantity ___ Amount $ ____ . _____

This aerial photo will give you an idea of the sprawling sandbars offshore at Big Sarasota Pass. The famous author, John McDonald, lived just inside the inlet in a stilt house with a tin roof on Sand Dollar Island.

BOCA GRANDE, SANIBEL & CAPTIVA

The entrance to the Boca Grande Harbor is very well marked. Use the 105-ft. tall lighthouse on Gasparilla Island as a bearing marker and the plant buildings on the end of the island coming in. If you're coming up from the south, watch out for the extending shoals of Johnson Bank. There is an extremely strong tide running in and out of the Boca Grande entrance. If there's an incoming tide, you may be set onto Johnson Shoal.

If you come into the Boca Grande Entrance between May and late June or July, watch out for the tarpon fishermen. They fish right in the channel entrance. One night when we came in, the channel was a mass of lights. But we left the mainsail up and the spreader lights on and the fishermen were courteous about getting out of our way. It's very similar to the fishermen on the Manesquant Inland on the Jersey Coast.

Once inside the Boca Grande Channel, you can pull into Johnson Shoal in the daylight. You can keep inside the main small

The great shelling beaches of Sanibel & Captiva.

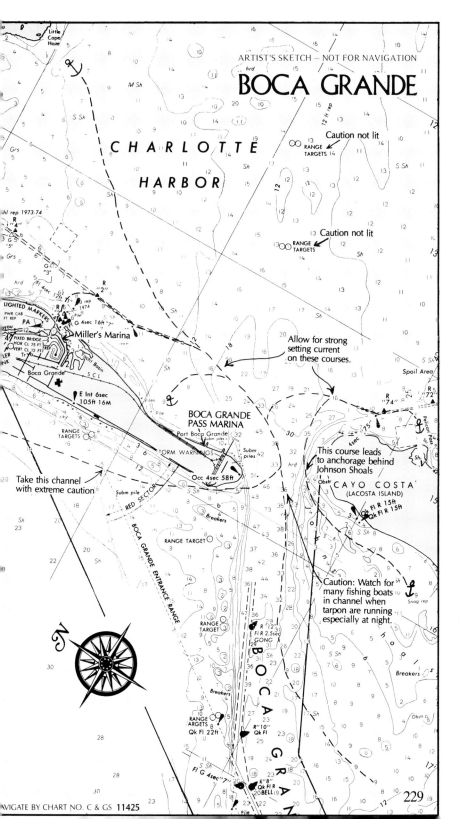

ARTIST'S SKETCH – NOT FOR NAVIGATION

BOCA GRANDE

Caution not lit

Caution not lit

CHARLOTTE

HARBOR

Miller's Marina

Allow for strong
setting current
on these courses.

BOCA GRANDE
PASS MARINA
Port Boca Grande

This course leads
to anchorage behind
Johnson Shoals

Take this channel
with extreme caution

STORM WARNINGS

CAYO COSTA
(LACOSTA ISLAND)

Caution: Watch for
many fishing boats
in channel when
tarpon are running
especially at night.

BOCA GRANDE ENTRANCE RANGE

229

islands (see chart on page 229) or keep on going just inside Gasparilla Island. There's an anchorage there, marked on the chart. As you travel further into Charlotte Harbor, watch out for the "Target Ranges", inside about ½ mile down the channel (see the chart). They're unlit and extremely dangerous at night.

The channel at the southern end of Cayo Costa Island is Captiva Pass. We've anchored and fished this area. We enjoyed the beautiful surroundings (despite a rather disappointing day of fishing). There is good dinghy exploring at Captiva Pass and up into Pigeon Cover and Safety Harbor. Neither of the adjoining islands are accessible by roads, so there aren't tourists to spoil the area.

On the east coast, and west of Rocky Channel, there are some fishing shacks built on stilts. We call the area Stiltsville. Behind Stiltsville is Bird Key, a bird sanctuary for the Pine Island Wildlife Refuge that's worth visiting.

Between North Captiva Island and Captiva lies Redfish Pass. Its mostly used by shallow draft vessels. Other boats may pass through, depending on the conditions. Listen to CB Channels 13 and 16 to check with local fishermen. We've had guides to take us in with 4½ ft. But in

This is an aerial photo showing the Boca Grande entrance, Gasparillia Island and Cayo Costa. Photo courtesy of N.O.A.A.

rough weather it's difficult to make the pass. You'll have to watch out for swells coming over the bar.

Just inside Redfish Pass, after you get into the intercoastal waterway, there's a well-marked channel. Come back in the channel to the South Seas Plantation Marina. You can take in 6 ft. here. But watch the turnoff in the intercoastal waterway. Don't let the current set you off course.

The South Seas Plantation Marina is very fancy. Golf, tennis and other amenities make it a very nice place to stay. You can reach Don Stands of the marina on VHF Channel 16.

As you travel north of Big Carlos Pass, we usually hold a course for the large 30-foot marker, a #1 4-second flashing green marker, which indicates the entrance to San Carlos Bay. When coming

in the channel, you can go in behind Estero Island, a very well marked channel between San Carlos Island and Fort Myers Beach proper. There are several nice marinas and a Coast Guard station up inside. But watch the current when coming around the main turn into the straight channel.

Olsen's and Hurricane Bay Marina in this area are geared mostly for repair and general boat work. Moss Marina and the Gulf Star have transient slips and a well marked channel coming in. There are several places to anchor in the channel. But watch the current that runs through the area.

Between Punta Rassa and Ybel Point, marked by a 98-foot light flashing 2-second, 10-second interval white light, you'll find a good entrance. It's espe-

The west coast of Florida is famous for shells.

232

On the way to Lake Okeechobee with the Ft. Myers Yacht Basin in the foreground.

cially good if the Gulf of Mexico is blowing up with winds in the direction that give you Sanibel Island on the lee. It's a well marked junction between the Caloosahatchee River, Matlacha Pass and the Pine Island Sound.

The Caloosahatchee River is the entrance to Fort Myers proper and the Okeechobee Waterway. We usually use this entrance to go into Fort Myers and stay at the Fort Myers City Marina. It's one of the nicest marinas on the West Coast, with excellent facilities and very considerate people. This also leads into the eastern side of Sanibel Island, where there's good shelling and beachcombing the Florida West Coast is known for. If you don't want to take a trip up to Pine Island Sound, there's the Sanibel Island Marina, just inside the southeastern tip of Sanibel Island.

NAPLES &
MARCO ISLAND

As you come up from Marco Island from the south, if your depth isn't too low, you can stay on the inside. Here you'll pass Rookery Bay, a great location for bird watching. Check with Marco or the Goodlands about the latest rules for visiting the over 4000-acre refuge sponsored by the Audubon Society. It's definitely worth seeing.

The docks at Naples Harbor.

Here is the break-water at Gordon Pass.

If you're coming into Naples from the Gulf of Mexico, you'll be going into Gordon Pass. We've taken in 6½ ft. there without any problems, staying on the starboard side of the channel coming in.

Keewaydin Island is privately owned by Mr. Norris, a Texaco Oil man. There's a restaurant there and a ferry boat that runs across from Port Royal at the Keewaydin dock. They have diesel fuel here. If you're coming by Gordon Pass this is a good place to slip in and pick up fuel and other supplies without going all the way to Naples. But going

Capri and Marco Pass sand bars in the center of the photograph.

up to Naples is a worthwhile trip.

If you have the time, Naples is one of the prettiest and cleanest towns we've stayed at on the west coast. It's alive with art festivals, swamp buggy races and several other events (at the city docks). We've also noticed a few boats anchored off. The City Marina suggests that you always make reservations when you come up, especially at the peak of the season.

The Cross Florida Cruise

Reader feedback picked up from boatshows and letters suggests showing an alternative route in returning from the Keys and Florida's coasts. It seems that, by and by, lots of cruising families have taken their boats on summer vacation cruises, and done a twenty to thirty day sail, using the Lake Okeechobee waterway as shown on the chart below. The only thing that might mess you up is a bridge height at port Mayaca of forty-eight feet on the eastern side of the lake.

Boaters from the eastern states trailer down to Stuart, Florida for a starting point, and sailors from as far as Texas put in at Fort Myers.

With kids on board, it's an education in itself, tricking them into nature's summer school. In order to maintain this beautiful environment, we must show the future generation how to enjoy and protect this wonderful gift. Not to mention, Mom and Dad can boogie and have a few beverages of their choice along the way.

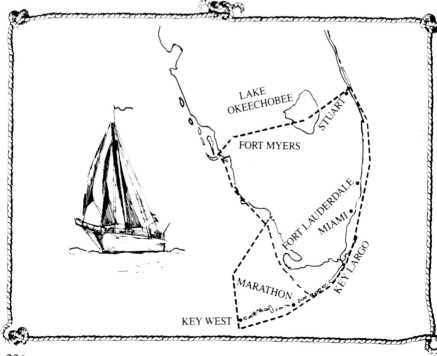

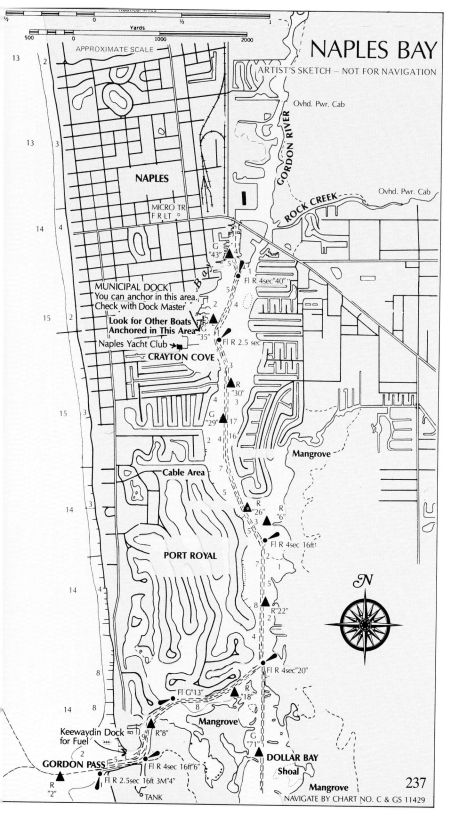

NAPLES BAY

ARTIST'S SKETCH — NOT FOR NAVIGATION

½ Nautical Miles
0 ½ 1

Yards
500 0 1000 2000

APPROXIMATE SCALE

13 2

13 3

NAPLES

14 4

MICRO TR
F R LT

Ovhd. Pwr. Cab

GORDON RIVER

ROCK CREEK

Ovhd. Pwr. Cab

G "43" 4
5

1
Fl R 4sec "40"

MUNICIPAL DOCK
You can anchor in this area.
Check with Dock Master

15 2

**Look for Other Boats
Anchored in This Area**

G "35"

Naples Yacht Club

CRAYTON COVE

Fl R 2.5 sec

5

2
4

R "30" 3

4

15 3

G "29"

17

2 4 16

Mangrove

Cable Area

5

R "26" R "6"
3
5

Fl R 4sec 16ft

14

PORT ROYAL

2
7 1
5

N

8 R "22"
2

4

14 4

Fl R 4sec "20"

8

Fl G "13"

R "18"

Mangrove

Keewaydin Dock
for Fuel

R "8"

9

G "71"

DOLLAR BAY
Shoal

14 8

2

GORDON PASS

Fl R 4sec 16ft "6"

R "2"

Fl R 2.5sec 16ft 3M "4"

TANK

Mangrove

237

NAVIGATE BY CHART NO. C & GS 11429

Cape Romano, the start of the beautiful sandy beaches of Florida's west coast.

As you sail up from the Cape Romano Shoals Light a large apartment building on Marco Island is usually the first landform you'll see. Knice Island is to the south and Cape Romano Island is to the north. This is Keewaydin, with five passes starting from the south; Caxambas Pass, Big Marco Pass, Capri Pass, Little Marco Pass and Hurricane Pass.

The safest pass is Capri Pass. Stay about 1½ miles off shore, using the large buildings for good bearing and you can pick up the sea buoy for Capri Pass marked C.P. Take up a heading about 80°, and you'll soon pick up Coconut Island. The channel is just to the north. When you get inside, use caution at the channel junction in the Big Marco River as you head up the river.

The first group of marinas on the southern side of the channel is Captain Jim's, where a Mr. Hornsby monitors VHF channels 16 and 68. The next marina, to the starboard, is the Marco River Marina, which also monitors VHF channel 16.

There's another nice marina with a well-marked channel close to the three stores and the restaurants there. If you're heading south to the keys, it's a good place to stock up on supplies—food, beer, rum, etc., because Everglade City and Flamingo are about the only two places to pick up provisions for the next 100 miles to the south. There's nothing worse than taking a trip without enough food and beverages.

Miami Harbor Entrance, Fla., 1995

Times and Heights of High and Low Waters

January

Day	Time	ft	cm
1 Su ●	0127	-0.7	-21
	0750	3.2	98
	1359	-0.2	-6
	2002	3.0	91
2 M	0218	-0.7	-21
	0840	3.2	98
	1450	-0.3	-9
	2054	3.0	91
3 Tu	0309	-0.6	-18
	0929	3.1	94
	1540	-0.3	-9
	2146	2.9	88
4 W	0358	-0.4	-12
	1017	3.0	91
	1630	-0.2	-6
	2237	2.8	85
5 Th	0448	-0.3	-9
	1104	2.8	85
	1720	-0.1	-3
	2330	2.6	79
6 F	0539	0.0	0
	1153	2.7	82
	1811	0.0	0
7 Sa	0024	2.4	73
	0631	0.2	6
	1242	2.5	76
	1903	0.1	3
8 Su	0120	2.3	70
	0725	0.3	9
	1333	2.3	70
	1957	0.1	3
9 M	0219	2.2	67
	0823	0.5	15
	1427	2.2	67
	2052	0.2	6
10 Tu	0318	2.2	67
	0922	0.5	15
	1521	2.1	64
	2146	0.1	3
11 W	0414	2.2	67
	1018	0.5	15
	1614	2.1	64
	2236	0.1	3
12 Th	0505	2.3	70
	1110	0.5	15
	1703	2.1	64
	2323	0.0	0
13 F	0551	2.3	70
	1156	0.4	12
	1749	2.2	67
14 Sa	0007	-0.1	-3
	0634	2.4	73
	1239	0.3	9
	1833	2.3	70
15 Su	0048	-0.2	-6
	0713	2.5	76
	1319	0.2	6
	1914	2.3	70
16 M ○	0128	-0.2	-6
	0751	2.6	79
	1357	0.1	3
	1954	2.4	73
17 Tu	0207	-0.3	-9
	0827	2.6	79
	1435	0.0	0
	2034	2.5	76
18 W	0246	-0.3	-9
	0904	2.6	79
	1513	-0.1	-3
	2115	2.5	76
19 Th	0326	-0.3	-9
	0941	2.6	79
	1552	-0.1	-3
	2158	2.5	76
20 F	0407	-0.2	-6
	1021	2.6	79
	1633	-0.2	-6
	2243	2.5	76
21 Sa	0452	-0.1	-3
	1103	2.5	76
	1719	-0.2	-6
	2333	2.4	73
22 Su	0541	0.0	0
	1150	2.4	73
	1810	-0.2	-6
23 M ◑	0029	2.4	73
	0636	0.1	3
	1243	2.4	73
	1907	-0.2	-6
24 Tu	0132	2.3	70
	0738	0.2	6
	1344	2.3	70
	2011	-0.2	-6
25 W	0239	2.4	73
	0846	0.2	6
	1450	2.3	70
	2117	-0.3	-9
26 Th	0347	2.4	73
	0955	0.1	3
	1558	2.4	73
	2223	-0.4	-12
27 F	0452	2.5	76
	1100	0.0	0
	1702	2.5	76
	2325	-0.5	-15
28 Sa	0551	2.7	82
	1200	-0.2	-6
	1802	2.6	79
29 Su	0022	-0.6	-18
	0645	2.8	85
	1254	-0.3	-9
	1858	2.7	82
30 M ●	0115	-0.7	-21
	0735	2.9	88
	1345	-0.4	-12
	1950	2.8	85
31 Tu	0204	-0.7	-21
	0822	2.9	88
	1433	-0.5	-15
	2039	2.8	85

February

Day	Time	ft	cm
1 W	0252	-0.7	-21
	0907	2.9	88
	1519	-0.5	-15
	2127	2.7	82
2 Th	0337	-0.5	-15
	0951	2.8	85
	1603	-0.5	-15
	2213	2.6	79
3 F	0422	-0.4	-12
	1033	2.6	79
	1647	-0.4	-12
	2259	2.5	76
4 Sa	0506	-0.2	-6
	1115	2.5	76
	1732	-0.2	-6
	2347	2.3	70
5 Su	0552	0.0	0
	1159	2.3	70
	1818	-0.1	-3
6 M	0036	2.2	67
	0640	0.2	6
	1244	2.1	64
	1907	0.0	0
7 Tu ◑	0130	2.0	61
	0733	0.4	12
	1335	2.0	61
	2000	0.1	3
8 W	0228	2.0	61
	0832	0.5	15
	1431	1.9	58
	2056	0.1	3
9 Th	0328	2.0	61
	0933	0.5	15
	1529	1.9	58
	2153	0.1	3
10 F	0424	2.0	61
	1030	0.4	12
	1626	1.9	58
	2247	0.0	0
11 Sa	0516	2.1	64
	1122	0.3	9
	1718	2.0	61
	2336	-0.1	-3
12 Su	0601	2.2	67
	1208	0.2	6
	1806	2.2	67
13 M	0021	-0.2	-6
	0642	2.4	73
	1249	0.0	0
	1850	2.3	70
14 Tu	0104	-0.3	-9
	0722	2.5	76
	1329	-0.1	-3
	1932	2.4	73
15 W ○	0144	-0.4	-12
	0759	2.6	79
	1408	-0.3	-9
	2014	2.5	76
16 Th	0225	-0.4	-12
	0837	2.6	79
	1447	-0.4	-12
	2056	2.6	79
17 F	0306	-0.4	-12
	0916	2.6	79
	1527	-0.5	-15
	2139	2.7	82
18 Sa	0348	-0.4	-12
	0957	2.6	79
	1610	-0.5	-15
	2225	2.6	79
19 Su	0434	-0.3	-9
	1041	2.6	79
	1657	-0.5	-15
	2315	2.6	79
20 M	0523	-0.2	-6
	1129	2.5	76
	1749	-0.4	-12
21 Tu	0011	2.5	76
	0618	0.0	0
	1223	2.4	73
	1847	-0.3	-9
22 W ◑	0113	2.4	73
	0720	0.1	3
	1326	2.3	70
	1952	-0.3	-9
23 Th	0221	2.3	70
	0830	2.3	70
	1435	2.3	70
	2102	-0.3	-9
24 F	0331	2.3	70
	0941	0.1	3
	1547	2.3	70
	2210	-0.3	-9
25 Sa	0438	2.4	73
	1048	0.0	0
	1654	2.4	73
	2314	-0.4	-12
26 Su	0537	2.5	76
	1147	-0.1	-3
	1754	2.5	76
27 M	0011	-0.5	-15
	0630	2.7	82
	1240	-0.3	-9
	1847	2.7	82
28 Tu	0102	-0.5	-15
	0717	2.7	82
	1327	-0.4	-12
	1936	2.7	82

March

Day	Time	ft	cm
1 W ●	0149	-0.5	-15
	0801	2.8	85
	1411	-0.5	-15
	2022	2.8	85
2 Th	0232	-0.5	-15
	0842	2.7	82
	1453	-0.5	-15
	2105	2.7	82
3 F	0314	-0.4	-12
	0921	2.7	82
	1533	-0.4	-12
	2147	2.7	82
4 Sa	0354	-0.2	-6
	1000	2.6	79
	1613	-0.4	-12
	2228	2.5	76
5 Su	0434	-0.1	-3
	1038	2.4	73
	1653	-0.2	-6
	2310	2.4	73
6 M	0515	0.1	3
	1117	2.3	70
	1734	-0.1	-3
	2354	2.2	67
7 Tu	0559	0.3	9
	1200	2.1	64
	1819	0.0	0
8 W	0043	2.1	64
	0648	0.4	12
	1247	2.0	61
	1909	0.2	6
9 Th ◑	0137	2.0	61
	0744	0.5	15
	1343	1.9	58
	2006	0.2	6
10 F	0237	2.0	61
	0846	0.5	15
	1445	1.9	58
	2107	0.2	6
11 Sa	0337	2.0	61
	0947	0.5	15
	1548	2.0	61
	2207	0.2	6
12 Su	0433	2.1	64
	1042	0.4	12
	1645	2.1	64
	2301	0.1	3
13 M	0522	2.3	70
	1131	0.2	6
	1736	2.3	70
	2350	-0.1	-3
14 Tu	0606	2.4	73
	1215	0.0	0
	1823	2.5	76
15 W	0035	-0.2	-6
	0648	2.6	79
	1257	-0.2	-6
	1907	2.7	82
16 Th ○	0119	-0.3	-9
	0728	2.7	82
	1338	-0.4	-12
	1951	2.8	85
17 F	0202	-0.4	-12
	0809	2.8	85
	1420	-0.5	-15
	2035	2.9	88
18 Sa	0245	-0.4	-12
	0851	2.8	85
	1504	-0.6	-18
	2121	3.0	91
19 Su	0330	-0.3	-9
	0934	2.8	85
	1549	-0.6	-18
	2209	2.9	88
20 M	0417	-0.2	-6
	1021	2.8	85
	1638	-0.5	-15
	2300	2.8	85
21 Tu	0508	-0.1	-3
	1112	2.7	82
	1731	-0.4	-12
	2355	2.7	82
22 W	0605	0.0	0
	1209	2.5	76
	1831	-0.3	-9
23 Th ◑	0058	2.6	79
	0708	0.2	6
	1314	2.4	73
	1937	-0.1	-3
24 F	0206	2.5	76
	0818	0.2	6
	1426	2.4	73
	2048	-0.1	-3
25 Sa	0315	2.5	76
	0929	0.2	6
	1538	2.4	73
	2158	0.0	0
26 Su	0421	2.5	76
	1034	0.1	3
	1645	2.5	76
	2301	-0.1	-3
27 M	0519	2.6	79
	1131	0.0	0
	1743	2.6	79
	2356	-0.1	-3
28 Tu	0609	2.7	82
	1221	-0.2	-6
	1834	2.7	82
29 W	0045	-0.2	-6
	0654	2.7	82
	1306	-0.3	-9
	1913	2.8	85
30 Th ●	0129	-0.2	-6
	0735	2.7	82
	1347	-0.3	-9
	2002	2.8	85
31 F	0210	-0.1	-3
	0814	2.7	82
	1425	-0.3	-9
	2041	2.8	85

Time meridian 75° W. 0000 is midnight. 1200 is noon.
Heights are referred to mean lower low water which is the chart datum of soundings.

Miami Harbor Entrance, Fla., 1995

Times and Heights of High and Low Waters

Time meridian 75° W. 0000 is midnight. 1200 is noon.
Heights are referred to mean lower low water which is the chart datum of soundings.

April

Day	Time	Height (ft)	Height (cm)
1 Sa	0248	-0.1	-3
	0851	2.7	82
	1503	-0.3	-9
	2120	2.8	85
2 Su	0326	0.0	0
	0927	2.6	79
	1539	-0.2	-6
	2158	2.7	82
3 M	0404	0.1	3
	1005	2.5	76
	1616	-0.1	-3
	2237	2.6	79
4 Tu	0442	0.3	9
	1041	2.4	73
	1655	0.0	0
	2318	2.4	73
5 W	0524	0.4	12
	1122	2.2	67
	1737	0.2	6
6 Th	0002	2.3	70
	0610	0.5	15
	1208	2.1	64
	1825	0.3	9
7 F	0053	2.2	67
	0703	0.6	18
	1302	2.0	61
	1921	0.4	12
8 Sa	0149	2.2	67
	0801	0.6	18
	1404	2.0	61
	2022	0.4	12
9 Su	0248	2.2	67
	0902	0.5	15
	1508	2.1	64
	2124	0.4	12
10 M	0345	2.3	70
	0958	0.4	12
	1609	2.3	70
	2222	0.3	9
11 Tu	0437	2.4	73
	1050	0.2	6
	1703	2.5	76
	2315	0.1	3
12 W	0525	2.5	76
	1138	0.0	0
	1753	2.7	82
13 Th	0004	0.0	0
	0611	2.7	82
	1224	-0.2	-6
	1841	2.9	88
14 F	0051	-0.1	-3
	0656	2.9	88
	1309	-0.4	-12
	1928	3.1	94
15 Sa	0137	-0.2	-6
	0741	3.0	91
	1355	-0.6	-18
	2015	3.2	98
16 Su	0224	-0.3	-9
	0827	3.0	91
	1441	-0.6	-18
	2103	3.2	98
17 M	0312	-0.2	-6
	0914	3.0	91
	1530	-0.6	-18
	2153	3.2	98
18 Tu	0402	-0.2	-6
	1005	2.9	88
	1622	-0.5	-15
	2245	3.1	94
19 W	0456	-0.1	-3
	1059	2.8	85
	1717	-0.4	-12
	2342	2.9	88
20 Th	0554	0.1	3
	1159	2.7	82
	1817	-0.2	-6
21 F	0043	2.8	85
	0657	0.2	6
	1305	2.5	76
	1923	0.0	0
22 Sa	0148	2.6	79
	0805	0.2	6
	1416	2.5	76
	2033	0.1	3
23 Su	0255	2.6	79
	0912	0.2	6
	1526	2.5	76
	2141	0.2	6
24 M	0357	2.6	79
	1014	0.1	3
	1630	2.6	79
	2242	0.2	6
25 Tu	0454	2.6	79
	1109	0.0	0
	1726	2.7	82
	2336	0.1	3
26 W	0543	2.6	79
	1157	-0.1	-3
	1815	2.7	82
27 Th	0023	0.1	3
	0626	2.6	79
	1240	-0.1	-3
	1859	2.8	85
28 F	0106	0.1	3
	0706	2.7	82
	1319	-0.2	-6
	1939	2.8	85
29 Sa	0145	0.1	3
	0744	2.6	79
	1356	-0.2	-6
	2016	2.8	85
30 Su	0223	0.2	6
	0820	2.6	79
	1432	-0.2	-6
	2053	2.8	85

May

Day	Time	Height (ft)	Height (cm)
1 M	0300	0.2	6
	0856	2.6	79
	1508	-0.1	-3
	2130	2.7	82
2 Tu	0337	0.3	9
	0932	2.5	76
	1545	0.0	0
	2208	2.6	79
3 W	0415	0.4	12
	1010	2.4	73
	1623	0.1	3
	2247	2.5	76
4 Th	0455	0.5	15
	1051	2.3	70
	1704	0.2	6
	2324	2.4	73
5 F	0539	0.5	15
	1137	2.2	67
	1750	0.3	9
6 Sa	0015	2.4	73
	0628	0.6	18
	1229	2.2	67
	1842	0.4	12
7 Su	0105	2.3	70
	0721	0.5	15
	1328	2.2	67
	1940	0.5	15
8 M	0200	2.3	70
	0818	0.5	15
	1430	2.2	67
	2041	0.4	12
9 Tu	0256	2.3	70
	0915	0.3	9
	1532	2.4	73
	2142	0.4	12
10 W	0351	2.5	76
	1010	0.1	3
	1629	2.6	79
	2239	0.2	6
11 Th	0444	2.6	79
	1102	-0.1	-3
	1723	2.8	85
	2332	0.1	3
12 F	0535	2.8	85
	1152	-0.3	-9
	1815	3.0	91
13 Sa	0023	0.0	0
	0625	2.9	88
	1242	-0.5	-15
	1905	3.2	98
14 Su	0114	-0.2	-6
	0715	3.0	91
	1332	-0.7	-21
	1955	3.3	101
15 M	0204	-0.2	-6
	0805	3.1	94
	1422	-0.7	-21
	2046	3.3	101
16 Tu	0255	-0.2	-6
	0857	3.1	94
	1514	-0.7	-21
	2137	3.2	98
17 W	0348	-0.2	-6
	0950	3.0	91
	1607	-0.5	-15
	2231	3.1	94
18 Th	0443	-0.1	-3
	1047	2.9	88
	1703	-0.4	-12
	2326	3.0	91
19 F	0540	0.0	0
	1147	2.7	82
	1802	-0.2	-6
20 Sa	0025	2.8	85
	0641	0.0	0
	1251	2.6	79
	1905	0.0	0
21 Su	0126	2.7	82
	0745	0.1	3
	1358	2.5	76
	2011	0.2	6
22 M	0227	2.6	79
	0848	0.1	3
	1505	2.5	76
	2115	0.3	9
23 Tu	0327	2.5	76
	0947	0.1	3
	1607	2.5	76
	2215	0.3	9
24 W	0421	2.5	76
	1040	0.0	0
	1702	2.5	76
	2309	0.3	9
25 Th	0510	2.5	76
	1128	0.0	0
	1751	2.6	79
	2357	0.3	9
26 F	0555	2.5	76
	1211	-0.1	-3
	1834	2.6	79
27 Sa	0040	0.3	9
	0635	2.5	76
	1250	-0.1	-3
	1914	2.7	82
28 Su	0119	0.3	9
	0714	2.5	76
	1328	-0.1	-3
	1952	2.7	82
29 M	0157	0.3	9
	0751	2.5	76
	1405	-0.1	-3
	2029	2.7	82
30 Tu	0235	0.3	9
	0828	2.4	73
	1441	-0.1	-3
	2105	2.7	82
31 W	0312	0.3	9
	0906	2.4	73
	1518	0.0	0
	2142	2.6	79

June

Day	Time	Height (ft)	Height (cm)
1 Th	0350	0.3	9
	0945	2.3	70
	1557	0.0	0
	2220	2.5	76
2 F	0429	0.3	9
	1026	2.3	70
	1637	0.1	3
	2259	2.5	76
3 Sa	0511	0.4	12
	1110	2.2	67
	1721	0.2	6
	2341	2.4	73
4 Su	0556	0.4	12
	1200	2.2	67
	1809	0.3	9
5 M	0027	2.4	73
	0645	0.3	9
	1255	2.2	67
	1903	0.4	12
6 Tu	0118	2.3	70
	0739	0.2	6
	1355	2.3	70
	2002	0.4	12
7 W	0213	2.4	73
	0835	0.1	3
	1457	2.4	73
	2104	0.3	9
8 Th	0310	2.4	73
	0933	-0.1	-3
	1558	2.5	76
	2204	0.2	6
9 F	0408	2.5	76
	1030	-0.3	-9
	1656	2.7	82
	2303	0.1	3
10 Sa	0504	2.7	82
	1125	-0.5	-15
	1751	2.9	88
	2359	0.0	0
11 Su	0600	2.8	85
	1219	-0.6	-18
	1845	3.1	94
12 M	0053	-0.2	-6
	0654	2.9	88
	1313	-0.7	-21
	1938	3.2	98
13 Tu	0147	-0.3	-9
	0748	3.0	91
	1406	-0.8	-24
	2030	3.2	98
14 W	0239	-0.3	-9
	0842	3.0	91
	1459	-0.7	-21
	2122	3.2	98
15 Th	0333	-0.3	-9
	0937	2.9	88
	1552	-0.6	-18
	2214	3.1	94
16 F	0427	-0.3	-9
	1033	2.8	85
	1647	-0.4	-12
	2307	3.0	91
17 Sa	0522	-0.2	-6
	1130	2.7	82
	1743	-0.2	-6
18 Su	0001	2.8	85
	0619	-0.1	-3
	1230	2.6	79
	1841	0.0	0
19 M	0057	2.6	79
	0717	-0.1	-3
	1333	2.5	76
	1941	0.2	6
20 Tu	0153	2.5	76
	0815	0.0	0
	1435	2.4	73
	2042	0.3	9
21 W	0249	2.4	73
	0912	0.0	0
	1536	2.3	70
	2141	0.4	12
22 Th	0343	2.3	70
	1006	0.0	0
	1632	2.4	73
	2236	0.4	12
23 F	0434	2.3	70
	1055	0.0	0
	1722	2.4	73
	2326	0.4	12
24 Sa	0521	2.3	70
	1140	0.0	0
	1806	2.5	76
25 Su	0011	0.4	12
	0604	2.3	70
	1221	-0.1	-3
	1848	2.5	76
26 M	0053	0.3	9
	0645	2.3	70
	1301	-0.1	-3
	1926	2.6	79
27 Tu	0132	0.3	9
	0725	2.3	70
	1339	-0.1	-3
	2004	2.6	79
28 W	0210	0.2	6
	0804	2.4	73
	1417	-0.1	-3
	2041	2.6	79
29 Th	0248	0.2	6
	0843	2.4	73
	1455	-0.1	-3
	2117	2.6	79
30 F	0325	0.2	6
	0923	2.5	76
	1533	-0.1	-3
	2153	2.5	76

Miami Harbor Entrance, Fla., 1995

Times and Heights of High and Low Waters

July

Day	Time	Height (ft)	Height (cm)
1 Sa	0403	0.2	6
	1003	2.3	70
	1613	0.0	0
	2231	2.5	76
2 Su	0442	0.2	6
	1046	2.3	70
	1655	0.1	3
	2310	2.4	73
3 M	0525	0.1	3
	1134	2.3	70
	1741	0.2	6
	2354	2.4	73
4 Tu	0612	0.1	3
	1226	2.3	70
	1832	0.2	6
5 W ☽	0042	2.4	73
	0704	0.0	0
	1324	2.3	70
	1930	0.3	9
6 Th	0137	2.4	73
	0802	-0.1	-3
	1427	2.4	73
	2032	0.3	9
7 F	0237	2.4	73
	0903	-0.2	-6
	1531	2.5	76
	2136	0.2	6
8 Sa	0339	2.5	76
	1004	-0.3	-9
	1633	2.7	82
	2239	0.1	3
9 Su	0441	2.6	79
	1104	-0.5	-15
	1732	2.8	85
	2339	0.0	0
10 M	0541	2.7	82
	1202	-0.6	-18
	1828	3.0	91
11 Tu	0036	-0.2	-6
	0638	2.9	88
	1258	-0.7	-21
	1922	3.1	94
12 W ○	0131	-0.3	-9
	0734	3.0	91
	1351	-0.7	-21
	2013	3.1	94
13 Th	0223	-0.4	-12
	0828	3.0	91
	1444	-0.7	-21
	2104	3.1	94
14 F	0315	-0.4	-12
	0921	3.0	91
	1535	-0.6	-18
	2153	3.1	94
15 Sa	0406	-0.4	-12
	1015	2.9	88
	1626	-0.4	-12
	2242	2.9	88
16 Su	0457	-0.3	-9
	1108	2.7	82
	1718	-0.2	-6
	2332	2.8	85
17 M	0549	-0.2	-6
	1203	2.6	79
	1811	0.0	0
18 Tu	0022	2.6	79
	0642	-0.1	-3
	1259	2.4	73
	1905	0.2	6
19 W ☽	0114	2.4	73
	0736	0.0	0
	1358	2.3	70
	2002	0.4	12
20 Th	0207	2.3	70
	0831	0.1	3
	1457	2.3	70
	2101	0.5	15
21 F	0302	2.2	67
	0926	0.1	3
	1555	2.3	70
	2159	0.5	15
22 Sa	0356	2.2	67
	1018	0.1	3
	1648	2.3	70
	2252	0.5	15
23 Su	0447	2.2	67
	1107	0.1	3
	1735	2.4	73
	2341	0.5	15
24 M	0535	2.2	67
	1152	0.0	0
	1819	2.5	76
25 Tu	0024	0.4	12
	0619	2.3	70
	1234	0.0	0
	1859	2.5	76
26 W	0105	0.3	9
	0701	2.4	73
	1315	-0.1	-3
	1937	2.6	79
27 Th ●	0144	0.2	6
	0741	2.5	76
	1354	-0.1	-3
	2013	2.7	82
28 F	0221	0.2	6
	0821	2.5	76
	1432	-0.1	-3
	2049	2.7	82
29 Sa	0258	0.1	3
	0900	2.6	79
	1510	-0.1	-3
	2125	2.7	82
30 Su	0335	0.0	1
	0941	2.6	79
	1550	0.0	0
	2202	2.7	82
31 M	0414	0.0	0
	1023	2.6	79
	1631	0.1	3
	2241	2.6	79

August

Day	Time	Height (ft)	Height (cm)
1 Tu	0456	0.0	0
	1110	2.6	79
	1716	0.2	6
	2324	2.6	79
2 W	0543	0.0	0
	1201	2.5	76
	1807	0.3	9
3 Th ○	0013	2.5	76
	0636	0.0	0
	1259	2.5	76
	1904	0.4	12
4 F	0109	2.5	76
	0735	0.0	0
	1402	2.5	76
	2008	0.4	12
5 Sa	0213	2.5	76
	0840	-0.1	-3
	1509	2.6	79
	2116	0.4	12
6 Su	0320	2.6	79
	0946	-0.1	-3
	1615	2.7	82
	2223	0.3	9
7 M	0426	2.7	82
	1050	-0.2	-6
	1717	2.9	88
	2325	0.1	3
8 Tu	0529	2.8	85
	1150	-0.3	-9
	1813	3.0	91
9 W	0022	0.0	0
	0627	3.0	91
	1245	-0.4	-12
	1906	3.1	94
10 Th ○	0115	-0.2	-6
	0722	3.1	94
	1337	-0.5	-15
	1955	3.2	98
11 F	0206	-0.3	-9
	0814	3.1	94
	1427	-0.4	-12
	2042	3.2	98
12 Sa	0254	-0.3	-9
	0904	3.1	94
	1515	-0.3	-9
	2128	3.1	94
13 Su	0341	-0.3	-9
	0952	3.1	94
	1602	-0.2	-6
	2134	3.0	91
14 M	0427	-0.2	-6
	1041	2.9	88
	1649	0.0	0
	2248	2.9	88
15 Tu	0514	0.0	0
	1130	2.8	85
	1737	0.3	9
	2343	2.7	82
16 W	0602	0.1	3
	1221	2.6	79
	1826	0.5	15
17 Th	0031	2.5	76
	0652	0.3	9
	1315	2.5	76
	1920	0.6	18
18 F	0122	2.4	73
	0745	0.4	12
	1412	2.4	73
	2018	0.8	24
19 Sa	0218	2.3	70
	0842	0.4	12
	1512	2.4	73
	2118	0.8	24
20 Su	0316	2.3	70
	0939	0.5	15
	1609	2.4	73
	2216	0.8	24
21 M	0413	2.3	70
	1032	0.4	12
	1700	2.5	76
	2307	0.7	21
22 Tu	0505	2.4	73
	1122	0.4	12
	1746	2.6	79
	2353	0.6	18
23 W	0552	2.5	76
	1207	0.3	9
	1827	2.7	82
24 Th	0034	0.5	15
	0636	2.7	82
	1248	0.2	6
	1905	2.8	85
25 F ●	0113	0.3	9
	0717	2.8	85
	1328	0.1	3
	1942	2.9	88
26 Sa	0150	0.2	6
	0757	2.9	88
	1407	0.1	3
	2019	3.0	91
27 Su	0228	0.1	3
	0837	3.0	91
	1447	0.1	3
	2056	3.0	91
28 M	0306	0.1	3
	0918	3.0	91
	1527	0.2	6
	2134	3.0	91
29 Tu	0346	0.0	0
	1002	3.0	91
	1609	0.2	6
	2215	3.0	91
30 W	0430	0.0	0
	1048	3.0	91
	1655	0.4	12
	2300	2.9	88
31 Th	0518	0.1	3
	1140	2.9	88
	1747	0.5	15
	2351	2.8	85

September

Day	Time	Height (ft)	Height (cm)
1 F	0613	0.2	6
	1239	2.9	88
	1846	0.6	18
2 Sa	0051	2.8	85
	0715	0.2	6
	1344	2.8	85
	1952	0.6	18
3 Su	0158	2.7	82
	0824	0.3	9
	1453	2.8	85
	2103	0.6	18
4 M	0309	2.8	85
	0933	0.2	6
	1601	2.9	88
	2211	0.5	15
5 Tu	0418	2.9	88
	1039	0.2	6
	1702	3.0	91
	2313	0.4	12
6 W	0521	3.1	94
	1139	0.1	3
	1758	3.2	98
	2359	0.6	18
7 Th	0008	0.2	6
	0618	3.2	98
	1233	0.0	0
	1848	3.3	101
8 F ○	0059	0.1	3
	0710	3.3	101
	1322	0.0	0
	1934	3.3	101
9 Sa	0145	0.0	0
	0758	3.4	104
	1409	0.0	0
	2018	3.3	101
10 Su	0230	-0.1	-3
	0843	3.4	104
	1453	0.1	3
	2100	3.3	101
11 M	0313	0.0	0
	0928	3.3	101
	1536	0.2	6
	2141	3.2	98
12 Tu	0355	0.1	3
	1011	3.2	98
	1618	0.4	12
	2222	3.0	91
13 W	0437	0.2	6
	1055	3.0	91
	1702	0.6	18
	2304	2.9	88
14 Th	0520	0.4	12
	1141	2.9	88
	1747	0.8	24
	2348	2.7	82
15 F	0606	0.6	18
	1231	2.7	82
	1837	0.9	27
16 Sa	0038	2.6	79
	0657	0.7	21
	1325	2.6	79
	1934	1.1	34
17 Su	0134	2.5	76
	0755	0.8	24
	1425	2.6	79
	2035	1.1	34
18 M	0236	2.5	76
	0855	0.8	24
	1524	2.6	79
	2135	1.1	34
19 Tu	0337	2.5	76
	0954	0.8	24
	1618	2.7	82
	2229	0.9	27
20 W	0433	2.7	82
	1047	0.7	21
	1706	2.8	85
	2316	0.8	24
21 Th	0522	2.8	85
	1135	0.6	18
	1749	3.0	91
	2359	0.6	18
22 F	0607	3.0	91
	1219	0.5	15
	1829	3.1	94
23 Sa	0039	0.5	15
	0650	3.2	98
	1300	0.4	12
	1908	3.2	98
24 Su ●	0118	0.3	9
	0732	3.3	101
	1341	0.4	12
	1947	3.3	101
25 M	0158	0.2	6
	0813	3.4	104
	1422	0.3	9
	2026	3.3	101
26 Tu	0239	0.1	3
	0856	3.5	107
	1505	0.4	12
	2108	3.3	101
27 W	0322	0.1	3
	0942	3.5	107
	1550	0.4	12
	2152	3.3	101
28 Th	0408	0.1	3
	1030	3.4	104
	1638	0.5	15
	2241	3.2	98
29 F	0459	0.2	6
	1123	3.3	101
	1732	0.7	21
	2336	3.1	94
30 Sa	0556	0.3	9
	1223	3.2	98
	1833	0.8	24

Time meridian 75° W. 0000 is midnight. 1200 is noon.
Heights are referred to mean lower low water which is the chart datum of soundings.

Miami Harbor Entrance, Fla., 1995

Times and Heights of High and Low Waters

October

Day	Time	h	cm	Day	Time	h	cm
1 Su	0039	3.0	91	16 M	0052	2.6	79
	0701	0.5	15		0708	1.0	30
	1328	3.1	94		1336	2.8	85
	1941	0.8	24		1951	1.2	37
2 M	0149	3.0	91	17 Tu	0154	2.6	79
	0811	0.6	18		0809	1.1	34
	1438	3.1	94		1434	2.8	85
	2052	0.8	24		2050	1.2	37
3 Tu	0302	3.0	91	18 W	0257	2.7	82
	0922	0.6	18		0910	1.0	30
	1545	3.1	94		1530	2.8	85
	2159	0.7	21		2145	1.0	30
4 W	0411	3.1	94	19 Th	0356	2.8	85
	1028	0.5	15		1007	1.0	30
	1646	3.2	98		1621	2.9	88
	2259	0.5	15		2235	0.9	27
5 Th	0513	3.3	101	20 F	0448	3.0	91
	1126	0.5	15		1058	0.8	24
	1739	3.3	101		1707	3.1	94
	2352	0.4	12		2320	0.7	21
6 F	0606	3.4	104	21 Sa	0536	3.2	98
	1218	0.4	12		1145	0.7	21
	1827	3.4	104		1751	3.2	98
7 Sa	0039	0.3	9	22 Su	0004	0.4	12
	0655	3.5	107		0621	3.4	104
	1305	0.4	12		1230	0.6	18
	1911	3.4	104		1833	3.3	101
8 Su	0123	0.2	6	23 M	0047	0.2	6
	0740	3.5	107		0706	3.6	110
	1348	0.4	12		1314	0.5	15
	1952	3.4	104		1916	3.4	104
9 M	0204	0.2	6	24 Tu	0130	0.1	3
	0822	3.5	107		0751	3.7	113
	1429	0.5	15		1359	0.4	12
	2031	3.3	101		2000	3.5	107
10 Tu	0244	0.2	6	25 W	0215	0.0	0
	0902	3.5	107		0836	3.7	113
	1509	0.6	18		1445	0.4	12
	2110	3.3	101		2046	3.5	107
11 W	0322	0.3	9	26 Th	0301	0.0	0
	0942	3.4	104		0924	3.7	113
	1549	0.7	21		1533	0.4	12
	2148	3.1	94		2134	3.5	107
12 Th	0401	0.5	15	27 F	0351	0.1	3
	1022	3.2	98		1015	3.6	110
	1629	0.9	27		1624	0.5	15
	2227	3.0	91		2227	3.4	104
13 F	0441	0.6	18	28 Sa	0444	0.2	6
	1104	3.1	94		1109	3.5	107
	1712	1.0	30		1720	0.6	18
	2310	2.9	88		2325	3.3	101
14 Sa	0525	0.8	24	29 Su	0543	0.4	12
	1150	3.0	91		1208	3.4	104
	1759	1.1	34		1822	0.7	21
	2357	2.7	82				
15 Su	0613	0.9	27	30 M	0029	3.1	94
	1240	2.8	85		0647	0.5	15
	1852	1.2	37		1312	3.2	98
					1929	0.7	21
				31 Tu	0140	3.1	94
					0757	0.6	18
					1419	3.2	98
					2038	0.7	21

November

Day	Time	h	cm	Day	Time	h	cm
1 W	0252	3.1	94	16 Th	0214	2.6	79
	0907	0.7	21		0823	1.0	30
	1524	3.1	94		1437	2.7	82
	2142	0.6	18		2058	0.8	24
2 Th	0359	3.1	94	17 F	0314	2.7	82
	1012	0.7	21		0922	0.9	27
	1623	3.2	98		1531	2.8	85
	2240	0.5	15		2151	0.7	21
3 F	0459	3.2	98	18 Sa	0411	2.9	88
	1109	0.7	21		1018	0.8	24
	1716	3.2	98		1623	2.9	88
	2332	0.4	12		2241	0.4	12
4 Sa	0551	3.3	101	19 Su	0503	3.1	94
	1200	0.6	18		1111	0.7	21
	1803	3.2	98		1712	3.1	94
					2330	0.2	6
5 Su	0018	0.3	9	20 M	0553	3.3	101
	0638	3.4	104		1201	0.5	15
	1245	0.6	18		1801	3.2	98
	1845	3.2	98				
6 M	0059	0.3	9	21 Tu	0018	0.0	0
	0720	3.4	104		0642	3.5	107
	1327	0.6	18		1249	0.4	12
	1925	3.2	98		1849	3.3	101
7 Tu	0139	0.3	9	22 W	0106	-0.2	-6
	0800	3.4	104		0730	3.6	110
	1406	0.6	18		1338	0.3	9
	2003	3.2	98		1938	3.4	104
8 W	0216	0.3	9	23 Th	0155	-0.3	-9
	0838	3.4	104		0819	3.7	113
	1444	0.7	21		1427	0.2	6
	2040	3.1	94		2028	3.4	104
9 Th	0253	0.4	12	24 F	0245	-0.3	-9
	0916	3.3	101		0909	3.6	110
	1522	0.8	24		1518	0.2	6
	2118	3.0	91		2120	3.4	104
10 F	0330	0.4	12	25 Sa	0337	-0.2	-6
	0953	3.2	98		1000	3.6	110
	1601	0.8	24		1611	0.2	6
	2156	2.9	88		2215	3.3	101
11 Sa	0409	0.6	18	26 Su	0431	-0.1	-3
	1033	3.1	94		1054	3.4	104
	1642	0.9	27		1707	0.3	9
	2237	2.8	85		2313	3.2	98
12 Su	0450	0.7	21	27 M	0529	0.1	3
	1114	3.0	91		1151	3.3	101
	1726	1.0	30		1807	0.4	12
	2323	2.7	82				
13 M	0535	0.8	24	28 Tu	0017	3.0	91
	1159	2.8	85		0637	0.3	9
	1814	1.0	30		1251	3.1	94
					1910	0.4	12
14 Tu	0014	2.6	79	29 W	0124	2.9	88
	0625	0.9	27		0737	0.5	15
	1249	2.8	85		1354	3.0	91
	1906	1.0	30		2015	0.4	12
15 W	0112	2.6	79	30 Th	0233	2.9	88
	0722	1.0	30		0844	0.6	18
	1342	2.7	82		1456	2.9	88
	2002	1.0	30		2118	0.4	12

December

Day	Time	h	cm	Day	Time	h	cm
1 F	0339	2.9	88	16 Sa	0232	2.5	76
	0948	0.6	18		0837	0.7	21
	1555	2.8	85		1443	2.5	76
	2215	0.3	9		2108	0.3	9
2 Sa	0438	2.9	88	17 Su	0333	2.6	79
	1046	0.6	18		0938	0.6	18
	1648	2.8	85		1541	2.6	79
	2307	0.3	9		2205	0.1	3
3 Su	0531	3.0	91	18 M	0431	2.8	85
	1138	0.6	18		1037	0.4	12
	1736	2.8	85		1638	2.7	82
	2353	0.2	6		2300	-0.1	-3
4 M	0617	3.0	91	19 Tu	0527	3.0	91
	1223	0.6	18		1133	0.3	9
	1819	2.8	85		1733	2.9	88
					2354	-0.3	-9
5 Tu	0035	0.1	3	20 W	0620	3.1	94
	0659	3.0	91		1227	0.1	3
	1305	0.6	18		1827	3.0	91
	1859	2.8	85				
6 W	0114	0.1	3	21 Th	0047	-0.5	-15
	0738	3.0	91		0712	3.3	101
	1344	0.5	15		1320	0.0	0
	1938	2.8	85		1921	3.1	94
7 Th	0152	0.1	3	22 F	0139	-0.6	-18
	0815	3.0	91		0803	3.4	104
	1422	0.5	15		1412	-0.2	-6
	2016	2.8	85		2014	3.2	98
8 F	0228	0.1	3	23 Sa	0231	-0.6	-18
	0852	3.0	91		0853	3.4	104
	1459	0.5	15		1504	-0.2	-6
	2053	2.7	82		2108	3.2	98
9 Sa	0305	0.2	6	24 Su	0323	-0.6	-18
	0928	2.9	88		0944	3.3	101
	1536	0.5	15		1556	-0.2	-6
	2131	2.6	79		2202	3.1	94
10 Su	0343	0.3	9	25 M	0417	-0.4	-12
	1005	2.8	85		1036	3.2	98
	1615	0.6	18		1650	-0.2	-6
	2211	2.6	79		2259	3.0	91
11 M	0422	0.4	12	26 Tu	0512	-0.2	-6
	1043	2.8	85		1130	3.0	91
	1655	0.6	18		1746	-0.1	-3
	2254	2.5	76		2358	2.8	85
12 Tu	0503	0.5	15	27 W	0609	0.0	0
	1123	2.7	82		1225	2.8	85
	1737	0.6	18		1844	0.0	0
	2341	2.4	73				
13 W	0549	0.6	18	28 Th	0100	2.7	82
	1206	2.6	79		0710	0.2	6
	1824	0.6	18		1322	2.7	82
					1944	0.0	0
14 Th	0033	2.4	73	29 F	0205	2.5	76
	0640	0.6	18		0813	0.3	9
	1254	2.6	79		1421	2.5	76
	1915	0.5	15		2045	0.1	3
15 F	0131	2.4	73	30 Sa	0309	2.5	76
	0734	0.7	21		0916	0.4	12
	1347	2.5	76		1520	2.4	73
	2011	0.4	12		2144	0.1	3
				31 Su	0411	2.5	76
					1016	0.5	15
					1615	2.4	73
					2238	0.1	3

Time meridian 75° W. 0000 is midnight. 1200 is noon.
Heights are referred to mean lower low water which is the chart datum of soundings.

Key West, Fla., 1995

Times and Heights of High and Low Waters

January

Day	Time	Height (ft)	Height (cm)
1 Su ●	0324	-0.5	-15
	1009	1.2	37
	1446	0.2	6
	2133	2.2	67
2 M	0410	-0.5	-15
	1050	1.3	40
	1538	0.1	3
	2223	2.1	64
3 Tu	0454	-0.4	-12
	1131	1.3	40
	1630	0.1	3
	2311	2.0	61
4 W	0536	-0.3	-9
	1211	1.3	40
	1705	0.1	3
	2358	1.8	55
5 Th	0616	-0.2	-6
	1252	1.4	43
	1823	0.2	6
6 F	0047	1.5	46
	0700	0.0	0
	1333	1.4	43
	1926	0.2	6
7 Sa	0139	1.3	40
	0744	0.1	3
	1417	1.4	43
	2035	0.2	6
8 ◐	0239	1.1	34
	0829	0.3	9
	1505	1.4	43
O	2150	0.2	6
9 M	0354	0.9	27
	0920	0.4	12
	1558	1.4	43
	2302	0.2	6
10 Tu	0525	0.8	24
	1014	0.5	15
	1655	1.5	46
11 W	0006	0.1	3
	0644	0.8	24
	1109	0.5	15
	1752	1.5	46
12 Th	0059	0.0	0
	0740	0.9	27
	1201	0.5	15
	1844	1.6	49
13 F	0145	-0.1	-3
	0821	0.9	27
	1248	0.4	12
	1930	1.7	52
14 Sa	0225	-0.2	-6
	0857	1.0	30
	1331	0.4	12
	2012	1.7	52
15 Su	0300	-0.2	-6
	0930	1.0	30
	1411	0.3	9
	2052	1.8	55
16 M O	0333	-0.3	-9
	1003	1.1	34
	1449	0.2	6
	2130	1.8	55
17 Tu	0404	-0.3	-9
	1036	1.1	34
	1529	0.2	6
	2209	1.8	55
18 W	0435	-0.3	-9
	1109	1.2	37
	1610	0.1	3
	2248	1.7	52
19 Th	0507	-0.3	-9
	1142	1.2	37
	1654	0.1	3
	2329	1.6	49
20 F	0540	-0.2	-6
	1216	1.3	40
	1743	0.0	0
21 Sa	0014	1.5	46
	0615	-0.1	-3
	1252	1.4	43
	1839	0.0	0
22 Su	0104	1.3	40
	0653	0.0	0
	1331	1.4	43
	1943	0.0	0
23 O	0205	1.1	34
	0736	0.1	3
	1418	1.5	46
	2057	0.0	0
24 Tu	0322	0.9	27
	0827	0.2	6
	1514	1.6	49
	2216	-0.1	-3
25 W	0458	0.8	24
	0928	0.3	9
	1621	1.6	49
	2332	-0.2	-6
26 Th	0628	0.8	24
	1036	0.3	9
	1734	1.7	52
27 F	0038	-0.3	-9
	0735	0.8	24
	1144	0.3	9
	1843	1.8	55
28 Sa	0135	-0.4	-12
	0826	0.9	27
	1247	0.2	6
	1945	1.9	58
29 Su	0224	-0.5	-15
	0909	1.0	30
	1345	0.1	3
	2039	1.9	58
30 M ●	0308	-0.5	-15
	0949	1.1	34
	1440	0.0	0
	2129	1.9	58
31 Tu	0349	-0.5	-15
	1025	1.2	37
	1532	-0.1	-3
	2216	1.8	55

February

Day	Time	Height (ft)	Height (cm)
1 W	0428	-0.4	-12
	1101	1.3	40
	1622	-0.1	-3
	2300	1.7	52
2 Th	0505	-0.3	-9
	1135	1.4	43
	1712	-0.2	-6
	2342	1.5	46
3 F	0541	-0.2	-6
	1208	1.4	43
	1803	-0.1	-3
4 Sa	0024	1.3	40
	0617	-0.1	-3
	1243	1.4	43
	1856	-0.1	-3
5 Su	0108	1.1	34
	0653	0.1	3
	1319	1.4	43
	1955	0.0	0
6 M	0157	0.9	27
	0731	0.2	6
	1401	1.4	43
	2101	0.1	3
7 Tu	0257	0.8	24
	0815	0.3	9
	1451	1.3	40
	2215	0.1	3
8 W O	0420	0.7	21
	0911	0.4	12
	1553	1.3	40
	2326	0.0	0
9 Th	0559	0.7	21
	1018	0.4	12
	1702	1.3	40
10 F	0028	0.0	0
	0707	0.7	21
	1123	0.4	12
	1809	1.4	43
11 Sa	0117	-0.1	-3
	0752	0.8	24
	1220	0.4	12
	1905	1.5	46
12 Su	0158	-0.2	-6
	0827	0.9	27
	1309	0.3	9
	1952	1.6	49
13 M	0232	-0.2	-6
	0900	1.0	30
	1353	0.2	6
	2035	1.6	49
14 Tu	0303	-0.3	-9
	0932	1.1	34
	1435	0.0	0
	2117	1.7	52
15 W O	0333	-0.3	-9
	1003	1.2	37
	1517	-0.1	-3
	2158	1.6	49
16 Th	0403	-0.3	-9
	1034	1.3	40
	1600	-0.2	-6
	2239	1.6	49
17 F	0434	-0.3	-9
	1106	1.4	43
	1645	-0.2	-6
	2323	1.5	46
18 Sa	0507	-0.2	-6
	1139	1.5	46
	1734	-0.3	-9
19 Su	0009	1.3	40
	0542	-0.1	-3
	1214	1.5	46
	1828	-0.3	-9
20 M	0100	1.1	34
	0620	0.0	0
	1255	1.6	49
	1929	-0.3	-9
21 Tu	0200	0.9	27
	0703	0.2	6
	1343	1.6	49
	2040	-0.2	-6
22 W O	0316	0.8	24
	0755	0.3	9
	1444	1.6	49
	2158	-0.2	-6
23 Th	0451	0.7	21
	0903	0.3	9
	1600	1.6	49
	2316	-0.2	-6
24 F	0617	0.8	24
	1022	0.3	9
	1724	1.6	49
25 Sa	0023	-0.3	-9
	0719	0.9	27
	1138	0.3	9
	1840	1.6	49
26 Su	0118	-0.3	-9
	0806	1.0	30
	1246	0.1	3
	1943	1.7	52
27 M	0204	-0.3	-9
	0846	1.1	34
	1344	0.0	0
	2037	1.7	52
28 Tu	0244	-0.3	-9
	0922	1.2	37
	1437	-0.1	-3
	2124	1.7	52

March

Day	Time	Height (ft)	Height (cm)
1 W ●	0321	-0.3	-9
	0954	1.4	43
	1525	-0.2	-6
	2207	1.6	49
2 Th	0356	-0.2	-6
	1025	1.4	43
	1611	-0.3	-9
	2247	1.5	46
3 F	0430	-0.1	-3
	1055	1.5	46
	1656	-0.3	-9
	2326	1.4	43
4 Sa	0503	0.0	0
	1125	1.5	46
	1740	-0.2	-6
5 Su	0003	1.2	37
	0535	0.1	3
	1156	1.5	46
	1826	-0.2	-6
6 M	0042	1.1	34
	0607	0.2	6
	1230	1.5	46
	1915	-0.1	-3
7 Tu	0125	0.9	27
	0640	0.3	9
	1310	1.4	43
	2013	0.0	0
8 W	0217	0.8	24
	0718	0.4	12
	1357	1.4	43
	2121	0.1	3
9 Th O	0326	0.7	21
	0809	0.5	15
	1457	1.3	40
	2236	0.1	3
10 F	0500	0.7	21
	0925	0.5	15
	1610	1.3	40
11 Sa	0619	0.8	24
	1047	0.5	15
	1727	1.3	40
12 Su	0035	0.0	0
	0709	0.9	27
	1154	0.4	12
	1833	1.4	43
13 M	0116	0.0	0
	0747	1.0	30
	1248	0.3	9
	1928	1.5	46
14 Tu	0150	-0.1	-3
	0820	1.1	34
	1335	0.1	3
	2016	1.5	46
15 W	0222	-0.1	-3
	0852	1.3	40
	1420	-0.1	-3
	2102	1.6	49
16 Th O	0253	-0.1	-3
	0923	1.4	43
	1504	-0.2	-6
	2146	1.6	49
17 F	0325	-0.1	-3
	0955	1.6	49
	1549	-0.4	-12
	2231	1.5	46
18 Sa	0359	-0.1	-3
	1028	1.7	52
	1635	-0.4	-12
	2317	1.4	43
19 Su	0434	0.0	0
	1104	1.8	55
	1724	-0.5	-15
20 M	0005	1.3	40
	0511	0.1	3
	1143	1.8	55
	1818	-0.4	-12
21 Tu	0058	1.1	34
	0552	0.2	6
	1228	1.8	55
	1917	-0.4	-12
22 W O	0159	1.0	30
	0639	0.3	9
	1321	1.8	55
	2025	-0.2	-6
23 Th	0312	0.9	27
	0738	0.4	12
	1426	1.7	52
	2140	-0.2	-6
24 F	0438	0.8	24
	0855	0.4	12
	1548	1.6	49
	2253	-0.1	-3
25 Sa	0554	0.9	27
	1021	0.4	12
	1718	1.5	46
	2357	-0.3	-9
26 Su	0652	1.1	34
	1141	0.3	9
	1836	1.5	46
27 M	0050	-0.1	-3
	0737	1.2	37
	1247	0.1	3
	1939	1.5	46
28 Tu	0133	-0.1	-3
	0815	1.4	43
	1343	0.0	0
	2031	1.5	46
29 W	0211	0.0	0
	0849	1.5	46
	1432	-0.1	-3
	2116	1.5	46
30 Th ●	0247	0.0	0
	0919	1.6	49
	1516	-0.2	-6
	2156	1.4	43
31 F	0320	0.1	3
	0948	1.7	52
	1557	-0.3	-9
	2234	1.4	43

Time meridian 75° W. 0000 is midnight. 1200 is noon.
Heights are referred to mean lower low water which is the chart datum of soundings

Key West, Fla., 1995

Times and Heights of High and Low Waters

April

Day	Time	h (ft)	cm		Day	Time	h (ft)	cm
1 Sa	0353	0.1	3		16 Su	0324	0.1	3
	1016	1.7	52			0956	2.0	61
	1638	-0.3	-9			1625	-0.6	-18
	2309	1.3	40			2311	1.4	43
2 Su	0424	0.2	6		17 M	0403	0.2	6
	1045	1.7	52			1037	2.1	64
	1717	-0.3	-9			1715	-0.6	-18
	2345	1.2	37					
3 M	0455	0.3	9		18 Tu	0001	1.3	40
	1116	1.7	52			0445	0.2	6
	1759	-0.2	-6			1121	2.1	64
						1808	-0.5	15
4 Tu	0022	1.1	34		19 W	0054	1.2	37
	0526	0.3	9			0532	0.3	9
	1151	1.6	49			1211	2.0	61
	1843	0.1	3			1906	0.4	12
5 W	0103	1.0	30		20 Th	0153	1.1	34
	0558	0.4	12			0626	0.4	12
	1230	1.6	49			1307	1.9	58
	1932	0.0	0			2009	-0.2	-6
6 Th	0152	0.9	27		21 F	0300	1.0	30
	0636	0.5	15			0733	0.5	15
	1316	1.5	46			1414	1.7	52
	2031	0.1	3		◑	2115	-0.1	-3
7 F	0253	0.8	24		22 Sa	0412	1.1	34
	0726	0.6	18			0856	0.5	15
	1411	1.4	43			1536	1.5	46
	2138	0.2	6			2221	0.0	0
8 Sa	0408	0.9	27		23 Su	0520	1.2	37
	0843	0.6	18			1024	0.4	12
	1521	1.3	40			1706	1.4	43
◐	2242	0.2	6			2320	0.1	3
9 Su	0521	0.9	27		24 M	0616	1.3	40
	1012	0.6	18			1141	0.3	9
	1640	1.3	40			1825	1.4	43
	2336	0.2	6					
10 M	0615	1.1	34		25 Tu	0010	0.2	6
	1127	0.5	15			0701	1.5	46
	1756	1.4	43			1245	0.1	3
						1929	1.4	43
11 Tu	0020	0.1	3		26 W	0054	0.2	6
	0656	1.2	37			0739	1.6	49
	1226	0.3	9			1337	0.0	0
	1900	1.4	43			2021	1.4	43
12 W	0058	0.1	3		27 Th	0132	0.2	6
	0732	1.4	43			0813	1.7	52
	1316	0.1	3			1423	-0.1	-3
	1955	1.5	46			2105	1.3	40
13 Th	0134	0.1	3		28 F	0208	0.3	9
	0807	1.6	49			0843	1.8	55
	1404	-0.1	-3			1504	-0.2	-6
	2046	1.5	46			2144	1.3	40
14 F	0210	0.1	3		29 Sa	0243	0.3	9
	0841	1.7	52			0912	1.8	55
	1450	-0.3	-9			1542	-0.3	-9
	2135	1.5	46		●	2220	1.3	40
15 Sa	0246	0.1	3		30 Su	0316	0.3	9
	0917	1.9	58			0942	1.8	55
	1537	-0.5	-15			1620	-0.3	-9
○	2222	1.4	43			2254	1.2	37

May

Day	Time	h (ft)	cm		Day	Time	h (ft)	cm
1 M	0348	0.4	12		16 Tu	0338	0.3	9
	1013	1.8	55			1018	2.3	70
	1658	-0.2	-6			1705	-0.6	-18
	2329	1.2	37			2352	1.2	37
2 Tu	0420	0.4	12		17 W	0426	0.3	9
	1046	1.8	55			1107	2.2	67
	1736	-0.2	-6			1756	-0.5	-15
3 W	0006	1.1	34		18 Th	0043	1.2	37
	0452	0.5	15			0519	0.3	9
	1122	1.8	55			1200	2.1	64
	1816	-0.1	-3			1850	-0.3	-9
4 Th	0047	1.1	34		19 F	0137	1.2	37
	0527	0.5	15			0619	0.4	12
	1201	1.7	52			1257	1.9	58
	1900	0.0	0			1946	-0.2	-6
5 F	0133	1.0	30		20 Sa	0235	1.2	37
	0607	0.6	18			0730	0.5	15
	1245	1.6	49			1402	1.7	52
	1949	0.1	3			2043	0.0	0
6 Sa	0227	1.0	30		21 Su	0336	1.3	40
	0700	0.6	18			0853	0.5	15
	1336	1.5	46			1518	1.4	43
	2042	0.2	6		○	2140	0.1	3
7 Su	0325	1.1	34		22 M	0436	1.4	43
	0814	0.7	21			1017	0.4	12
	1439	1.4	43			1643	1.3	40
◑	2137	0.2	6			2235	0.2	6
8 M	0424	1.1	34		23 Tu	0531	1.5	46
	0940	0.6	18			1132	0.3	9
	1555	1.3	40			1805	1.2	37
	2230	0.2	6			2324	0.3	9
9 Tu	0516	1.3	40		24 W	0618	1.6	49
	1058	0.5	15			1234	0.1	3
	1717	1.3	40			1913	1.2	37
	2318	0.3	9					
10 W	0601	1.4	43		25 Th	0010	0.4	12
	1201	0.2	6			0659	1.7	52
	1831	1.3	40			1325	0.0	0
						2007	1.2	37
11 Th	0002	0.3	9		26 F	0051	0.4	12
	0642	1.6	49			0736	1.8	55
	1256	0.0	0			1410	-0.1	-3
	1935	1.3	40			2051	1.2	37
12 F	0045	0.3	9		27 Sa	0130	0.4	12
	0723	1.8	55			0809	1.8	55
	1347	-0.2	-6			1450	-0.2	-6
	2032	1.3	40			2130	1.2	37
13 Sa	0127	0.4	12		28 Su	0207	0.4	12
	0804	2.0	61			0842	1.9	58
	1436	-0.4	-12			1527	-0.2	-6
	2124	1.3	40			2204	1.2	37
14 Su	0209	0.3	9		29 M	0242	0.4	12
	0846	2.1	64			0915	1.9	58
	1525	-0.6	-18			1604	-0.2	-6
○	2213	1.3	40			2238	1.2	37
15 M	0253	0.3	9		30 Tu	0317	0.4	12
	0931	2.2	67			0949	1.9	58
	1614	-0.6	-18			1640	-0.2	-6
	2302	1.3	40			2313	1.1	34
					31 W	0351	0.5	15
						1025	1.9	58
						1716	-0.2	-6
						2349	1.1	34

June

Day	Time	h (ft)	cm		Day	Time	h (ft)	cm
1 Th	0426	0.5	15		16 F	0022	1.3	40
	1101	1.8	55			0510	0.3	9
	1753	-0.1	-3			1151	2.0	61
						1828	-0.3	-9
2 F	0029	1.1	34		17 Sa	0110	1.3	40
	0505	0.5	15			0612	0.3	9
	1140	1.8	55			1245	1.8	55
	1831	-0.1	-3			1916	-0.1	-3
3 Sa	0111	1.1	34		18 Su	0200	1.4	43
	0549	0.6	18			0721	0.4	12
	1222	1.6	49			1344	1.6	49
	1911	0.0	0			2005	0.0	0
4 Su	0155	1.2	37		19 M	0251	1.4	43
	0643	0.6	18			0838	0.4	12
	1309	1.5	46			1451	1.3	40
	1953	0.1	3		○	2055	0.2	6
5 M	0242	1.2	37		20 Tu	0345	1.5	46
	0751	0.6	18			0957	0.3	9
	1407	1.4	43			1610	1.1	34
	2039	0.2	6			2145	0.3	9
6 Tu	0329	1.3	40		21 W	0439	1.6	49
	0911	0.5	15			1111	0.2	6
	1518	1.3	40			1735	1.0	30
◑	2128	0.3	9			2234	0.4	12
7 W	0418	1.4	43		22 Th	0531	1.7	52
	1029	0.4	12			1214	0.2	6
	1642	1.2	37			1850	1.0	30
	2219	0.3	9			2325	0.5	15
8 Th	0507	1.6	49		23 F	0618	1.7	52
	1137	0.1	3			1307	0.1	3
	1806	1.1	34			1948	1.0	30
	2310	0.4	12					
9 F	0556	1.8	55		24 Sa	0012	0.5	15
	1237	-0.1	-3			0701	1.8	55
	1919	1.1	34			1353	0.0	0
						2033	1.0	30
10 Sa	0000	0.4	12		25 Su	0056	0.5	15
	0645	2.0	61			0741	1.8	55
	1332	-0.3	-9			1434	-0.1	-3
	2019	1.2	37			2111	1.1	34
11 Su	0050	0.4	12		26 M	0136	0.5	15
	0735	2.1	64			0819	1.9	58
	1424	-0.5	-15			1511	-0.1	-3
	2113	1.2	37			2145	1.1	34
12 M	0139	0.3	9		27 Tu	0215	0.5	15
	0826	2.3	70			0856	1.9	58
	1514	-0.5	-15			1547	-0.1	-3
○	2202	1.2	37		●	2218	1.1	34
13 Tu	0229	0.3	9		28 W	0253	0.5	15
	0916	2.3	70			0932	1.9	58
	1603	-0.6	-18			1621	-0.2	-6
	2249	1.2	37			2251	1.2	37
14 W	0320	0.3	9		29 Th	0330	0.4	12
	1007	2.3	70			1009	1.9	58
	1651	-0.5	-15			1654	-0.1	-3
	2336	1.3	40			2326	1.2	37
15 Th	0413	0.3	9		30 F	0408	0.4	12
	1058	2.2	67			1046	1.9	58
	1740	-0.4	-12			1726	-0.1	-3

Time meridian 75° W. 0000 is midnight. 1200 is noon.
Heights are referred to mean lower low water which is the chart datum of soundings.

Key West, Fla., 1995
Times and Heights of High and Low Waters

July

Day	Time	ft	cm	Day	Time	ft	cm
1 Sa	0002	1.2	37	16 Su	0034	1.5	46
	0449	0.5	15		0600	0.2	6
	1124	1.8	55		1229	1.7	52
	1759	-0.1	-3		1839	0.0	0
2 Su	0039	1.3	40	17 M	0116	1.6	49
	0535	0.5	15		0703	0.3	9
	1205	1.7	52		1321	1.5	46
	1833	0.0	0		1921	0.2	6
3 M	0116	1.3	40	18 Tu	0200	1.6	49
	0628	0.5	15		0811	0.3	9
	1251	1.5	46		1419	1.3	40
	1910	0.1	3		2006	0.3	9
4 Tu	0156	1.4	43	19 W ◐	0248	1.6	49
	0731	0.4	12		0924	0.3	9
	1346	1.4	43		1527	1.1	34
	1950	0.2	6		2054	0.5	15
5 W ◐	0238	1.5	46	20 Th	0340	1.7	52
	0844	0.4	12		1038	0.3	9
	1453	1.2	37		1653	1.0	30
	2036	0.3	9		2147	0.6	18
6 Th	0327	1.6	49	21 F	0438	1.7	52
	1002	0.3	9		1146	0.3	9
	1617	1.1	34		1819	1.0	30
	2129	0.4	12		2243	0.6	18
7 F	0421	1.8	55	22 Sa	0536	1.7	52
	1115	0.1	3		1244	0.2	6
	1749	1.0	30		1923	1.0	30
	2226	0.5	15		2337	0.6	18
8 Sa	0520	1.9	58	23 Su	0630	1.8	55
	1221	-0.1	-3		1333	0.1	3
	1907	1.0	30		2008	1.0	30
	2325	0.5	15				
9 Su	0620	2.1	64	24 M	0027	0.6	18
	1319	-0.2	-6		0717	1.9	58
	2008	1.1	34		1414	0.1	3
					2045	1.1	34
10 M	0024	0.4	12	25 Tu	0113	0.6	18
	0719	2.2	67		0800	1.9	58
	1412	-0.4	-12		1451	0.0	0
	2059	1.1	34		2118	1.2	37
11 Tu	0120	0.4	12	26 W	0155	0.5	15
	0815	2.3	70		0839	2.0	61
	1501	-0.4	-12		1524	0.0	0
	2145	1.2	37		2149	1.2	37
12 W ○	0216	0.3	9	27 Th ●	0235	0.5	15
	0909	2.3	70		0917	2.0	61
	1548	-0.4	-12		1554	0.0	0
	2229	1.3	40		2221	1.3	40
13 Th	0310	0.2	6	28 F	0314	0.4	12
	1000	2.3	70		0955	2.0	61
	1632	-0.4	-12		1624	0.0	0
	2310	1.4	43		2254	1.4	43
14 F	0405	0.2	6	29 Sa	0354	0.4	12
	1050	2.2	67		1033	1.9	58
	1715	-0.3	-9		1653	0.0	0
	2352	1.5	46		2328	1.5	46
15 Sa	0501	0.2	6	30 Su	0437	0.4	12
	1139	2.0	61		1112	1.9	58
	1757	-0.1	-3		1723	0.1	3
					2359	1.5	46
				31 M	0522	0.3	9
					1154	1.7	52
					1755	0.2	6

August

Day	Time	ft	cm	Day	Time	ft	cm
1 Tu	0033	1.6	49	16 W	0107	1.8	55
	0614	0.3	9		0736	0.4	12
	1240	1.6	49		1345	1.4	43
	1830	0.3	9		1916	0.6	18
2 W	0110	1.7	52	17 Th	0150	1.8	55
	0713	0.3	9		0843	0.4	12
	1333	1.4	43		1443	1.2	37
	1909	0.4	12		2001	0.7	21
3 Th ◐	0153	1.8	55	18 F	0241	1.8	55
	0822	0.3	9		0956	0.5	15
	1439	1.2	37		1600	1.1	34
	1954	0.5	15		2056	0.8	24
4 F	0244	1.8	55	19 Sa	0342	1.8	55
	0939	0.2	6		1109	0.5	15
	1605	1.1	34		1735	1.1	34
	2050	0.6	18		2201	0.8	24
5 Sa	0346	1.9	58	20 Su	0451	1.8	55
	1057	0.2	6		1213	0.4	12
	1739	1.0	30		1847	1.1	34
	2156	0.6	18		2307	0.8	24
6 Su	0457	2.0	61	21 M	0557	1.8	55
	1206	0.1	3		1304	0.4	12
	1856	1.1	34		1934	1.2	37
	2305	0.6	18				
7 M	0608	2.1	64	22 Tu	0005	0.8	24
	1306	0.0	0		0652	1.9	58
	1954	1.2	37		1345	0.3	9
					2010	1.3	40
8 Tu	0012	0.5	15	23 W ●	0054	0.7	21
	0713	2.2	67		0739	2.0	61
	1357	-0.1	-3		1420	0.3	9
	2040	1.3	40		2042	1.4	43
9 W	0113	0.4	12	24 Th	0139	0.6	18
	0811	2.3	70		0821	2.0	61
	1443	-0.1	-3		1450	0.2	6
	2122	1.4	43		2113	1.5	46
10 Th	0210	0.3	9	25 F	0220	0.5	15
	0904	2.3	70		0901	2.1	64
	1525	-0.1	-3		1519	0.2	6
	2201	1.5	46		2144	1.6	49
11 F	0305	0.2	6	26 Sa	0300	0.4	12
	0953	2.2	67		0941	2.1	64
	1605	-0.1	-3		1547	0.2	6
	2238	1.7	52		2214	1.7	52
12 Sa	0358	0.2	6	27 Su	0341	0.3	9
	1040	2.1	64		1020	2.0	61
	1644	0.0	0		1616	0.3	9
	2315	1.8	55		2245	1.8	55
13 Su	0450	0.2	6	28 M	0424	0.3	9
	1125	1.9	58		1102	1.9	58
	1721	0.2	6		1646	0.3	9
	2351	1.8	55		2317	1.9	58
14 M	0542	0.2	6	29 Tu	0510	0.2	6
	1210	1.7	52		1145	1.8	55
	1758	0.3	9		1719	0.4	12
					2352	2.0	61
15 Tu	0028	1.8	55	30 W	0600	0.2	6
	0637	0.3	9		1233	1.6	49
	1256	1.5	46		1754	0.5	15
	1836	0.4	12				
				31 Th	0030	2.0	61
					0657	0.3	9
					1328	1.5	46
					1835	0.6	18

September

Day	Time	ft	cm	Day	Time	ft	cm
1 F	0116	2.1	64	16 Sa ○	0148	1.9	58
	0804	0.3	9		0908	0.6	18
	1435	1.3	40		1512	1.3	40
	1923	0.7	21		2004	1.0	30
2 Sa	0213	2.1	64	17 Su	0249	1.9	58
	0921	0.3	9		1023	0.7	21
	1601	1.2	37		1640	1.3	40
	2025	0.8	24		2120	1.0	30
3 Su	0324	2.1	64	18 M	0403	1.8	55
	1040	0.3	9		1130	0.7	21
	1731	1.2	37		1758	1.3	40
	2142	0.8	24		2239	1.0	30
4 M	0446	2.1	64	19 Tu	0518	1.9	58
	1150	0.3	9		1222	0.6	18
	1841	1.3	40		1849	1.4	43
	2301	0.8	24		2344	0.9	27
5 Tu	0605	2.2	67	20 W	0622	1.9	58
	1248	0.2	6		1303	0.6	18
	1933	1.4	43		1926	1.5	46
6 W	0012	0.6	18	21 Th	0036	0.8	24
	0712	2.2	67		0714	2.0	61
	1336	0.2	6		1337	0.5	15
	2015	1.6	49		1959	1.7	52
7 Th	0113	0.5	15	22 F	0122	0.7	21
	0809	2.3	70		0800	2.1	64
	1418	0.2	6		1407	0.5	15
	2053	1.8	55		2031	1.8	55
8 F ○	0209	0.4	12	23 Sa	0204	0.5	15
	0900	2.2	67		0844	2.1	64
	1456	0.2	6		1436	0.5	15
	2129	1.9	58		2101	2.0	61
9 Sa	0300	0.3	9	24 Su ●	0245	0.4	12
	0946	2.2	67		0926	2.1	64
	1533	0.3	9		1506	0.5	15
	2202	2.0	61		2133	2.1	64
10 Su	0348	0.2	6	25 M	0327	0.2	6
	1029	2.1	64		1009	2.0	61
	1608	0.4	12		1537	0.5	15
	2235	2.1	64		2205	2.2	67
11 M	0435	0.2	6	26 Tu	0411	0.2	6
	1110	1.9	58		1053	2.0	61
	1643	0.5	15		1610	0.6	18
	2307	2.1	64		2240	2.3	70
12 Tu	0521	0.2	6	27 W	0457	0.1	3
	1150	1.8	55		1139	1.8	55
	1717	0.6	18		1646	0.6	18
	2341	2.1	64		2317	2.3	70
13 W	0609	0.3	9	28 Th	0548	0.2	6
	1231	1.6	49		1228	1.7	52
	1752	0.7	21		1725	0.7	21
14 Th	0017	2.1	64	29 F	0000	2.4	73
	0700	0.4	12		0644	0.2	6
	1314	1.5	46		1325	1.5	46
	1828	0.8	24		1810	0.8	24
15 F	0058	2.0	61	30 Sa	0051	2.3	70
	0759	0.6	18		0749	0.3	9
	1405	1.4	43		1432	1.4	43
	1910	0.9	27		1905	0.9	27

Time meridian 75° W. 0000 is midnight. 1200 is noon.
Heights are referred to mean lower low water which is the chart datum of soundings

247

Key West, Fla., 1995

Times and Heights of High and Low Waters

October

Day	Time	h	cm	Day	Time	h	cm
1 Su ◐	0154	2.2	67	**16** M ◑	0202	1.9	58
	0902	0.4	12		0926	0.7	21
	1553	1.4	43		1546	1.4	43
	2016	1.0	30		2038	1.1	34
2 M	0312	2.2	67	**17** Tu	0312	1.8	55
	1018	0.5	15		1031	0.7	21
	1712	1.5	46		1658	1.5	46
	2143	0.9	27		2206	1.1	34
3 Tu	0441	2.1	64	**18** W	0430	1.8	55
	1125	0.5	15		1124	0.7	21
	1815	1.6	49		1753	1.6	49
	2306	0.8	24		2318	1.0	30
4 W	0602	2.1	64	**19** Th	0543	1.8	55
	1219	0.5	15		1207	0.7	21
	1904	1.7	52		1835	1.7	52
5 Th	0016	0.7	21	**20** F	0014	0.8	24
	0709	2.1	64		0645	1.9	58
	1305	0.5	15		1243	0.7	21
	1945	1.9	58		1911	1.9	58
6 F	0115	0.5	15	**21** Sa	0102	0.6	18
	0805	2.1	64		0738	1.9	58
	1345	0.5	15		1317	0.7	21
	2022	2.0	61		1945	2.0	61
7 Sa	0206	0.4	12	**22** Su	0146	0.4	12
	0854	2.1	64		0826	2.0	61
	1422	0.6	18		1350	0.7	21
	2055	2.2	67		2019	2.2	67
8 Su ○	0253	0.2	6	**23** M ●	0229	0.2	6
	0937	2.0	61		0913	2.0	61
	1508	0.6	18		1425	0.6	18
	2127	2.2	67		2054	2.3	70
9 M	0336	0.2	6	**24** Tu	0313	0.1	3
	1017	1.9	58		0958	1.9	58
	1532	0.7	21		1500	0.7	21
	2157	2.3	70		2131	2.5	76
10 Tu	0418	0.2	6	**25** W	0359	0.0	0
	1055	1.9	58		1044	1.8	55
	1606	0.7	21		1538	0.7	21
	2228	2.3	70		2211	2.5	76
11 W	0500	0.2	6	**26** Th	0447	0.0	0
	1131	1.7	52		1132	1.7	52
	1639	0.8	24		1619	0.7	21
	2301	2.3	70		2254	2.5	76
12 Th	0542	0.3	9	**27** F	0537	0.0	0
	1208	1.6	49		1223	1.6	49
	1712	0.9	27		1704	0.7	21
	2337	2.2	67		2343	2.5	76
13 F	0627	0.4	12	**28** Sa	0633	0.1	3
	1248	1.5	46		1318	1.6	49
	1747	0.9	27		1755	0.8	24
14 Sa	0017	2.1	64	**29** Su	0038	2.4	73
	0718	0.6	18		0733	0.3	9
	1336	1.5	46		1421	1.5	46
	1827	1.0	30		1858	0.9	27
15 Su	0105	2.0	61	**30** M ◐	0143	2.2	67
	0818	0.7	21		0839	0.4	12
	1434	1.4	43		1530	1.5	46
	1920	1.1	34		2017	0.9	27
				31 Tu	0301	2.0	61
					0946	0.5	15
					1640	1.6	49
					2146	0.9	27

November

Day	Time	h	cm	Day	Time	h	cm
1 W	0431	1.9	58	**16** Th	0339	1.6	49
	1048	0.6	18		1012	0.7	21
	1739	1.7	52		1650	1.6	49
	2308	0.7	21		2243	0.8	24
2 Th	0554	1.8	55	**17** F	0459	1.6	49
	1142	0.6	18		1100	0.7	21
	1829	1.9	58		1737	1.7	52
					2346	0.6	18
3 F	0016	0.6	18	**18** Sa	0613	1.6	49
	0703	1.8	55		1144	0.7	21
	1228	0.6	18		1819	1.9	58
	1912	2.0	61				
4 Sa	0112	0.4	12	**19** Su	0039	0.4	12
	0759	1.8	55		0716	1.6	49
	1309	0.7	21		1225	0.7	21
	1949	2.1	64		1900	2.1	64
5 Su	0200	0.3	9	**20** M	0127	0.2	6
	0846	1.8	55		0810	1.6	49
	1347	0.7	21		1306	0.6	18
	2023	2.2	67		1941	2.2	67
6 M	0243	0.2	6	**21** Tu	0214	0.0	0
	0928	1.7	52		0900	1.6	49
	1424	0.7	21		1347	0.6	18
	2055	2.3	70		2023	2.4	73
7 Tu ○	0324	0.1	3	**22** W	0301	-0.2	-6
	1005	1.7	52		0948	1.6	49
	1459	0.7	21		1430	0.6	18
	2126	2.3	70		2107	2.5	76
8 W	0402	0.1	3	**23** Th	0348	-0.3	-9
	1040	1.6	49		1035	1.6	49
	1533	0.7	21		1514	0.5	15
	2158	2.3	70		2153	2.5	76
9 Th	0441	0.2	6	**24** F	0436	-0.3	-9
	1114	1.6	49		1122	1.5	46
	1607	0.8	24		1600	0.5	15
	2232	2.2	67		2241	2.5	76
10 F	0520	0.2	6	**25** Sa	0526	-0.2	-6
	1149	1.5	46		1211	1.5	46
	1641	0.8	24		1651	0.5	15
	2308	2.2	67		2333	2.4	73
11 Sa	0601	0.3	9	**26** Su	0618	-0.1	-3
	1227	1.5	46		1302	1.5	46
	1717	0.9	27		1748	0.6	18
	2348	2.1	64				
12 Su	0644	0.4	12	**27** M	0029	2.2	67
	1311	1.4	43		0712	0.1	3
	1757	0.9	27		1356	1.5	46
					1855	0.6	18
13 M	0032	2.0	61	**28** Tu	0132	2.0	61
	0732	0.5	15		0808	0.2	6
	1401	1.4	43		1455	1.5	46
	1849	1.0	30		2014	0.6	18
14 Tu	0123	1.8	55	**29** W ◐	0246	1.7	52
	0824	0.6	18		0906	0.4	12
	1457	1.4	43		1556	1.6	49
	2000	1.0	30				
15 W ◑	0225	1.7	52	**30** Th	0411	1.6	49
	0919	0.6	18		1003	0.5	15
	1556	1.5	46		1655	1.7	52
	2126	0.9	27		2300	0.5	15

December

Day	Time	h	cm	Day	Time	h	cm
1 F	0538	1.4	43	**16** Sa	0416	1.2	37
	1057	0.6	18		0951	0.5	15
	1749	1.8	55		1636	1.6	49
					2313	0.3	9
2 Sa	0008	0.3	9	**17** Su	0542	1.2	37
	0651	1.4	43		1044	0.5	15
	1147	0.6	18		1728	1.8	55
	1836	1.9	58				
3 Su	0103	0.2	6	**18** M	0015	0.1	3
	0750	1.4	43		0656	1.2	37
	1232	0.6	18		1136	0.5	15
	1917	2.0	61		1820	1.9	58
4 M	0150	0.1	3	**19** Tu	0109	-0.1	-3
	0837	1.4	43		0757	1.2	37
	1314	0.6	18		1227	0.5	15
	1955	2.0	61		1911	2.1	64
5 Tu	0232	0.0	0	**20** W	0200	-0.3	-9
	0917	1.4	43		0849	1.2	37
	1354	0.6	18		1317	0.4	12
	2030	2.1	64		2002	2.2	67
6 W	0311	0.0	0	**21** Th	0249	-0.4	-12
	0952	1.4	43		0937	1.3	40
	1431	0.6	18		1407	0.3	9
	2104	2.1	64		2053	2.3	70
7 Th	0348	0.0	0	**22** F	0337	-0.5	-15
	1024	1.4	43		1022	1.3	40
	1507	0.6	18		1458	0.3	9
	2138	2.1	64		2144	2.3	70
8 F	0424	0.0	0	**23** Sa	0424	-0.5	-15
	1056	1.3	40		1106	1.3	40
	1543	0.6	18		1550	0.2	6
	2213	2.0	61		2235	2.3	70
9 Sa	0500	0.0	0	**24** Su	0510	-0.4	-12
	1130	1.3	40		1150	1.4	43
	1618	0.6	18		1645	0.2	6
	2250	2.0	61		2327	2.1	64
10 Su	0536	0.1	3	**25** M	0557	-0.3	-9
	1205	1.3	40		1235	1.4	43
	1656	0.6	18		1743	0.2	6
	2328	1.9	58				
11 M	0612	0.1	3	**26** Tu	0021	1.9	58
	1244	1.3	40		0643	-0.1	-3
	1738	0.6	18		1322	1.4	43
					1848	0.2	6
12 Tu	0009	1.8	55	**27** W	0119	1.6	49
	0650	0.2	6		0731	0.0	0
	1325	1.3	40		1412	1.5	46
	1828	0.7	21		2001	0.3	9
13 W	0054	1.6	49	**28** Th	0224	1.4	43
	0729	0.3	9		0821	0.2	6
	1409	1.3	40		1506	1.5	46
	1929	0.7	21		2120 ○	0.2	6
14 Th	0148	1.5	46	**29** F	0343	1.2	37
	0812	0.4	12		0913	0.3	9
	1456	1.4	43		1603	1.6	49
	2044	0.6	18		2239	0.2	6
15 F	0254	1.3	40	**30** Sa	0512	1.0	30
	0900	0.4	12		1009	0.4	12
	1545	1.5	46		1701	1.6	49
	2203 ○	0.5	15		2349	0.1	3
				31 Su	0634	1.0	30
					1104	0.5	15
					1757	1.7	52

Time meridian 75° W. 0000 is midnight. 1200 is noon.
Heights are referred to mean lower low water which is the chart datum of soundings

248

Miami Harbor Entrance, Fla., 1996

Times and Heights of High and Low Waters

January

Day	Time	ft	cm	Day	Time	ft	cm
1 M	0506	2.5	76	16 Tu	0405	2.5	76
	1111	0.4	12		1011	0.2	6
	1708	2.4	73		1613	2.4	73
	2327	0.0	0		2237	-0.4	-12
2 Tu	0554	2.5	76	17 W	0505	2.6	79
	1159	0.4	12		1113	0.0	0
	1754	2.4	73		1714	2.6	79
					2336	-0.6	-18
3 W	0011	0.0	0	18 Th	0602	2.8	85
	0637	2.6	79		1210	-0.2	-6
	1242	0.4	12		1813	2.8	85
	1836	2.4	73				
4 Th	0051	-0.1	-3	19 F	0032	-0.7	-21
	0716	2.6	79		0656	3.0	91
	1322	0.3	9		1305	-0.4	-12
	1916	2.4	73		1909	2.9	88
5 F ○	0130	-0.1	-3	20 Sa ●	0126	-0.8	-24
	0753	2.6	79		0748	3.1	94
	1400	0.2	6		1358	-0.5	-15
	1954	2.4	73		2003	3.0	91
6 Sa	0207	-0.1	-3	21 Su	0218	-0.9	-27
	0829	2.7	82		0838	3.1	94
	1436	0.2	6		1449	-0.6	-18
	2032	2.4	73		2056	3.0	91
7 Su	0243	-0.1	-3	22 M	0310	-0.8	-24
	0904	2.6	79		0927	3.1	94
	1512	0.2	6		1539	-0.6	-18
	2110	2.4	73		2148	2.9	88
8 M	0320	-0.1	-3	23 Tu	0401	-0.7	-21
	0939	2.6	79		1016	3.0	91
	1549	0.2	6		1630	-0.6	-18
	2149	2.4	73		2241	2.8	85
9 Tu	0358	0.0	0	24 W	0452	-0.5	-15
	1015	2.5	76		1106	2.8	85
	1626	0.1	3		1722	-0.5	-15
	2229	2.3	70		2335	2.6	79
10 W	0437	0.1	3	25 Th	0545	-0.3	-9
	1052	2.4	73		1156	2.6	79
	1705	0.1	3		1815	-0.3	-9
	2312	2.3	70				
11 Th	0519	0.2	6	26 F	0032	2.5	76
	1132	2.4	73		0640	0.0	0
	1749	0.1	3		1249	2.4	73
					1910	-0.2	-6
12 F	0000	2.2	67	27 Sa	0131	2.3	70
	0606	0.3	9		0738	0.2	6
	1217	2.3	70		1344	2.2	67
	1837	0.1	3	○	2008	-0.1	-3
13 Sa ○	0055	2.2	67	28 Su	0233	2.2	67
	0700	0.3	9		0839	0.3	9
	1308	2.3	70		1442	2.1	64
	1933	0.0	0		2106	0.0	0
14 Su	0156	2.3	70	29 M	0335	2.1	64
	0801	0.3	9		0941	0.4	12
	1406	2.3	70		1540	2.0	61
	2033	-0.1	-3		2218	0.0	0
15 M	0300	2.3	70	30 Tu	0433	2.1	64
	0906	0.3	9		1039	0.4	12
	1509	2.3	70		1635	2.0	61
	2136	-0.2	-6		2256	0.0	0
				31 W	0524	2.2	67
					1130	0.3	9
					1726	2.1	64
					2343	-0.1	-3

February

Day	Time	ft	cm	Day	Time	ft	cm
1 Th	0609	2.3	70	16 F	0545	2.7	82
	1216	0.2	6		1154	-0.3	-9
	1811	2.1	64		1801	2.7	82
2 F	0026	-0.2	-6	17 Sa	0019	-0.7	-21
	0650	2.3	70		0640	2.8	85
	1257	0.1	3		1249	-0.5	-15
	1853	2.2	67		1857	2.8	85
3 Sa	0106	-0.2	-6	18 Su ●	0113	-0.8	-24
	0727	2.4	73		0731	2.9	88
	1334	0.0	0		1341	-0.6	-18
	1933	2.3	70		1950	2.9	88
4 Su ○	0145	-0.3	-9	19 M	0204	-0.8	-24
	0803	2.5	76		0819	3.0	91
	1411	0.0	0		1430	-0.7	-21
	2011	2.3	70		2041	3.0	91
5 M	0222	-0.3	-9	20 Tu	0253	-0.8	-24
	0838	2.5	76		0906	3.0	91
	1446	-0.1	-3		1518	-0.7	-21
	2049	2.4	73		2130	2.9	88
6 Tu	0258	-0.3	-9	21 W	0341	-0.6	-18
	0912	2.5	76		0952	2.9	88
	1521	-0.2	-6		1605	-0.7	-21
	2126	2.4	73		2219	2.8	85
7 W	0335	-0.2	-6	22 Th	0428	-0.5	-15
	0946	2.4	73		1037	2.7	82
	1557	-0.2	-6		1652	-0.5	-15
	2205	2.4	73		2308	2.6	79
8 Th	0413	-0.1	-3	23 F	0516	-0.2	-6
	1022	2.4	73		1123	2.5	76
	1635	-0.2	-6		1740	-0.4	-12
	2247	2.3	70		2359	2.4	73
9 F	0454	-0.1	-3	24 Sa	0606	0.0	0
	1101	2.3	70		1211	2.3	70
	1717	-0.2	-6		1830	-0.2	-6
	2333	2.3	70				
10 Sa	0539	0.0	0	25 Su	0052	2.3	70
	1145	2.3	70		0659	0.2	6
	1805	-0.2	-6		1302	2.1	64
					1924	0.0	0
11 Su	0026	2.2	67	26 M	0150	2.1	64
	0631	0.1	3		0757	0.4	12
	1237	2.2	67		1359	2.0	61
	1901	-0.2	-6	○	2022	0.1	3
12 M	0126	2.2	67	27 Tu	0251	2.0	61
	0732	0.2	6		0859	0.4	12
	1337	2.2	67		1459	1.9	58
○	2004	-0.2	-6		2122	0.1	3
13 Tu	0233	2.2	67	28 W	0352	2.0	61
	0840	0.2	6		1001	0.4	12
	1444	2.2	67		1600	1.9	58
	2111	-0.3	-9		2219	0.1	3
14 W	0341	2.3	70	29 Th	0447	2.1	64
	0949	0.1	3		1056	0.4	12
	1553	2.3	70		1655	2.0	61
	2218	-0.4	-12		2311	0.1	3
15 Th	0446	2.5	76				
	1055	-0.1	-3				
	1700	2.5	76				
	2321	-0.5	-15				

March

Day	Time	ft	cm	Day	Time	ft	cm
1 F	0535	2.2	67	16 Sa	0528	2.7	82
	1144	0.3	9		1139	-0.2	-6
	1744	2.1	64		1750	2.7	82
	2358	0.0	0				
2 Sa	0617	2.3	70	17 Su	0006	-0.4	-12
	1226	0.1	3		0621	2.8	85
	1828	2.2	67		1233	-0.4	-12
					1845	2.9	88
3 Su	0040	-0.1	-3	18 M	0058	-0.5	-15
	0656	2.4	73		0711	2.9	88
	1304	0.0	0		1322	-0.5	-15
	1908	2.4	73		1935	3.0	91
4 M	0119	-0.2	-6	19 Tu ●	0147	-0.5	-15
	0732	2.5	76		0757	3.0	91
	1340	-0.1	-3		1409	-0.6	-18
	1947	2.5	76		2023	3.0	91
5 Tu ○	0157	-0.2	-6	20 W	0234	-0.5	-15
	0807	2.5	76		0841	2.9	88
	1416	-0.2	-6		1454	-0.6	-18
	2025	2.6	79		2109	3.0	91
6 W	0234	-0.2	-6	21 Th	0319	-0.4	-12
	0842	2.6	79		0924	2.9	88
	1452	-0.3	-9		1537	-0.5	-15
	2103	2.6	79		2154	2.9	88
7 Th	0312	-0.2	-6	22 F	0403	-0.2	-6
	0918	2.6	79		1007	2.7	82
	1529	-0.3	-9		1621	-0.4	-12
	2143	2.6	79		2239	2.7	82
8 F	0351	-0.2	-6	23 Sa	0447	0.0	0
	0955	2.5	76		1050	2.5	76
	1609	-0.3	-9		1705	-0.2	-6
	2226	2.6	79		2325	2.6	79
9 Sa	0432	-0.1	-3	24 Su	0533	0.2	6
	1036	2.5	76		1134	2.4	73
	1652	-0.3	-9		1750	0.0	0
	2312	2.5	76				
10 Su	0519	0.0	0	25 M	0014	2.4	73
	1122	2.4	73		0622	0.4	12
	1742	-0.3	-9		1222	2.2	67
					1840	0.2	6
11 M	0005	2.4	73	26 Tu	0106	2.2	67
	0612	0.1	3		0716	0.5	15
	1216	2.3	70		1317	2.1	64
	1838	-0.2	-6	○	1936	0.3	9
12 Tu	0105	2.4	73	27 W	0204	2.1	64
	0714	0.2	6		0816	0.6	18
	1319	2.3	70		1417	2.0	61
○	1944	-0.1	-3		2036	0.4	12
13 W	0212	2.4	73	28 Th	0304	2.1	64
	0823	0.3	9		0918	0.6	18
	1429	2.3	70		1521	2.0	61
	2054	-0.1	-3		2137	0.4	12
14 Th	0322	2.4	73	29 F	0401	2.2	67
	0934	0.1	3		1014	0.5	15
	1542	2.4	73		1619	2.1	64
	2204	-0.2	-6		2233	0.3	9
15 F	0428	2.5	76	30 Sa	0452	2.2	67
	1040	0.0	0		1104	0.4	12
	1649	2.5	76		1711	2.2	67
	2308	-0.3	-9		2322	0.2	6
				31 Su	0537	2.4	73
					1148	0.2	6
					1757	2.4	73

Time meridian 75° W. 0000 is midnight. 1200 is noon.
Heights are referred to mean lower low water which is the chart datum of soundings.

249

Miami Harbor Entrance, Fla., 1996

Times and Heights of High and Low Waters

April

Day	Time (h m)	ft	cm	Day	Time (h m)	ft	cm
1 M	0007	0.1	3	16 Tu	0042	-0.2	-6
	0617	2.5	76		0648	2.9	88
	1228	0.0	0		1301	-0.4	-12
	1839	2.6	79		1919	3.0	91
2 Tu	0049	0.0	0	17 W ●	0129	-0.2	-6
	0656	2.6	79		0733	2.9	88
	1306	-0.1	-3		1346	-0.4	-12
	1920	2.7	82		2004	3.1	94
3 W ○	0129	-0.1	-3	18 Th	0213	-0.1	-3
	0733	2.7	82		0815	2.9	88
	1344	-0.2	-6		1428	-0.4	-12
	2000	2.8	85		2047	3.0	91
4 Th	0208	-0.1	-3	19 F	0255	-0.1	-3
	0811	2.7	82		0856	2.8	85
	1423	-0.3	-9		1509	-0.3	-9
	2040	2.9	88		2129	2.9	88
5 F	0248	-0.1	-3	20 Sa	0337	0.0	0
	0850	2.8	85		0937	2.7	82
	1503	-0.4	-12		1550	-0.2	-6
	2123	2.9	88		2211	2.8	85
6 Sa	0330	0.0	0	21 Su	0419	0.2	6
	0932	2.7	82		1018	2.5	76
	1546	-0.4	-12		1631	-0.1	-3
	2207	2.9	88		2253	2.7	82
7 Su	0415	0.0	0	22 M	0502	0.3	9
	1017	2.7	82		1100	2.4	73
	1633	-0.3	-9		1714	0.1	3
	2256	2.8	85		2338	2.5	76
8 M	0504	0.1	3	23 Tu	0548	0.5	15
	1107	2.6	79		1146	2.3	70
	1725	-0.2	-6		1800	0.3	9
	2350	2.7	82				
9 Tu	0600	0.2	6	24 W	0025	2.4	73
	1204	2.5	76		0638	0.6	18
	1824	-0.1	-3		1238	2.1	64
					1852	0.4	12
10 W ◑	0050	2.6	79	25 Th	0118	2.3	70
	0703	0.2	6		0733	0.6	18
	1309	2.5	76		1336	2.1	64
	1930	0.0	0		1949 ○	0.5	15
11 Th	0156	2.6	79	26 F	0214	2.2	67
	0811	0.3	9		0831	0.6	18
	1421	2.5	76		1438	2.1	64
	2041	0.0	0		2050	0.5	15
12 F	0305	2.6	79	27 Sa	0310	2.2	67
	0920	0.2	6		0927	0.5	15
	1533	2.5	76		1538	2.2	67
	2150	0.0	0		2148	0.5	15
13 Sa	0409	2.6	79	28 Su	0402	2.3	70
	1025	0.0	0		1018	0.4	12
	1639	2.7	82		1632	2.3	70
	2254	0.0	0		2241	0.4	12
14 Su	0508	2.7	82	29 M	0450	2.4	73
	1122	-0.1	-3		1105	0.2	6
	1738	2.8	85		1721	2.5	76
	2350	-0.1	-3		2329	0.3	9
15 M	0600	2.8	85	30 Tu	0534	2.5	76
	1214	-0.3	-9		1148	0.0	0
	1831	3.0	91		1807	2.7	82

May

Day	Time (h m)	ft	cm	Day	Time (h m)	ft	cm
1 W ○	0015	0.2	6	16 Th	0108	0.1	3
	0617	2.6	79		0707	2.7	82
	1231	-0.2	-6		1322	-0.3	-9
	1850	2.9	88		1944	2.9	88
2 Th	0058	0.1	3	17 F	0151	0.1	3
	0659	2.8	85		0749	2.7	82
	1313	-0.3	-9		1403	-0.3	-9
	1934	3.0	91		2025	2.9	88
3 F	0142	0.0	0	18 Sa	0232	0.1	3
	0742	2.8	85		0829	2.6	79
	1356	-0.4	-12		1442	-0.2	-6
	2018	3.1	94		2105	2.8	85
4 Sa	0226	-0.1	-3	19 Su	0312	0.2	6
	0826	2.9	88		0909	2.6	79
	1441	-0.5	-15		1521	-0.1	-3
	2104	3.1	94		2144	2.7	82
5 Su	0312	-0.1	-3	20 M	0353	0.3	9
	0912	2.9	88		0949	2.5	76
	1528	-0.5	-15		1601	0.0	0
	2151	3.1	94		2224	2.6	79
6 M	0401	0.0	0	21 Tu	0434	0.3	9
	1002	2.8	85		1030	2.3	70
	1618	-0.4	-12		1642	0.1	3
	2242	3.0	91		2305	2.5	76
7 Tu	0453	0.0	0	22 W	0517	0.4	12
	1056	2.7	82		1115	2.2	67
	1713	-0.3	-9		1725	0.2	6
	2337	2.9	88		2348	2.4	73
8 W	0550	0.1	3	23 Th	0603	0.5	15
	1156	2.6	79		1203	2.2	67
	1813	-0.1	-3		1813	0.4	12
9 Th	0037	2.8	85	24 F	0032	2.3	70
	0652	0.1	3		0652	0.5	15
	1302	2.6	79		1257	2.1	64
	1918	0.0	0		1905	0.5	15
10 F	0140	2.7	82	25 Sa	0125	2.3	70
	0758	0.1	3		0744	0.5	15
	1411	2.6	79		1355	2.1	64
	2027 ○	0.1	3		2002	0.5	15
11 Sa	0245	2.6	79	26 Su	0217	2.3	70
	0904	0.1	3		0838	0.4	12
	1521	2.6	79		1453	2.2	67
	2134	0.1	3		2100	0.5	15
12 Su	0347	2.6	79	27 M	0309	2.3	70
	1006	0.0	0		0930	0.3	9
	1625	2.7	82		1550	2.3	70
	2236	0.1	3		2156	0.4	12
13 M	0444	2.7	82	28 Tu	0400	2.4	73
	1102	-0.1	-3		1021	0.1	3
	1722	2.8	85		1643	2.5	76
	2332	0.1	3		2249	0.3	9
14 Tu	0536	2.7	82	29 W	0450	2.5	76
	1153	-0.2	-6		1109	-0.1	-3
	1814	2.9	88		1733	2.7	82
					2339	0.2	6
15 W	0022	0.1	3	30 Th	0539	2.6	79
	0624	2.7	82		1157	-0.3	-9
	1239	-0.3	-9		1821	2.8	85
	1901	2.9	88				
				31 F	0028	0.1	3
					0627	2.7	82
					1245	-0.5	-15
					1909	3.0	91

June

Day	Time (h m)	ft	cm	Day	Time (h m)	ft	cm
1 Sa ○	0117	-0.1	-3	16 Su	0210	0.2	6
	0716	2.8	85		0804	2.4	73
	1333	-0.6	-18		1418	-0.2	-6
	1957	3.1	94		2041	2.7	82
2 Su	0205	-0.1	-3	17 M	0249	0.2	6
	0805	2.9	88		0844	2.4	73
	1422	-0.6	-18		1456	-0.1	-3
	2046	3.1	94		2119	2.6	79
3 M	0255	-0.2	-6	18 Tu	0327	0.2	6
	0856	2.9	88		0923	2.4	73
	1512	-0.6	-18		1534	-0.1	-3
	2136	3.1	94		2156	2.6	79
4 Tu	0347	-0.2	-6	19 W	0406	0.2	6
	0949	2.9	88		1004	2.3	70
	1605	-0.5	-15		1613	0.0	0
	2228	3.1	94		2234	2.5	76
5 W	0441	-0.2	-6	20 Th	0446	0.3	9
	1046	2.8	85		1046	2.2	67
	1701	-0.4	-12		1654	0.1	3
	2323	2.9	88		2313	2.4	73
6 Th	0537	-0.1	-3	21 F	0527	0.3	9
	1146	2.7	82		1130	2.2	67
	1800	-0.2	-6		1737	0.2	6
					2355	2.3	70
7 F	0020	2.8	85	22 Sa	0612	0.3	9
	0637	-0.1	-3		1219	2.1	64
	1249	2.6	79		1825	0.3	9
	1902	-0.1	-3				
8 Sa ○	0120	2.7	82	23 Su	0039	2.3	70
	0740	-0.1	-3		0659	0.3	9
	1356	2.6	79		1312	2.1	64
	2007	0.1	3		1917	0.4	12
9 Su	0221	2.6	79	24 M ◑	0128	2.2	67
	0842	-0.1	-3		0750	0.2	6
	1503	2.5	76		1409	2.2	67
	2112	0.2	6		2013	0.4	12
10 M	0321	2.5	76	25 Tu	0220	2.2	67
	0943	-0.1	-3		0844	0.1	3
	1606	2.6	79		1508	2.3	70
	2214	0.2	6		2112	0.4	12
11 Tu	0418	2.5	76	26 W	0315	2.3	70
	1039	-0.2	-6		0939	0.0	0
	1703	2.6	79		1606	2.4	73
	2310	0.2	6		2211	0.3	9
12 W	0510	2.5	76	27 Th	0411	2.4	73
	1129	-0.2	-6		1034	-0.2	-6
	1754	2.6	79		1701	2.6	79
					2307	0.2	6
13 Th	0001	0.2	6	28 F	0507	2.5	76
	0558	2.5	76		1128	-0.4	-12
	1216	-0.2	-6		1755	2.8	85
	1841	2.7	82				
14 F	0047	0.2	6	29 Sa	0001	0.0	0
	0643	2.5	76		0601	2.7	82
	1259	-0.2	-6		1221	-0.6	-18
	1923	2.7	82		1847	2.9	88
15 Sa ●	0129	0.2	6	30 Su ○	0054	-0.1	-3
	0724	2.5	76		0655	2.8	85
	1339	-0.2	-6		1313	-0.7	-21
	2003	2.7	82		1938	3.1	94

Time meridian 75° W. 0000 is midnight. 1200 is noon.
Heights are referred to mean lower low water which is the chart datum of soundings.

Miami Harbor Entrance, Fla., 1996

Times and Heights of High and Low Waters

July

Day	Time (h m)	Height (ft)	Height (cm)
1	0146	-0.3	-9
	0748	2.9	88
	1406	-0.7	-21
	2028	3.1	94
2	0238	-0.4	-12
	0842	3.0	91
	1458	-0.7	-21
	2119	3.1	94
3	0331	-0.4	-12
	0937	3.0	91
	1551	-0.6	-18
	2211	3.1	94
4	0424	-0.4	-12
	1032	2.9	88
	1646	-0.5	-15
	2304	3.0	91
5	0519	-0.4	-12
	1130	2.8	85
	1742	-0.3	-9
	2358	2.8	85
6	0616	-0.3	-9
	1231	2.7	82
	1841	-0.1	-3
7	0054	2.7	82
	0715	-0.2	-6
	1334	2.5	76
	1943	0.1	3
8	0153	2.5	76
	0815	-0.1	-3
	1438	2.5	76
	2046	0.2	6
9	0252	2.4	73
	0915	-0.1	-3
	1541	2.4	73
	2148	0.3	9
10	0349	2.3	70
	1012	-0.1	-3
	1639	2.4	73
	2245	0.3	9
11	0444	2.3	70
	1104	-0.1	-3
	1732	2.5	76
	2338	0.3	9
12	0534	2.3	70
	1152	-0.1	-3
	1819	2.5	76
13	0024	0.3	9
	0619	2.3	70
	1236	-0.1	-3
	1901	2.6	79
14	0107	0.3	9
	0702	2.4	73
	1316	-0.1	-3
	1939	2.6	79
15	0146	0.2	6
	0742	2.4	73
	1355	-0.1	-3
	2016	2.6	79
16 Tu	0224	0.2	6
	0821	2.4	73
	1432	-0.1	-3
	2052	2.6	79
17 W	0301	0.2	6
	0859	2.4	73
	1509	-0.1	-3
	2128	2.6	79
18 Th	0337	0.1	3
	0938	2.4	73
	1547	0.0	0
	2203	2.5	76
19 F	0414	0.2	6
	1018	2.4	73
	1625	0.1	3
	2239	2.5	76
20 Sa	0452	0.2	6
	1059	2.3	70
	1705	0.2	6
	2317	2.4	73
21 Su	0533	0.2	6
	1144	2.3	70
	1749	0.3	9
	2358	2.4	73
22 M	0617	0.2	6
	1234	2.3	70
	1838	0.4	12
23	0045	2.3	70
	0708	0.1	3
	1330	2.3	70
	1933	0.5	15
24	0138	2.3	70
	0804	0.1	3
	1431	2.3	70
	2035	0.4	12
25 Th	0238	2.4	73
	0904	0.0	0
	1533	2.5	76
	2138	0.4	12
26 F	0340	2.5	76
	1006	-0.2	-6
	1634	2.6	79
	2240	0.2	6
27 Sa	0442	2.6	79
	1105	-0.3	-9
	1732	2.8	85
	2339	0.1	3
28 Su	0542	2.8	85
	1202	-0.5	-15
	1827	3.0	91
29 M	0035	-0.1	-3
	0639	2.9	88
	1257	-0.6	-18
	1919	3.1	94
30 Tu	0128	-0.3	-9
	0734	3.1	94
	1351	-0.7	-21
	2010	3.2	98
31 W	0220	-0.4	-12
	0828	3.2	98
	1443	-0.6	-18
	2100	3.3	101

August

Day	Time (h m)	Height (ft)	Height (cm)
1 Th	0312	-0.5	-15
	0921	3.2	98
	1535	-0.6	-18
	2150	3.2	98
2 F	0403	-0.4	-12
	1015	3.1	94
	1627	-0.4	-12
	2240	3.1	94
3 Sa	0455	-0.4	-12
	1110	3.0	91
	1720	-0.2	-6
	2331	2.9	88
4 Su	0549	-0.2	-6
	1206	2.8	85
	1815	0.1	3
5 M	0025	2.7	82
	0644	-0.1	-3
	1305	2.7	82
	1913	0.3	9
6 Tu	0120	2.6	79
	0743	0.0	0
	1407	2.5	76
	2015	0.4	12
7 W	0219	2.4	73
	0842	0.1	3
	1510	2.5	76
	2117	0.5	15
8 Th	0319	2.3	70
	0942	0.2	6
	1611	2.4	73
	2218	0.6	18
9 F	0416	2.3	70
	1037	0.2	6
	1705	2.5	76
	2312	0.6	18
10 Sa	0509	2.4	73
	1127	0.2	6
	1752	2.5	76
	2359	0.5	15
11 Su	0556	2.4	73
	1211	0.2	6
	1834	2.6	79
12 M	0041	0.4	12
	0639	2.5	76
	1252	0.1	3
	1912	2.7	82
13 Tu	0120	0.3	9
	0720	2.6	79
	1331	0.1	3
	1948	2.7	82
14 W	0156	0.3	9
	0758	2.6	79
	1408	0.1	3
	2023	2.8	85
15 Th	0231	0.2	6
	0835	2.7	82
	1444	0.1	3
	2057	2.8	85
16 F	0306	0.2	6
	0913	2.7	82
	1520	0.2	6
	2131	2.7	82
17 Sa	0341	0.2	6
	0950	2.7	82
	1557	0.3	9
	2206	2.7	82
18 Su	0418	0.2	6
	1030	2.7	82
	1636	0.4	12
	2242	2.7	82
19 M	0457	0.2	6
	1113	2.6	79
	1718	0.5	15
	2323	2.6	79
20 Tu	0542	0.2	6
	1202	2.6	79
	1807	0.6	18
21 W	0011	2.6	79
	0633	0.3	9
	1258	2.6	79
	1903	0.6	18
22 Th	0107	2.5	76
	0732	0.3	9
	1400	2.6	79
	2007	0.6	18
23 F	0211	2.6	79
	0837	0.2	6
	1507	2.7	82
	2114	0.6	18
24 Sa	0319	2.7	82
	0944	0.1	3
	1612	2.8	85
	2220	0.4	12
25 Su	0426	2.8	85
	1048	0.0	0
	1712	3.0	91
	2321	0.1	3
26 M	0528	3.0	91
	1147	-0.2	-6
	1808	3.2	98
27 Tu	0018	0.0	0
	0626	3.2	98
	1243	-0.3	-9
	1900	3.3	101
28 W	0111	-0.2	-6
	0721	3.4	104
	1335	-0.3	-9
	1950	3.4	104
29 Th	0201	-0.3	-9
	0813	3.5	107
	1426	-0.3	-9
	2038	3.5	107
30 F	0250	-0.3	-9
	0904	3.5	107
	1515	-0.2	-6
	2126	3.4	104
31 Sa	0339	-0.3	-9
	0954	3.4	104
	1605	-0.1	-3
	2213	3.3	101

September

Day	Time (h m)	Height (ft)	Height (cm)
1 Su	0428	-0.2	-6
	1045	3.3	101
	1654	0.1	3
	2302	3.1	94
2 M	0518	0.0	0
	1138	3.1	94
	1746	0.4	12
	2352	2.9	88
3 Tu	0610	0.2	6
	1233	2.9	88
	1841	0.6	18
4 W	0045	2.7	82
	0706	0.4	12
	1331	2.7	82
	1940	0.8	24
5 Th	0143	2.6	79
	0805	0.5	15
	1433	2.6	79
	2043	0.9	27
6 F	0245	2.5	76
	0906	0.6	18
	1535	2.6	79
	2145	0.9	27
7 Sa	0346	2.5	76
	1004	0.6	18
	1630	2.6	79
	2240	0.9	27
8 Su	0442	2.5	76
	1057	0.6	18
	1719	2.7	82
	2328	0.8	24
9 M	0531	2.6	79
	1143	0.5	15
	1801	2.8	85
10 Tu	0010	0.7	21
	0614	2.8	85
	1225	0.5	15
	1840	2.9	88
11 W	0048	0.5	15
	0654	2.9	88
	1304	0.4	12
	1916	3.0	91
12 Th	0124	0.4	12
	0732	3.0	91
	1341	0.4	12
	1950	3.0	91
13 F	0159	0.4	12
	0810	3.1	94
	1418	0.4	12
	2025	3.1	94
14 Sa	0234	0.3	9
	0847	3.1	94
	1454	0.4	12
	2059	3.1	94
15 Su	0310	0.3	9
	0925	3.1	94
	1531	0.5	15
	2134	3.0	91
16 M	0347	0.3	9
	1005	3.1	94
	1611	0.6	18
	2213	3.0	91
17 Tu	0428	0.3	9
	1048	3.1	94
	1654	0.7	21
	2256	2.9	88
18 W	0514	0.4	12
	1137	3.0	91
	1744	0.8	24
	2346	2.9	88
19 Th	0607	0.5	15
	1234	2.9	88
	1842	0.8	24
20 F	0046	2.8	85
	0709	0.5	15
	1338	2.9	88
	1948	0.9	27
21 Sa	0154	2.8	85
	0818	0.5	15
	1446	3.0	91
	2058	0.8	24
22 Su	0306	2.9	88
	0928	0.5	15
	1552	3.1	94
	2205	0.6	18
23 M	0415	3.1	94
	1034	0.4	12
	1653	3.2	98
	2306	0.4	12
24 Tu	0518	3.3	101
	1134	0.2	6
	1749	3.4	104
25 W	0001	0.2	6
	0614	3.5	107
	1228	0.1	3
	1840	3.5	107
26 Th	0052	0.0	0
	0707	3.6	110
	1319	0.1	3
	1928	3.6	110
27 F	0141	-0.1	-3
	0756	3.7	113
	1407	0.1	3
	2015	3.6	110
28 Sa	0227	-0.1	-3
	0845	3.7	113
	1454	0.2	6
	2100	3.5	107
29 Su	0313	0.0	0
	0932	3.6	110
	1541	0.3	9
	2145	3.4	104
30 M	0359	0.1	3
	1019	3.5	107
	1628	0.5	15
	2230	3.2	98

ne meridian 75° W. 0000 is midnight. 1200 is noon.
ghts are referred to mean lower low water which is the chart datum of soundings.

Miami Harbor Entrance, Fla., 1996

Times and Heights of High and Low Waters

October

Day	Time	ft	cm	Day	Time	ft	cm
1 Tu	0446	0.3	9	**16** W	0405	0.3	9
	1107	3.3	101		1029	3.4	104
	1716	0.7	21		1636	0.8	24
	2318	3.1	94		2237	3.2	98
2 W	0534	0.5	15	**17** Th	0454	0.4	12
	1158	3.1	94		1119	3.3	101
	1807	0.9	27		1729	0.8	24
					2331	3.1	94
3 Th	0009	2.9	88	**18** F	0550	0.5	15
	0626	0.7	21		1216	3.2	98
	1252	2.9	88		1828	0.9	27
	1903	1.0	30				
4 F	0105	2.7	82	**19** Sa	0034	3.0	91
	0722	0.9	27		0654	0.6	18
	1350	2.8	85		1320	3.1	94
	2004	1.1	34		1905	0.9	27
5 Sa	0207	2.6	79	**20** Su	0144	3.0	91
	0824	1.0	30		0804	0.7	21
	1450	2.8	85		1427	3.1	94
	2106	1.1	34		2044	0.8	24
6 Su	0310	2.6	79	**21** M	0257	3.1	94
	0924	1.0	30		0914	0.7	21
	1547	2.8	85		1533	3.2	98
	2202	1.1	34		2150	0.6	18
7 M	0409	2.7	82	**22** Tu	0405	3.2	98
	1020	0.9	27		1020	0.6	18
	1638	2.9	88		1634	3.3	101
	2251	0.9	27		2250	0.5	15
8 Tu	0459	2.8	85	**23** W	0506	3.4	104
	1109	0.9	27		1119	0.5	15
	1722	3.0	91		1729	3.4	104
	2334	0.8	24		2314	0.3	9
9 W	0544	3.0	91	**24** Th	0602	3.6	110
	1153	0.8	24		1213	0.4	12
	1802	3.1	94		1819	3.5	107
10 Th	0013	0.7	21	**25** F	0033	0.1	3
	0625	3.1	94		0652	3.7	113
	1234	0.7	21		1302	0.4	12
	1839	3.1	94		1906	3.5	107
11 F	0050	0.5	15	**26** Sa	0120	0.0	0
	0704	3.3	101		0740	3.7	113
	1312	0.6	18		1349	0.4	12
	1916	3.2	98		1951	3.5	107
12 Sa	0126	0.4	12	**27** Su	0205	0.0	0
	0743	3.4	104		0825	3.7	113
	1350	0.6	18		1434	0.4	12
	1952	3.3	101		2034	3.5	107
13 Su	0203	0.3	9	**28** M	0248	0.1	3
	0821	3.4	104		0909	3.6	110
	1429	0.6	18		1518	0.5	15
	2029	3.3	101		2117	3.3	101
14 M	0241	0.3	9	**29** Tu	0331	0.2	6
	0901	3.5	107		0953	3.5	107
	1508	0.6	18		1601	0.7	21
	2108	3.3	101		2201	3.2	98
15 Tu	0322	0.3	9	**30** W	0414	0.4	12
	0943	3.4	104		1037	3.3	101
	1550	0.7	21		1646	0.8	24
	2150	3.2	98		2245	3.0	91
				31 Th	0459	0.6	18
					1123	3.1	94
					1734	0.9	27
					2333	2.8	85

November

Day	Time	ft	cm	Day	Time	ft	cm
1 F	0546	0.8	24	**16** Sa	0537	0.3	9
	1211	3.0	91		1201	3.2	98
	1825	1.0	30		1816	0.6	18
2 Sa	0026	2.7	82	**17** Su	0024	3.0	91
	0639	0.9	27		0640	0.5	15
	1304	2.9	88		1303	3.1	94
	1921	1.1	34		1921	0.6	18
3 Su	0125	2.6	79	**18** M	0134	3.0	91
	0736	1.0	30		0748	0.6	18
	1400	2.8	85		1407	3.1	94
	2019	1.1	34		2027	0.5	15
4 M	0227	2.6	79	**19** Tu	0244	3.0	91
	0837	1.1	34		0858	0.6	18
	1456	2.8	85		1512	3.1	94
	2115	1.0	30		2132	0.4	12
5 Tu	0327	2.7	82	**20** W	0352	3.1	94
	0935	1.0	30		1003	0.6	18
	1548	2.8	85		1612	3.1	94
	2206	0.9	27		2231	0.3	9
6 W	0421	2.8	85	**21** Th	0453	3.2	98
	1028	1.0	30		1102	0.5	15
	1635	2.9	88		1707	3.1	94
	2252	0.7	21		2325	0.1	3
7 Th	0509	3.0	91	**22** F	0547	3.3	101
	1116	0.9	27		1156	0.5	15
	1719	3.0	91		1758	3.2	98
	2334	0.6	18				
8 F	0553	3.1	94	**23** Sa	0014	0.0	0
	1159	0.8	24		0637	3.4	104
	1800	3.1	94		1245	0.4	12
					1844	3.2	98
9 Sa	0014	0.4	12	**24** Su	0100	0.0	0
	0635	3.3	101		0723	3.4	104
	1241	0.7	21		1330	0.4	12
	1840	3.2	98		1929	3.2	98
10 Su	0055	0.3	9	**25** M	0144	0.0	0
	0716	3.4	104		0806	3.4	104
	1323	0.6	18		1414	0.4	12
	1921	3.2	98		2011	3.1	94
11 M	0135	0.1	3	**26** Tu	0225	0.0	0
	0757	3.5	107		0848	3.3	101
	1404	0.5	15		1456	0.5	15
	2002	3.3	101		2052	3.0	91
12 Tu	0217	0.1	3	**27** W	0306	0.1	3
	0840	3.5	107		0928	3.2	98
	1448	0.5	15		1537	0.5	15
	2046	3.3	101		2134	2.9	88
13 W	0302	0.1	3	**28** Th	0346	0.3	9
	0925	3.5	107		1009	3.1	94
	1534	0.5	15		1619	0.6	18
	2133	3.3	101		2216	2.8	85
14 Th	0349	0.1	3	**29** F	0427	0.4	12
	1013	3.4	104		1050	2.9	88
	1623	0.5	15		1702	0.7	21
	2224	3.2	98		2300	2.6	79
15 F	0441	0.2	6	**30** Sa	0511	0.5	15
	1105	3.3	101		1133	2.8	85
	1717	0.6	18		1748	0.8	24
	2321	3.1	94		2349	2.5	76

December

Day	Time	ft	cm	Day	Time	ft	cm
1 Su	0557	0.7	21	**16** M	0012	2.9	88
	1219	2.7	82		0625	0.1	3
	1837	0.8	24		1243	2.9	88
					1902	0.1	3
2 M	0041	2.4	73	**17** Tu	0118	2.8	85
	0649	0.8	24		0730	0.3	9
	1308	2.6	79		1344	2.8	85
	1929	0.8	24		2006	0.1	3
3 Tu	0139	2.4	73	**18** W	0226	2.7	82
	0745	0.9	27		0837	0.3	9
	1400	2.5	76		1446	2.7	82
	2022	0.7	21		2109	0.1	3
4 W	0238	2.5	76	**19** Th	0333	2.7	82
	0843	0.9	27		0942	0.4	12
	1453	2.5	76		1547	2.7	82
	2115	0.6	18		2210	0.0	0
5 Th	0335	2.5	76	**20** F	0435	2.8	85
	0940	0.8	24		1043	0.4	12
	1544	2.6	79		1644	2.7	82
	2205	0.5	15		2305	-0.1	-3
6 F	0428	2.7	82	**21** Sa	0531	2.8	85
	1033	0.7	21		1138	0.3	9
	1633	2.7	82		1737	2.7	82
	2253	0.3	9		2355	-0.1	-3
7 Sa	0517	2.8	85	**22** Su	0621	2.9	88
	1123	0.6	18		1228	0.3	9
	1721	2.8	85		1824	2.7	82
	2340	0.1	3				
8 Su	0604	3.0	91	**23** M	0041	-0.2	-6
	1210	0.5	15		0706	2.9	88
	1807	2.9	88		1313	0.3	9
					1909	2.7	82
9 M	0025	-0.1	-3	**24** Tu	0124	-0.2	-6
	0650	3.2	98		0748	2.9	88
	1256	0.3	9		1355	0.2	6
	1854	3.0	91		1951	2.7	82
10 Tu	0111	-0.2	-6	**25** W	0204	-0.2	-6
	0735	3.3	101		0827	2.9	88
	1343	0.2	6		1435	0.2	6
	1941	3.1	94		2031	2.6	79
11 W	0158	-0.3	-9	**26** Th	0243	-0.1	-3
	0822	3.3	101		0905	2.8	85
	1430	0.1	3		1513	0.2	6
	2030	3.1	94		2110	2.6	79
12 Th	0246	-0.3	-9	**27** F	0321	0.0	0
	0909	3.3	101		0942	2.8	85
	1518	0.1	3		1552	0.3	9
	2120	3.1	94		2150	2.5	76
13 F	0336	-0.3	-9	**28** Sa	0400	0.1	3
	0958	3.3	101		1019	2.7	82
	1609	0.0	0		1631	0.3	9
	2214	3.1	94		2231	2.4	73
14 Sa	0429	-0.2	-6	**29** Su	0439	0.2	6
	1050	3.2	98		1057	2.6	79
	1703	0.1	3		1711	0.3	9
	2311	3.0	91		2314	2.3	70
15 Su	0525	0.0	0	**30** M	0521	0.3	9
	1144	3.1	94		1137	2.4	73
	1801	0.1	3		1753	0.3	9
				31 Tu	0001	2.2	67
					0606	0.4	12
					1219	2.3	70
					1839	0.3	9

Time meridian 75° W. 0000 is midnight. 1200 is noon.
Heights are referred to mean lower low water which is the chart datum of soundings.

Key West, Fla., 1996

Times and Heights of High and Low Waters

January

Day	Time (h m)	Height (ft)	(cm)	Day	Time (h m)	Height (ft)	(cm)
1 M	0047	0.0	0	16 Tu	0640	0.9	27
	0733	1.0	30		1102	0.4	12
	1200	0.5	15		1752	1.7	52
	1850	1.7	52				
2 Tu	0136	-0.1	-3	17 W	0051	-0.3	-9
	0821	1.0	30		0744	0.9	27
	1247	0.4	12		1203	0.3	9
	1933	1.8	55		1854	1.9	58
3 W	0219	-0.1	-3	18 Th	0145	-0.5	-15
	0900	1.1	34		0836	1.0	30
	1330	0.4	12		1301	0.2	6
	2012	1.8	55		1952	2.0	61
4 Th	0257	-0.2	-6	19 F	0235	-0.6	-18
	0933	1.1	34		0921	1.1	34
	1411	0.4	12		1357	0.1	3
	2049	1.8	55		2047	2.1	64
5 F ○	0332	-0.2	-6	20 Sa ●	0322	-0.6	-18
	1003	1.1	34		1004	1.2	37
	1449	0.3	9		1451	0.0	0
	2125	1.8	55		2139	2.1	64
6 Sa	0406	-0.2	-6	21 Su	0406	-0.6	-18
	1034	1.1	34		1045	1.3	40
	1526	0.3	9		1545	-0.1	-3
	2201	1.8	55		2229	2.0	61
7 Su	0439	-0.2	-6	22 M	0449	-0.5	-15
	1106	1.2	37		1125	1.3	40
	1603	0.3	9		1639	-0.1	-3
	2236	1.8	55		2319	1.8	55
8 M	0510	-0.2	-6	23 Tu	0531	-0.4	-12
	1139	1.2	37		1206	1.4	43
	1641	0.3	9		1736	-0.1	-3
	2313	1.7	52				
9 Tu	0541	-0.1	-3	24 W	0009	1.6	49
	1213	1.2	37		0613	-0.2	-6
	1722	0.3	9		1247	1.4	43
	2352	1.6	49		1835	-0.1	-3
10 W	0613	-0.1	-3	25 Th	0101	1.4	43
	1248	1.2	37		0655	-0.1	-3
	1808	0.3	9		1330	1.4	43
					1939	0.0	0
11 Th	0035	1.4	43	26 F	0158	1.1	34
	0647	0.0	0		0739	0.1	3
	1325	1.3	40		1417	1.4	43
	1903	0.3	9		2050	0.0	0
12 F	0124	1.3	40	27 Sa ○	0305	0.9	27
	0725	0.1	3		0828	0.2	6
	1405	1.3	40		1510	1.4	43
	2009	0.2	6		2205	0.0	0
13 Sa ○	0225	1.1	34	28 Su	0431	0.8	24
	0808	0.2	6		0924	0.3	9
	1452	1.4	43		1611	1.4	43
	2124	0.2	6		2318	0.0	0
14 Su	0343	0.9	27	29 M	0603	0.7	21
	0900	0.3	9		1025	0.4	12
	1546	1.5	46		1716	1.4	43
	2241	0.0	0				
15 M	0516	0.9	27	30 Tu	0022	0.0	0
	0959	0.4	12		0713	0.8	24
	1647	1.6	49		1126	0.4	12
	2350	-0.1	-3		1818	1.5	46
				31 W	0115	-0.1	-3
					0801	0.8	24
					1222	0.4	12
					1910	1.5	46

February

Day	Time (h m)	Height (ft)	(cm)	Day	Time (h m)	Height (ft)	(cm)
1 Th	0159	-0.2	-6	16 F	0128	-0.4	-12
	0837	0.9	27		0817	1.0	30
	1310	0.3	9		1252	0.1	3
	1954	1.6	49		1947	1.8	55
2 F	0237	-0.2	-6	17 Sa	0216	-0.5	-15
	0908	0.9	27		0859	1.1	34
	1354	0.2	6		1351	0.0	0
	2034	1.6	49		2043	1.9	58
3 Sa	0311	-0.3	-9	18 Su ●	0300	-0.5	-15
	0937	1.0	30		0938	1.2	37
	1434	0.2	6		1447	-0.2	-6
	2112	1.6	49		2134	1.8	55
4 Su ○	0342	-0.3	-9	19 M	0341	-0.5	-15
	1006	1.1	34		1016	1.4	43
	1512	0.1	3		1539	-0.3	-9
	2148	1.6	49		2223	1.8	55
5 M	0410	-0.3	-9	20 Tu	0420	-0.4	-12
	1036	1.1	34		1052	1.5	46
	1549	0.0	0		1631	-0.3	-9
	2224	1.6	49		2310	1.6	49
6 Tu	0439	-0.2	-6	21 W	0459	-0.3	-9
	1106	1.2	37		1129	1.5	46
	1628	0.0	0		1723	-0.3	-9
	2301	1.5	46		2356	1.4	43
7 W	0507	-0.2	-6	22 Th	0537	-0.1	-3
	1137	1.3	40		1206	1.5	46
	1708	0.0	0		1816	-0.3	-9
	2340	1.4	43				
8 Th	0536	-0.1	-3	23 F	0043	1.2	37
	1208	1.3	40		0615	0.0	0
	1753	-0.1	-3		1244	1.5	46
					1912	-0.2	-6
9 F	0022	1.3	40	24 Sa	0132	1.0	30
	0608	0.0	0		0655	0.1	3
	1241	1.3	40		1325	1.5	46
	1844	-0.1	-3		2014	-0.1	-3
10 Sa	0110	1.1	34	25 Su	0228	0.8	24
	0643	0.1	3		0739	0.3	9
	1318	1.4	43		1412	1.4	43
	1944	-0.1	-3		2123	0.0	0
11 Su	0208	0.9	27	26 M ◐	0342	0.7	21
	0724	0.2	6		0834	0.4	12
	1404	1.4	43		1510	1.3	40
	2055	-0.1	-3		2237	0.0	0
12 M ○	0324	0.8	24	27 Tu	0519	0.7	21
	0816	0.3	9		0942	0.4	12
	1501	1.5	46		1623	1.3	40
	2213	-0.1	-3		2346	0.0	0
13 Tu	0500	0.7	21	28 W	0638	0.7	21
	0921	0.3	9		1055	0.4	12
	1612	1.5	46		1739	1.3	40
	2328	-0.2	-6				
14 W	0626	0.6	18	29 Th	0043	0.0	0
	1036	0.3	9		0727	0.8	24
	1731	1.6	49		1159	0.4	12
					1842	1.4	43
15 Th	0033	-0.3	-9				
	0729	0.8	24				
	1147	0.2	6				
	1843	1.7	52				

March

Day	Time (h m)	Height (ft)	(cm)	Day	Time (h m)	Height (ft)	(cm)
1 F	0129	-0.1	-3	16 Sa	0103	-0.2	-6
	0802	0.9	27		0751	1.1	34
	1253	0.3	9		1251	0.1	3
	1932	1.4	43		1943	1.7	52
2 Sa	0206	-0.1	-3	17 Su	0149	-0.2	-6
	0833	1.0	30		0831	1.3	40
	1338	0.2	6		1349	-0.1	-3
	2015	1.5	46		2039	1.7	52
3 Su	0238	-0.1	-3	18 M	0231	-0.2	-6
	0901	1.1	34		0908	1.5	46
	1419	0.1	3		1443	-0.3	-9
	2055	1.5	46		2129	1.7	52
4 M	0307	-0.2	-6	19 Tu	0310	-0.2	-6
	0930	1.2	37		0943	1.6	49
	1457	0.0	0		1532	-0.4	-12
	2133	1.5	46		2215	1.6	49
5 Tu ○	0334	-0.2	-6	20 W	0347	-0.1	-3
	0959	1.3	40		1018	1.7	52
	1535	-0.1	-3		1620	-0.4	-12
	2212	1.5	46		2259	1.5	46
6 W	0401	-0.1	-3	21 Th	0424	0.0	0
	1029	1.4	43		1051	1.7	52
	1614	-0.2	-6		1707	-0.4	-12
	2251	1.5	46		2342	1.3	40
7 Th	0430	-0.1	-3	22 F	0500	0.1	3
	1058	1.5	46		1125	1.7	52
	1654	-0.3	-9		1754	-0.3	-9
	2332	1.4	43				
8 F	0500	0.0	0	23 Sa	0024	1.2	37
	1129	1.5	46		0536	0.2	6
	1739	-0.3	-9		1201	1.7	52
					1844	-0.2	-6
9 Sa	0015	1.2	37	24 Su	0108	1.0	30
	0533	0.1	3		0614	0.3	9
	1203	1.6	49		1239	1.6	49
	1829	-0.3	-9		1938	-0.1	-3
10 Su	0105	1.1	34	25 M	0157	0.9	27
	0610	0.2	6		0656	0.4	12
	1242	1.6	49		1324	1.6	49
	1926	-0.2	-6		2039	0.0	0
11 M	0203	0.9	27	26 Tu ◐	0258	0.8	24
	0653	0.3	9		0748	0.5	15
	1330	1.6	49		1418	1.4	43
	2034	-0.2	-6		2149	0.1	3
12 Tu ○	0318	0.8	24	27 W	0418	0.8	24
	0749	0.4	12		0900	0.6	18
	1432	1.6	49		1527	1.3	40
	2150	-0.2	-6		2258	0.1	3
13 W	0448	0.8	24	28 Th	0541	0.8	24
	0902	0.4	12		1024	0.5	15
	1552	1.6	49		1649	1.3	40
	2305	-0.2	-6		2356	0.1	3
14 Th	0608	0.9	27	29 F	0636	0.9	27
	1026	0.4	12		1135	0.5	15
	1720	1.6	49		1803	1.3	40
15 F	0010	-0.2	-6	30 Sa	0043	0.1	3
	0706	1.0	30		0715	1.1	34
	1144	0.3	9		1232	0.3	9
	1838	1.6	49		1902	1.4	43
				31 Su	0120	0.1	3
					0748	1.2	37
					1319	0.2	6
					1951	1.4	43

Time meridian 75° W. 0000 is midnight. 1200 is noon.
Heights are referred to mean lower low water which is the chart datum of soundings.

Key West, Fla., 1996

Times and Heights of High and Low Waters

April

Day	Time	ft	cm		Day	Time	ft	cm
1 M	0152	0.1	3		16 Tu	0156	0.1	3
	0818	1.3	40			0836	1.7	52
	1401	0.1	3			1437	-0.3	-9
	2035	1.5	46			2122	1.5	46
2 Tu	0222	0.1	3		17 W ●	0235	0.1	3
	0849	1.5	46			0911	1.8	55
	1440	-0.1	-3			1523	-0.3	-9
	2117	1.5	46			2206	1.4	43
3 W ○	0251	0.1	3		18 Th	0312	0.2	6
	0919	1.6	49			0944	1.9	58
	1519	-0.2	-6			1607	-0.4	-12
	2158	1.5	46			2248	1.4	43
4 Th	0321	0.1	3		19 F	0349	0.2	6
	0950	1.7	52			1017	1.9	58
	1559	-0.3	-9			1650	-0.4	-12
	2241	1.4	43			2327	1.3	40
5 F	0353	0.1	3		20 Sa	0425	0.3	9
	1022	1.8	55			1050	1.9	58
	1641	-0.4	-12			1733	-0.3	-9
	2324	1.3	40					
6 Sa	0427	0.2	6		21 Su	0006	1.2	37
	1057	1.8	55			0501	0.4	12
	1727	-0.4	-12			1125	1.8	55
						1818	-0.2	-6
7 Su	0011	1.2	37		22 M	0046	1.1	34
	0504	0.3	9			0538	0.4	12
	1135	1.9	58			1203	1.7	52
	1817	-0.4	-12			1905	-0.1	-3
8 M	0103	1.1	34		23 Tu	0131	1.0	30
	0546	0.3	9			0619	0.5	15
	1219	1.8	55			1247	1.6	49
	1914	-0.3	-9			1959	0.1	3
9 Tu	0202	1.0	30		24 W	0223	1.0	30
	0635	0.4	12			0710	0.6	18
	1312	1.8	55			1337	1.5	46
	2018	-0.2	-6			2058	0.2	6
10 W ○	0313	1.0	30		25 Th ○	0326	1.0	30
	0738	0.5	15			0821	0.6	18
	1418	1.7	52			1439	1.4	43
	2129	-0.1	-3			2159	0.2	6
11 Th	0430	1.0	30		26 F	0434	1.0	30
	0900	0.5	15			0948	0.6	18
	1541	1.6	49			1554	1.3	40
	2238	0.0	0			2255	0.3	9
12 F	0539	1.1	34		27 Sa	0532	1.1	34
	1028	0.4	12			1105	0.5	15
	1713	1.5	46			1713	1.3	40
	2338	0.0	0			2342	0.3	9
13 Sa	0634	1.2	37		28 Su	0617	1.2	37
	1146	0.3	9			1205	0.4	12
	1833	1.5	46			1823	1.3	40
14 Su	0030	0.0	0		29 M	0022	0.3	9
	0720	1.4	43			0655	1.4	43
	1251	0.1	3			1255	0.2	6
	1938	1.5	46			1921	1.3	40
15 M	0115	0.0	0		30 Tu	0058	0.3	9
	0800	1.6	49			0731	1.5	46
	1347	-0.1	-3			1338	0.0	0
	2033	1.5	46			2012	1.4	43

May

Day	Time	ft	cm		Day	Time	ft	cm
1 W	0132	0.3	9		16 Th	0200	0.3	9
	0805	1.7	52			0841	1.9	58
	1420	-0.1	-3			1512	-0.3	-9
	2059	1.4	43			2156	1.3	40
2 Th	0206	0.3	9		17 F ●	0239	0.3	9
	0839	1.8	55			0915	2.0	61
	1501	-0.3	-9			1553	-0.3	-9
	2145	1.4	43			2235	1.2	37
3 F ○	0242	0.3	9		18 Sa	0317	0.4	12
	0915	2.0	61			0948	2.0	61
	1544	-0.4	-12			1633	-0.3	-9
	2231	1.4	43			2311	1.2	37
4 Sa	0319	0.3	9		19 Su	0353	0.4	12
	0953	2.0	61			1023	1.9	58
	1629	-0.5	-15			1713	-0.2	-6
	2317	1.3	40			2347	1.2	37
5 Su	0358	0.3	9		20 M	0430	0.4	12
	1033	2.1	64			1059	1.9	58
	1717	-0.5	-15			1754	-0.2	-6
6 M	0006	1.2	37		21 Tu	0025	1.1	34
	0442	0.3	9			0509	0.5	15
	1118	2.1	64			1137	1.8	55
	1807	-0.4	-12			1836	-0.1	-3
7 Tu	0057	1.2	37		22 W	0106	1.1	34
	0530	0.4	12			0551	0.6	18
	1207	2.0	61			1219	1.7	52
	1902	-0.3	-9			1920	0.0	0
8 W	0154	1.1	34		23 Th	0151	1.1	34
	0627	0.5	15			0641	0.6	18
	1304	1.8	55			1305	1.5	46
	2001	-0.2	-6			2007	0.1	3
9 Th	0256	1.1	34		24 F	0241	1.1	34
	0738	0.5	15			0746	0.6	18
	1412	1.7	52			1400	1.4	43
	2103	-0.1	-3			2057	0.2	6
10 F	0401	1.2	37		25 Sa	0335	1.2	37
	0903	0.5	15			0906	0.6	18
	1533	1.5	46			1505	1.3	40
	2204	0.1	3			2146	0.3	9
11 Sa	0503	1.3	40		26 Su	0427	1.3	40
	1029	0.4	12			1025	0.5	15
	1702	1.4	43			1621	1.2	37
	2300	0.1	3			2233	0.3	9
12 Su	0558	1.5	46		27 M	0516	1.4	43
	1145	0.2	6			1130	0.4	12
	1824	1.3	40			1740	1.2	37
	2351	0.2	6			2318	0.4	12
13 M	0645	1.6	49		28 Tu	0600	1.5	46
	1248	0.0	0			1225	0.2	6
	1931	1.3	40			1850	1.2	37
14 Tu	0037	0.2	6		29 W	0001	0.4	12
	0727	1.8	55			0642	1.7	52
	1341	-0.1	-3			1313	0.0	0
	2026	1.3	40			1950	1.2	37
15 W	0120	0.3	9		30 Th	0042	0.4	12
	0805	1.9	58			0723	1.9	58
	1429	-0.2	-6			1359	-0.2	-6
	2114	1.3	40			2042	1.2	37
					31 F	0124	0.4	12
						0804	2.0	61
						1445	-0.4	-12
						2131	1.3	40

June

Day	Time	ft	cm		Day	Time	ft	cm
1 Sa ○	0207	0.3	9		16 Su	0250	0.4	12
	0847	2.1	64			0928	2.0	61
	1530	-0.5	-15			1617	-0.2	-6
	2219	1.3	40			2252	1.1	34
2 Su	0251	0.3	9		17 M	0329	0.4	12
	0932	2.2	67			1003	1.9	58
	1617	-0.5	-15			1654	-0.2	-6
	2306	1.2	37			2325	1.2	37
3 M	0337	0.3	9		18 Tu	0407	0.4	12
	1019	2.2	67			1040	1.9	58
	1705	-0.5	-15			1730	-0.1	-3
	2353	1.2	37					
4 Tu	0427	0.3	9		19 W	0000	1.2	37
	1109	2.2	67			0447	0.5	15
	1754	-0.4	-12			1117	1.8	55
						1806	-0.1	-3
5 W	0042	1.3	40		20 Th	0036	1.2	37
	0522	0.3	9			0529	0.5	15
	1201	2.0	61			1157	1.7	52
	1845	-0.3	-9			1842	0.0	0
6 Th	0133	1.3	40		21 F	0115	1.2	37
	0625	0.4	12			0617	0.5	15
	1259	1.8	55			1240	1.6	49
	1937	-0.2	-6			1919	0.1	3
7 F	0228	1.3	40		22 Sa	0157	1.3	40
	0738	0.4	12			0714	0.6	18
	1404	1.6	49			1328	1.4	43
	2031	0.0	0			1958	0.2	6
8 Sa ○	0325	1.4	43		23 Su	0241	1.3	40
	0900	0.4	12			0823	0.5	15
	1520	1.4	43			1426	1.3	40
	2125	0.1	3			2040	0.3	9
9 Su	0422	1.5	46		24 M	0328	1.4	43
	1022	0.3	9			0939	0.5	15
	1647	1.2	37			1536	1.1	34
	2219	0.2	6			2126	0.4	12
10 M	0518	1.6	49		25 Tu	0416	1.5	46
	1136	0.2	6			1050	0.3	9
	1810	1.1	34			1659	1.1	34
	2311	0.3	9			2216	0.4	12
11 Tu	0609	1.8	55		26 W	0506	1.6	49
	1239	0.0	0			1153	0.2	6
	1920	1.1	34			1821	1.0	30
						2308	0.5	15
12 W	0000	0.4	12		27 Th	0557	1.8	55
	0656	1.8	55			1249	0.0	0
	1332	-0.1	-3			1929	1.1	34
	2017	1.1	34			2359	0.4	12
13 Th	0046	0.4	12		28 F	0648	2.0	61
	0738	1.9	58			1340	-0.2	-6
	1418	-0.2	-6			2026	1.1	34
	2103	1.1	34					
14 F	0130	0.4	12		29 Sa	0050	0.4	12
	0816	1.9	58			0739	2.1	64
	1500	-0.2	-6			1429	-0.4	-12
	2143	1.1	34			2116	1.2	37
15 Sa ●	0211	0.4	12		30 Su ○	0141	0.4	12
	0853	2.0	61			0830	2.2	67
	1539	-0.2	-6			1516	-0.4	-12
	2218	1.1	34			2202	1.2	37

Time meridian 75° W. 0000 is midnight. 1200 is noon.
Heights are referred to mean lower low water which is the chart datum of soundings.

Key West, Fla., 1996

Times and Heights of High and Low Waters

July

Day	Time	ft	cm	Day	Time	ft	cm
1 M	0232	0.3	9	16 Tu	0311	0.4	12
	0920	2.3	70		0949	1.9	58
	1602	-0.5	-15		1630	-0.1	-3
	2247	1.3	40		2256	1.3	40
2 Tu	0324	0.2	6	17 W	0350	0.4	12
	1011	2.3	70		1024	1.9	58
	1648	-0.5	-15		1701	0.0	0
	2331	1.3	40		2327	1.3	40
3 W	0419	0.2	6	18 Th	0429	0.4	12
	1102	2.2	67		1101	1.8	55
	1734	-0.4	-12		1732	0.0	0
4 Th	0016	1.4	43	19 F	0000	1.4	43
	0516	0.2	6		0510	0.4	12
	1155	2.0	61		1139	1.7	52
	1820	-0.2	-6		1802	0.1	3
5 F	0102	1.5	46	20 Sa	0035	1.4	43
	0619	0.2	6		0555	0.5	15
	1251	1.8	55		1219	1.6	49
	1906	-0.1	-3		1833	0.2	6
6 Sa	0151	1.6	49	21 Su	0111	1.5	46
	0729	0.3	9		0646	0.5	15
	1352	1.5	46		1304	1.5	46
	1954	0.1	3		1907	0.3	9
7 Su	0242	1.6	49	22 M	0149	1.5	46
	0846	0.3	9		0746	0.5	15
	1502	1.3	40		1357	1.3	40
	2044	0.3	9		1945	0.4	12
8 M	0338	1.7	52	23 Tu	0232	1.6	49
	1005	0.2	6		0857	0.4	12
	1625	1.1	34		1504	1.2	37
	2137	0.4	12		2030	0.5	15
9 Tu	0436	1.7	52	24 W	0322	1.7	52
	1119	0.2	6		1012	0.3	9
	1753	1.0	30		1629	1.1	34
	2233	0.5	15		2125	0.6	18
10 W	0534	1.8	55	25 Th	0419	1.8	55
	1223	0.1	3		1123	0.2	6
	1906	1.0	30		1759	1.0	30
	2327	0.5	15		2226	0.6	18
11 Th	0627	1.8	55	26 F	0522	1.9	58
	1318	0.0	0		1226	0.0	0
	2003	1.0	30		1912	1.1	34
					2328	0.6	18
12 F	0018	0.5	15	27 Sa	0624	2.1	64
	0715	1.9	58		1321	-0.1	-3
	1404	0.0	0		2008	1.2	37
	2047	1.1	34				
13 Sa	0106	0.5	15	28 Su	0029	0.5	15
	0758	1.9	58		0724	2.2	67
	1445	-0.1	-3		1411	-0.2	-6
	2123	1.1	34		2055	1.3	40
14 Su	0150	0.5	15	29 M	0126	0.4	12
	0837	2.0	61		0820	2.3	70
	1522	-0.1	-3		1458	-0.3	-9
	2155	1.2	37		2139	1.4	43
15 M	0231	0.5	15	30 Tu	0222	0.3	9
	0913	2.0	61		0913	2.3	70
	1557	-0.1	-3		1542	-0.3	-9
	2225	1.2	37		2220	1.5	46
				31 W	0317	0.2	6
					1005	2.3	70
					1625	-0.2	-6
					2301	1.6	49

August

Day	Time	ft	cm	Day	Time	ft	cm
1 Th	0412	0.1	3	16 F	0413	0.4	12
	1056	2.2	67		1046	1.9	58
	1707	-0.1	-3		1653	0.2	6
	2342	1.7	52		2320	1.6	49
2 F	0509	0.1	3	17 Sa	0452	0.4	12
	1147	2.0	61		1124	1.8	55
	1748	0.0	0		1721	0.3	9
					2351	1.7	52
3 Sa	0024	1.8	55	18 Su	0534	0.4	12
	0608	0.2	6		1204	1.7	52
	1239	1.7	52		1750	0.4	12
	1831	0.2	6				
4 Su	0109	1.8	55	19 M	0024	1.7	52
	0712	0.2	6		0622	0.4	12
	1335	1.5	46		1248	1.6	49
	1915	0.3	9		1823	0.5	15
5 M	0156	1.8	55	20 Tu	0100	1.8	55
	0822	0.3	9		0717	0.4	12
	1439	1.3	40		1340	1.4	43
	2002	0.5	15		1900	0.6	18
6 Tu	0249	1.8	55	21 W	0143	1.8	55
	0937	0.3	9		0824	0.4	12
	1558	1.1	34		1446	1.3	40
	2056	0.6	18		1947	0.7	21
7 W	0350	1.8	55	22 Th	0236	1.9	58
	1052	0.3	9		0941	0.4	12
	1729	1.1	34		1612	1.2	37
	2157	0.7	21		2047	0.8	24
8 Th	0456	1.8	55	23 F	0343	2.0	61
	1206	0.3	9		1057	0.3	9
	1846	1.1	34		1744	1.2	37
	2300	0.7	21		2159	0.8	24
9 F	0600	1.9	58	24 Sa	0458	2.0	61
	1257	0.3	9		1204	0.2	6
	1941	1.1	34		1853	1.2	37
	2358	0.7	21		2312	0.7	21
10 Sa	0655	1.9	58	25 Su	0611	2.2	67
	1344	0.2	6		1301	0.1	3
	2021	1.2	37		1945	1.4	43
11 Su	0050	0.6	18	26 M	0020	0.6	18
	0741	2.0	61		0716	2.3	70
	1423	0.2	6		1349	0.0	0
	2054	1.3	40		2029	1.5	46
12 M	0136	0.6	18	27 Tu	0120	0.4	12
	0822	2.0	61		0815	2.3	70
	1458	0.2	6		1433	0.0	0
	2123	1.3	40		2110	1.7	52
13 Tu	0218	0.5	15	28 W	0217	0.3	9
	0859	2.0	61		0908	2.3	70
	1529	0.1	3		1515	0.0	0
	2151	1.4	43		2148	1.8	55
14 W	0257	0.5	15	29 Th	0311	0.2	6
	0934	2.0	61		0958	2.3	70
	1558	0.2	6		1555	0.1	3
	2220	1.5	46		2226	2.0	61
15 Th	0335	0.4	12	30 F	0405	0.1	3
	1010	2.0	61		1047	2.1	64
	1626	0.2	6		1634	0.2	6
	2250	1.6	49		2305	2.0	61
				31 Sa	0457	0.1	3
					1135	2.0	61
					1713	0.3	9
					2344	2.1	64

September

Day	Time	ft	cm	Day	Time	ft	cm
1 Su	0552	0.1	3	16 M	0516	0.3	9
	1224	1.8	55		1153	1.8	55
	1753	0.5	15		1712	0.6	18
					2343	2.1	64
2 M	0025	2.1	64	17 Tu	0603	0.3	9
	0649	0.2	6		1239	1.6	49
	1315	1.6	49		1747	0.7	21
	1834	0.6	18				
3 Tu	0109	2.1	64	18 W	0020	2.1	64
	0751	0.4	12		0657	0.4	12
	1412	1.4	43		1332	1.5	46
	1920	0.7	21		1827	0.8	24
4 W	0159	2.0	61	19 Th	0106	2.1	64
	0901	0.5	15		0801	0.4	12
	1524	1.3	40		1440	1.4	43
	2016	0.8	24		1918	0.9	27
5 Th	0300	1.9	58	20 F	0204	2.1	64
	1016	0.5	15		0916	0.5	15
	1654	1.2	37		1603	1.3	40
	2123	0.9	27		2026	0.9	27
6 F	0412	1.9	58	21 Sa	0319	2.1	64
	1127	0.5	15		1032	0.5	15
	1814	1.3	40		1726	1.4	43
	2236	0.9	27		2149	0.9	27
7 Sa	0527	1.9	58	22 Su	0444	2.1	64
	1226	0.5	15		1139	0.4	12
	1907	1.3	40		1829	1.5	46
	2342	0.9	27		2309	0.8	24
8 Su	0630	1.9	58	23 M	0604	2.2	67
	1312	0.5	15		1234	0.4	12
	1945	1.4	43		1918	1.7	52
9 M	0036	0.8	24	24 Tu	0019	0.6	18
	0720	2.0	61		0712	2.2	67
	1350	0.5	15		1321	0.3	9
	2015	1.5	46		2000	1.8	55
10 Tu	0123	0.7	21	25 W	0119	0.5	15
	0803	2.0	61		0810	2.3	70
	1423	0.4	12		1403	0.4	12
	2044	1.6	49		2038	2.0	61
11 W	0204	0.6	18	26 Th	0214	0.3	9
	0841	2.1	64		0903	2.2	67
	1452	0.4	12		1443	0.4	12
	2112	1.7	52		2115	2.2	67
12 Th	0243	0.5	15	27 F	0305	0.1	3
	0918	2.1	64		0951	2.2	67
	1519	0.4	12		1521	0.4	12
	2140	1.8	55		2152	2.3	70
13 F	0319	0.4	12	28 Sa	0355	0.1	3
	0955	2.0	61		1038	2.1	64
	1546	0.5	15		1559	0.5	15
	2209	1.9	58		2228	2.3	70
14 Sa	0356	0.4	12	29 Su	0443	0.1	3
	1032	2.0	61		1122	1.9	58
	1613	0.5	15		1637	0.6	18
	2239	2.0	61		2306	2.3	70
15 Su	0435	0.3	9	30 M	0532	0.2	6
	1111	1.9	58		1207	1.8	55
	1641	0.6	18		1716	0.7	21
	2310	2.0	61		2344	2.3	70

Time meridian 75° W. 0000 is midnight. 1200 is noon.
Heights are referred to mean lower low water which is the chart datum of soundings.

Key West, Fla., 1996

Times and Heights of High and Low Waters

October

Day	Time	ft	cm
1 Tu	0623	0.3	9
	1253	1.6	49
	1756	0.8	24
2 W	0026	2.2	67
	0719	0.4	12
	1344	1.5	46
	1841	0.9	27
3 Th	0113	2.1	64
	0822	0.6	18
	1446	1.4	43
	1936	1.0	30
4 F ○	0210	2.0	61
	0932	0.7	21
	1603	1.4	43
	2049	1.1	34
5 Sa	0321	1.9	58
	1042	0.7	21
	1722	1.4	43
	2211	1.1	34
6 Su	0442	1.9	58
	1141	0.7	21
	1818	1.5	46
	2323	1.0	30
7 M	0554	1.9	58
	1228	0.7	21
	1857	1.6	49
8 Tu	0020	0.9	27
	0651	1.9	58
	1306	0.7	21
	1929	1.7	52
9 W	0107	0.7	21
	0738	2.0	61
	1338	0.6	18
	2000	1.9	58
10 Th	0148	0.6	18
	0820	2.0	61
	1407	0.6	18
	2029	2.0	61
11 F	0225	0.5	15
	0900	2.0	61
	1436	0.6	18
	2059	2.1	64
12 Sa ●	0302	0.3	9
	0940	2.0	61
	1504	0.7	21
	2130	2.2	67
13 Su	0340	0.3	9
	1020	1.9	58
	1534	0.9	27
	2201	2.3	70
14 M	0419	0.2	6
	1101	1.9	58
	1606	0.7	21
	2235	2.3	70
15 Tu	0502	0.2	6
	1145	1.8	55
	1640	0.8	24
	2311	2.3	70

Day	Time	ft	cm
16 W	0549	0.2	6
	1233	1.6	49
	1719	0.8	24
	2353	2.3	70
17 Th	0642	0.3	9
	1328	1.5	46
	1805	0.9	27
18 F	0044	2.3	70
	0744	0.4	12
	1433	1.5	46
	1904	1.0	30
19 Sa ○	0146	2.2	67
	0852	0.4	12
	1547	1.5	46
	2021	1.0	30
20 Su	0305	2.1	64
	1003	0.5	15
	1658	1.6	49
	2149	0.9	27
21 M	0435	2.0	61
	1106	0.5	15
	1757	1.7	52
	2311	0.8	24
22 Tu	0559	2.0	61
	1200	0.5	15
	1846	1.9	58
23 W	0020	0.6	18
	0708	2.0	61
	1247	0.5	15
	1928	2.1	64
24 Th	0118	0.4	12
	0806	2.0	61
	1329	0.6	18
	2007	2.2	67
25 F	0210	0.2	6
	0857	2.0	61
	1410	0.6	18
	2045	2.3	70
26 Sa ○	0258	0.1	3
	0944	1.9	58
	1449	0.6	18
	2121	2.4	73
27 Su	0344	0.0	0
	1028	1.9	58
	1527	0.7	21
	2157	2.4	73
28 M	0428	0.1	3
	1109	1.8	55
	1605	0.7	21
	2233	2.4	73
29 Tu	0513	0.1	3
	1150	1.7	52
	1643	0.8	24
	2311	2.3	70
30 W	0559	0.2	6
	1231	1.6	49
	1723	0.8	24
	2351	2.2	67
31 Th	0648	0.4	12
	1315	1.5	46
	1807	0.9	27

November

Day	Time	ft	cm
1 F	0035	2.1	64
	0741	0.5	15
	1406	1.4	43
	1900	1.0	30
2 Sa	0126	1.9	58
	0841	0.6	18
	1507	1.4	43
	2011	1.0	30
3 Su ○	0229	1.8	55
	0944	0.7	21
	1613	1.5	46
	2137	1.0	30
4 M	0344	1.7	52
	1041	0.7	21
	1711	1.5	46
	2254	0.9	27
5 Tu	0503	1.7	52
	1130	0.7	21
	1758	1.6	49
	2355	0.8	24
6 W	0612	1.7	52
	1210	0.7	21
	1837	1.8	55
7 Th	0044	0.6	18
	0709	1.7	52
	1246	0.7	21
	1912	1.9	58
8 F	0126	0.5	15
	0757	1.7	52
	1319	0.7	21
	1947	2.0	61
9 Sa ○	0206	0.3	9
	0842	1.7	52
	1351	0.7	21
	2021	2.2	67
10 Su	0244	0.1	3
	0925	1.7	52
	1424	0.7	21
	2056	2.3	70
11 M	0324	0.0	0
	1008	1.7	52
	1459	0.7	21
	2132	2.4	73
12 Tu	0406	0.0	0
	1052	1.7	52
	1537	0.7	21
	2211	2.4	73
13 W	0450	-0.1	-3
	1137	1.6	49
	1617	0.7	21
	2253	2.4	73
14 Th	0538	0.0	0
	1225	1.5	46
	1703	0.7	21
	2307	2.3	70
15 F	0629	0.1	3
	1318	1.5	46
	1756	0.8	24

Day	Time	ft	cm
16 Sa	0034	2.2	67
	0725	0.2	6
	1416	1.5	46
	1901	0.8	24
17 Su	0138	2.0	61
	0826	0.3	9
	1518	1.5	46
	2021	0.8	24
18 M	0256	1.8	55
	0927	0.4	12
	1622	1.6	49
	2149	0.7	21
19 Tu	0425	1.7	52
	1027	0.5	15
	1720	1.8	55
	2310	0.5	15
20 W	0551	1.6	49
	1121	0.5	15
	1811	1.9	58
21 Th	0017	0.3	9
	0703	1.6	49
	1210	0.6	18
	1858	2.1	64
22 F	0114	0.2	6
	0802	1.6	49
	1256	0.6	18
	1940	2.2	67
23 Sa	0204	0.0	0
	0852	1.6	49
	1339	0.6	18
	2019	2.2	67
24 Su ○	0250	-0.1	-3
	0937	1.6	49
	1420	0.6	18
	2057	2.3	70
25 M	0333	-0.1	-3
	1017	1.5	46
	1459	0.6	18
	2134	2.3	70
26 Tu	0414	-0.1	-3
	1055	1.5	46
	1539	0.6	18
	2210	2.2	67
27 W	0455	0.0	0
	1131	1.4	43
	1618	0.6	18
	2247	2.1	64
28 Th	0536	0.1	3
	1207	1.4	43
	1658	0.7	21
	2325	2.0	61
29 F	0618	0.2	6
	1245	1.4	43
	1741	0.7	21
30 Sa	0007	1.9	58
	0702	0.3	9
	1328	1.3	40
	1831	0.8	24

December

Day	Time	ft	cm
1 Su	0053	1.8	55
	0748	0.4	12
	1415	1.3	40
	1933	0.8	24
2 M	0146	1.6	49
	0838	0.5	15
	1506	1.4	43
	2050	0.8	24
3 Tu ○	0250	1.5	46
	0928	0.5	15
	1600	1.4	43
	2210	0.7	21
4 W	0405	1.5	46
	1018	0.6	18
	1652	1.5	46
	2317	0.6	18
5 Th	0525	1.3	40
	1104	0.6	18
	1739	1.7	52
6 F	0013	0.4	12
	0636	1.3	40
	1147	0.6	18
	1823	1.8	55
7 Sa	0100	0.2	6
	0734	1.3	40
	1228	0.6	18
	1905	1.9	58
8 Su	0144	0.0	0
	0825	1.4	43
	1309	0.6	18
	1947	2.1	64
9 M	0227	-0.1	-3
	0911	1.4	43
	1350	0.5	15
	2029	2.2	67
10 Tu	0309	-0.3	-9
	0955	1.4	43
	1432	0.5	15
	2112	2.3	70
11 W	0353	-0.3	-9
	1039	1.4	43
	1516	0.4	12
	2157	2.3	70
12 Th	0438	-0.3	-9
	1123	1.4	43
	1604	0.4	12
	2245	2.3	70
13 F	0524	-0.3	-9
	1209	1.4	43
	1655	0.4	12
	2335	2.1	64
14 Sa	0612	-0.2	-6
	1256	1.4	43
	1753	0.4	12
15 Su	0030	2.0	61
	0702	-0.1	-3
	1347	1.4	43
	1900	0.4	12

Day	Time	ft	cm
16 M	0132	1.7	52
	0754	0.1	3
	1441	1.5	46
	2017	0.4	12
17 Tu ○	0244	1.5	46
	0848	0.2	6
	1539	1.6	49
	2141	0.3	9
18 W	0410	1.3	40
	0944	0.4	12
	1638	1.7	52
	2300	0.2	6
19 Th	0539	1.2	37
	1040	0.4	12
	1736	1.8	55
20 F	0009	0.1	3
	0656	1.2	37
	1135	0.5	15
	1829	1.9	58
21 Sa	0107	-0.1	-3
	0756	1.2	37
	1225	0.5	15
	1917	1.9	58
22 Su	0156	-0.2	-6
	0846	1.2	37
	1313	0.5	15
	2001	2.0	61
23 M	0241	-0.2	-6
	0927	1.2	37
	1357	0.4	12
	2041	2.0	61
24 Tu	0321	-0.2	-6
	1004	1.2	37
	1439	0.4	12
	2118	2.0	61
25 W	0359	-0.2	-6
	1037	1.2	37
	1520	0.4	12
	2154	1.9	58
26 Th	0436	-0.2	-6
	1108	1.2	37
	1559	0.4	12
	2230	1.9	58
27 F	0512	-0.1	-3
	1140	1.2	37
	1639	0.4	12
	2307	1.8	55
28 Sa	0548	-0.1	-3
	1213	1.2	37
	1721	0.4	12
	2345	1.7	52
29 Su	0623	0.0	0
	1248	1.2	37
	1806	0.4	12
30 M	0027	1.5	46
	0658	0.2	6
	1327	1.3	40
	1858	0.4	12
31 Tu	0113	1.4	43
	0735	0.2	6
	1409	1.3	40
	2001	0.4	12

Time meridian 75° W. 0000 is midnight. 1200 is noon.
Heights are referred to mean lower low water which is the chart datum of soundings.